AROUND THE WORLD

'WHERE EVERY PROSPECT PLEASES' — COLOMBO

AROUND THE WORLD

A Friendly Guide for the World Traveler

BY

ROBERT FROTHINGHAM

WITH ILLUSTRATIONS

BOSTON AND NEW YORK
HOUGHTON MIFFLIN COMPANY
The Riverside Press Cambridge
1925

𝕿𝖍𝖊 𝕽𝖎𝖛𝖊𝖗𝖘𝖎𝖉𝖊 𝕻𝖗𝖊𝖘𝖘

CAMBRIDGE · MASSACHUSETTS

PRINTED IN THE U.S.A.

TO

'MOTHER' AND DOROTHY

MY TWO PALS

ON THE ORIENT TRAIL

'Fear not, little mother, there may be a region
Where poets have only to smile and keep still.
The click of the typewriter there will be useless,
But there will be need of a motherkin still.'

CONTENTS

INTRODUCTION	xi
I. BLUE PETER AT THE FORE	1
II. UNDER NIPPON'S SKIES	14
III. NIKKO'S SUNNY SPLENDOR	35
IV. ANCIENT KYOTO	51
V. KOREA — JAPAN'S UNHAPPY VASSAL	75
VI. CHINA — THE SURVIVAL OF THE UNFIT	88
VII. CHINA'S GREAT WALL	114
VIII. CANTON — THE HOME OF 'JOHN CHINAMAN'	126
IX. THE LURE OF THE PHILIPPINES	144
X. CRUISING AMONG THE ISLANDS	156
XI. IN THE SULU SEA	174
XII. SANDAKAN — HELL'S OWN TOWN	190
XIII. IN THE STRAITS AT SINGAPORE	209
XIV. INDIA — ANCIENT OF DAYS	222
XV. TAJ MAHAL — THE INCOMPARABLE	236
XVI. IN RAJPUTANA	253
XVII. BOMBAY TO CEYLON'S ISLE	268
XVIII. EGYPT AND THE HOME TRAIL	291
INDEX	309

ILLUSTRATIONS

'Where every prospect pleases' — Colombo
Frontispiece

The Frail Sisterhood of Yoshiwara 32

Nikko's Ancient Colonnade of Buddhas 40

Great Torii on the Sacred Island of Miyajima 72

Outside the An Ting Gate — Peking City Wall 90

China's Great Wall 114

Ruins of the Famous Yellow Temple on the Peking Plain 122

The Most Distinctive Pagoda in All China 126

One of the Gates in the Ancient City Wall of Manila and a Native 'Taxi' 150

Philippine Aspirants for Independence 164

In the Suburbs of Zamboanga 178

Two Distinguished Sulu Moros 186

Great Shwe Dagon Pagoda — Rangoon, Burmah 212

'Elephints a-pilin' teak' — Rangoon 216

Indulging in the 'Whackin' White Cheroot' in the Rangoon Bazaar 216

Burning Ghats on the Banks of the Ganges at Benares 228

Taj Mahal — The Most Beautiful Building in the World — Agra 236

'Friday Mosque' or Sabbath Services in the Jamma Masjid — Delhi   250

The Maharana's Palace on Lake Pichola, Udaipur   260

Dravidian Temple to Siva — Tanjore   276

Dravidian Temple to Siva and Minakshi — Madura   280

When the Monsoon Blows — Colombo   284

Hour of Prayer in the Desert   296

Ruins of Memphis   296

Temple at Philæ   300

Rock-Hewn Temple at Abu Simbel   304

INTRODUCTION

DEAR COMRADE OF THE RESTLESS FOOT

Now that you have made up your mind to take a trip round the world, just bear with me while I utter a brief preachment about 'Seeing America First.' There's something more in that expression than a mere advertising slogan. And, considering the fact that you will doubtless cross the United States in a railway train, there is much to be said in favor of your doing that at the start instead of at the finish. If, like most of our trans-atlantic travelers, you have never been west of Chicago, you have, in the vernacular of the day, 'something coming to you.' If you leave that until the end of your journey, you'll take it all from the car window because of the probability of your being 'fed-up' on scenery and the inevitable pull on the heartstrings as you draw nearer your own hearthstone, wherever it may happen to be. And — while there is more to be seen from the car window in the United States and Canada than in any other country on the face of the earth, that's no reason why you should be contented with a 'half loaf' only to regret later on that you did not do the thing right when you had the opportunity.

Let us assume, therefore, that you will sail from some Pacific Coast port for Japan, and that, given the necessary inducement, you might provide for an additional ten days or two weeks in advance of your sailing date 'for to admire an' for to see' some of the natural wonders of your own land. For be advised, you will meet with a goodly number of Occidental travelers in the Orient who may have more than a speaking acquaintance with these very marvels.

Considering, therefore, that you will have at least fifteen days at sea between San Francisco and Yokohama, including an eight to ten hours' stop-over at Honolulu, you could do much worse than indulge a bit of browsing around on your own native soil with a view to familiarizing yourself with a few of its sublimities. And what is more — you'll be glad you did it.

There are five steamship lines plying between Pacific Coast ports and Japan all of which are served by transcontinental railway systems, as follows: Pacific Mail, Dollar Line, and Toyo Kisen Kaisha from San Francisco; Admiral-Oriental from Seattle and the Canadian Pacific from Vancouver, British Columbia. It takes fifteen, twelve, and ten days, respectively, to make the run from the three ports in the order given. All San Francisco lines call at Honolulu; the others go direct to Yokohama by a more northerly course. The two trunk lines that run into San Francisco are the Southern Pacific and the Atchison, Topeka & Santa Fé; the Northern Pacific and the Great Northern into Seattle; the Canadian Pacific and the Canadian National into Vancouver. All of these railway systems have a multitude of connections with other lines over which the traveler may be routed with the same convenience and comfort he would enjoy within a fifty-mile radius of his home town.

In round numbers it's a three-thousand-mile jaunt from the Atlantic to the Pacific Coast by any one of these many lines, all of which make the run in approximately five days and for the same fare, including sleeping-car accommodations. And now — without suggesting a hard-and-fast programme, let us see what can be accomplished with an additional ten days or two weeks to your transcontinental schedule. We will start with the southernmost road and take them in their order as we go north.

A journey of two days to historic New Orleans, via any one of three or four different routes, connects us with the Southern Pacific Railway, direct for Los Angeles and San Francisco. Glimpses of moss-festooned trees surrounding little hamlets which have dotted the diked Louisiana landscape, unchanged since the Civil War, meet the traveler's eye as the train enters those vast stretches of lowland so characteristic of the country. It is still the country of *mañana* and carries its own peculiar interest to the sightseer. Through Texas and its limitless prairies, over the Rio Grande River, with a brief glance at the changing scenery in New Mexico, and we find ourselves in Globe, Arizona, on the third day out, at the gateway of the famous Apache Trail. Here, still traveling on our regular ticket, we may leave the train and, for a few dollars extra, take an enthralling motor trip of one hundred and twenty-five miles to Roosevelt Dam, Tonto Cliff Dwellings, Salt River Gorge, and the Superstition Mountains. Nine hours later, after an experience of a lifetime amid the most brilliantly painted landscape imaginable, we rejoin the railroad at Phœnix and continue our journey. Shortly after nightfall finds us in that great metropolis of the Pacific Coast, Los Angeles, with its population of over a million. Here we may follow any one of a half-dozen different programmes. A motor drive south along the seashore to lovely San Diego and over the mountains into Imperial Valley, with its six hundred thousand acres of irrigated land under the most efficient cultivation, is richly worth while. It may interest you to know that this garden spot, with a concrete motor highway running its full length, was once the bottom of a vast prehistoric inland sea and in earlier days was known as the 'Salton Sink' because it is several hundred feet below sealevel. You wouldn't care to live there, but it's a place to see, with thousands of acres of garden truck and fruit lying side by side with sagebrush desert as yet not under irrigation, the principal product of which is 'Spanish Bayonet.' It is worth a day or two to take a look at the ancient waterline still to be seen high up on the mountainous cliffs and to get into an argument with your friend as to whether that beautiful expanse a mile or so to the side is really water or a mirage. You'll have at least one satisfaction in knowing that others have been as certain as you that it was a lake and didn't hesitate to leave the car and walk toward it with a view to proving their case — only to see it recede as they apparently drew nearer. Emerging from the desert, the road crosses the mountains near Riverside and leads back to Los Angeles. Now you may either take the train or you may motor all the way to San Francisco for the price of your train fare, running for the greater part along the beach and visiting California's ancient capital, Monterey, with its stark, staring, stunted, and altogether picturesque cypresses along the shore. Also, you will have a chance to call at several of the ancient Franciscan Missions along that old-time trail, 'El Camino Real,' the King's Highway, now one of the most attractive and comfortable motor roads in the Golden State. Lacking a visit to one of these exquisite old missions, you will not have seen California. And — if you're not careful, you'll miss your steamer — that's precisely what California means — and it has taken you less than a week to gather in impressions that will last a lifetime.

The Santa Fé Route lies next to the north. Like most of these great across-the-West lines, it starts at Chicago, only we are going to do it differently on this particular jaunt. We will take either the Burlington, the Union Pacific, or the Rock Island to Denver, thence over the Denver & Rio Grande to Colorado Springs where we will have one day at

Pike's Peak and one in the Garden of the Gods. Resuming our journey we catch the Santa Fé at La Junta, thence into the very eye of the West. If there's any desert scenery on the face of the earth to rival that of the Santa Fé in New Mexico and Arizona, I don't know where it is. Believe me, you won't read any novels while passing through that country. A few miles from the little station siding at Adamana, Arizona, will be found in great profusion the brilliantly colored, petrified trunks of prehistoric trees, familiarly known as the 'Petrified Forest.' Many millions of years ago, this portion of that wondrous country, including thousands of acres of forest land, being subjected to a shrinking of the earth's crust, caved in to an estimated depth of ten thousand feet and the sea flowed in. Being covered with a deposit of silt and silica for a few millions of years following, the trees became petrified. And then, old Dame Nature reversed herself. She just pushed that great sunken area, covering about three hundred thousand square miles, back into its original position and the sea flowed out into what is now the Pacific Ocean. The action of the elements in the æons that followed swept the greater part of the silt deposit away and left these beautifully colored stone trees exposed. They are composed of agate and carnelian — and, before the National Government set the place aside as a public park, a number of Arizona's enterprising citizens carried away tons of the colorful material which was later made into table-tops and put on the market. Take it from me — they are worth seeing as they lie there on the ground beneath the entrancing blue of an Arizona sky.

Just a few hours westward from Adamana brings us to Williams, junction point for the most wonderful and terrific natural upheaval in the world: the Grand Cañon of the Colorado, formed by the same cataclysm that created the Petrified Forest. This is no place to attempt any description of that unspeakable gorge, two hundred and fifty miles long, from eight to thirteen miles wide, and over a mile deep. Light and shadow are its divinities and colors are created there that have no existence in any other portion of the known world. To pass that spot by on your way to the Coast would be an indictment of your sanity. Better one brief day on its indescribably wonderful and terrifying marge than to miss seeing it altogether. Having 'done' Los Angeles and Southern California while on the Southern Pacific, we will stay right on the main line of the Santa Fé until we get to Madera, a brief twenty-four hours. Here, through the Wawona Gateway, we are ushered into the workshop of the Almighty Himself: the oldest living things in the world: the Mariposa Grove or Sequoias, or the Big Trees, many of which are known by scientists to be over three thousand years old. The overpowering magnificence of these Godlike trees, which tower between three and four hundred feet in the air, is so tremendously impressive that the metaphor used above is not at all out of place. You almost expect to hear —

> ... the rushing garments of the Lord
> Sweep through the silent air, ascending heavenward.

Yea, verily — 'a day in Thy courts is better than a thousand.' And — one day is all you can give to it; then that ravishingly beautiful 'Horse-Shoe' motor trip through the forest of the Sierra, to Yosemite Valley — that exquisite gem of the California wilderness. Two days, at least, here, my friend, and then, once more the Santa Fé at Merced Station for a night's ride into San Francisco. The same itinerary may be duplicated on the Southern Pacific, and the sum total of extra time you have given to this little diversion from an otherwise unbroken trip on either road is seven days. Think it over and ruminate upon the un-escapable fact that you'll be a long time dead.

In event of your already having visited these scenic glories, you might like to touch at Salt Lake City on your way west. With Denver as your starting-point, you can take the Denver & Rio Grande road for a thrilling trip through the Royal Gorge of the Arkansas River, south of Pueblo, over a hanging bridge where the railway tracks are suspended over the rushing river from either side of the narrowed gorge, where there is about enough room for a railway train to pass. An eerie place where the roar of the torrent drowns that of the train. A stop-over of one day at the Mormon Zion is mightily worth while, thence across Salt Lake (America's Dead Sea) on one of the most cele-brated railway trestles in the world — the Lucin Cut-Off of the Southern Pacific — and you start climbing the Sierra Nevada, stopping a few miles short of the summit at the little town of Truckee. Here you leave the steel highway for a glorious three-day motor trip amongst the mountain peaks, around Lake Tahoe, sixty-three hundred feet above sea-level, down into the Tuolumne Grove of Big Trees and into Yosemite Valley, thence to San Francisco, and all planned in advance, with tickets issued accordingly.

Now, let us assume you never have seen the mighty Co-lumbia River or the pigmented waters of Crater Lake in Oregon. The Union Pacific Road will start you either at Chicago or Denver for an unbroken run through Colorado, Wyoming, into the heart of the Sawtooth Mountains in Idaho, through the Cascade Range in Oregon, and will deposit you at Portland after a two hundred and twenty-five mile ride through the majestic cañon of the Columbia, with the river on one side and the famous motor highway on the other. Thence you may proceed south for a twenty-seven hours' ride over the Shasta Route of the Southern

Pacific for San Francisco, exclusive of a brief two days for a motor trip to one of the wonder spots of the West — Crater Lake. You leave the rails at Medford where a big comfortable motor awaits all trains, and are whisked off into the mountains, spending the night at the Lake Chalet, picking up the train service next day at Klamath Falls. This wonderful body of water, with its startling blue and green and violet coloring, lies in a great pit created by the wrecking in prehistoric times of the volcano Mount Mazama which, according to the geologists, once had an altitude of fourteen thousand feet above sea-level and eight thousand feet above the surrounding country. One day, many æons ago, about six thousand feet of the peak crumpled into its crater, probably on account of the withdrawal of the lava in the interior. The crater, which now stands about two thousand feet above the tableland, is six miles long by four wide. No one knows where the water comes from that fills it. It has a depth, however, of two thousand feet and is surrounded by walls from six hundred to two thousand feet high. Despite its great elevation, it has never been known to freeze. And, while it has no visible outlet, it's waters are always fresh. Yes — it's very much worth while seeing.

Even Yellowstone Park with its mighty geysers may be included in just such an itinerary as we are discussing. There are several ways of reaching this wonderland. One from Cody, Wyoming, via the Colorado & Southern Railway, north from Denver. This is a most interesting ride through the Bad Lands of Wyoming. Another entrance is from the west via the Union Pacific lines from Pocatello, Idaho. The most direct route, however, is over the Northern Pacific, starting from St. Paul. You can be dropped from your car at the very gateway of the park itself, at

Gardiner. Take your five-day 'round trip and resume your journey to the Coast. The railway trip through the Cascade Range itself is worth all it costs and you can finish in Portland, via the Columbia River Cañon, or go direct to Seattle, with the same facilities for continuing your journey as have already been set forth.

A few hundred miles southeast of Yellowstone Park lies the Rocky Mountain National Park in Colorado, where the Rockies attain their most imposing magnificence. You may be surprised to learn that, of the fifty-five known mountain peaks in the United States which have an altitude of fourteen thousand feet, forty-two are in Colorado. A most satisfactory tour of this remarkable reservation of natural beauty can be made in three days as you go north from Denver on the Colorado & Southern to finish your last lap for the Coast over the Northern Pacific.

Doubtless you have read about the glories of Glacier National Park without being sufficiently interested to learn precisely where it is. Know, then, that this inspiring aggregation of 'heaven-kissing hills' lies in the extreme northern part of Montana, right up against the Canadian boundary. In fact, it is part of the Canadian Rocky Mountains, which is to say that there is nothing within the borders of the United States to which this amazingly beautiful spot can be compared. The Great Northern Railway, which practically parallels and is owned by the Northern Pacific, will take you aboard one of its overland trains at Duluth, Minneapolis, St. Louis, or Kansas City and drop you at the Glacier Park Station, for a three days' special kind of a holiday different from anything you may have previously undertaken, see that you are brought back to the station on schedule time, and will land you a little over twenty-four hours later at either Seattle, Tacoma, or Everett, whence you may follow your inclinations, either direct to

Japan from Seattle, north to Vancouver, or south to San Francisco. In any case, there's one thing to keep in mind: Mount Rainier. There is simply no such thing as exaggerating the majesty and the individuality of this tremendous volcano — for that is what it is, though dormant. Standing there in its isolated magnificence, nearly fifteen thousand feet above sea-level, visible for a radius of one hundred and fifty miles, with its twenty-eight separate glaciers radiating from its truncated peak, it is a sight for gods and men, a gorgeous spectacle of the first magnitude. Sixty miles distant from Seattle and forty-two from Tacoma, it is a simple one-day's motor ride which will send you on your way to the Orient with a more exalted opinion of the natural glories of your own land than you ever dreamed of.

This symposium of suggestions would be incomplete without some reference to the two great railway systems of our Canadian sister across the border — a boundary in name only: for 'the communion of saints' that is found amongst Nature-lovers admits neither 'border nor breed nor birth.' A leisurely ride of six days from New York to Vancouver, via Montreal on the Canadian Pacific or the Canadian National Railways will give you enough wonderful scenery from the car window to make you wish you could give a month to it. Or, if you care little for Canada's vast wheat-fields, you can take a short cut to Winnipeg via the 'Soo Line' from Chicago and be in the mountains *pronto*, on either line. A two or three days' stop-over at Banff on the C.P.R. or at Jasper on the C.N.R. would be time mightily well spent in the very heart of the Rockies. And the balance of the run to the Coast along the rushing Fraser River and its magnificent cañons would furnish enough thrills for a lifetime. From Vancouver you would have a pleasant railway journey of eleven hundred and twenty-seven miles down the Coast to San Francisco which would take forty-two hours, with plenty of reasons for stopping off here and there as already suggested. Or — you might take the boat to Seattle through Puget Sound — a nine-hour ride from early morn till dewy eve. Any way you figure it, starting from any point in the United States, you would not have to add more than a fortnight at the outside to give you a prideful foretaste of the natural wonders of your own country that would add zest to your globe-trotting and bring you back home with the determination to make a virtue of your former detestation and 'See America First' from A to Z. And — you'll be glad of it.

ROBERT FROTHINGHAM

AROUND THE WORLD

CHAPTER I

BLUE PETER AT THE FORE

The days are sick and cold and the skies are grey and old,
And the twice-breathed airs blow damp;
And I'd sell my tired soul for the bucking beam-sea roll
 Of a black Bilbao tramp,
 With her load-line over her hatch, dear lass,
 And a drunken Dago crew,
 And her nose held down on the old trail, our own trail, the out
 trail
From Cadiz south on the Long Trail — the trail that is always new.
                                                        KIPLING

FROM the time that ancient Israel's aged leader climbed to
the summit of Mount Nebo for a last, long look over into
the Promised Land from which Jehovah had barred him,
down to Stevenson's cheerful acknowledgment that 'to
travel hopefully is a better thing than to arrive,' a goodly
portion of mankind has been infected with a restless
foot. We shall never know how much that famous old
missionary hymn 'Greenland's Icy Mountains' has contributed to the love of travel. One cannot lightly discuss
such momentous topics as India's coral strand without
taking a long chance on disturbing the noiseless tenor of
the family circle. Equally unwise would it be even to
whisper about the alleged spicy breezes blowing soft o'er
Ceylon's Isle unless we have our steamer reservations
signed, sealed, and delivered and not subject to cancella-
tion. What a flat, stale, and unprofitable old world it would
be if it were not for the Seven Seas and the Wanderlust.

When Masefield cries out,

> I must go down to the seas again,

one feels a lump rising in his throat. When Hovey, that gallant spirit cut down before his prime, proclaims,

> I am tired of four walls and a ceiling,
> I have need of the sky —
> I have business with the grass,

we turn and look out at the window lest some one note the telltale humidness in the corner of our eye. When Knibbs, that 'God's darling' of the West, sings,

> Out there, somewhere, we'll ride the range,
>   A-looking for the new and strange —
> My feet are tired and need a change —
>   Come on, it's up to you —

we simply get up and leave home, for there's 'nothing to do but go.' And — what more eloquent parable was ever dedicated to those who are bound upon the Wheel than penned by that apostle of sublimated common sense and mysticism, Don Marquis. Hear ye! Hear ye!

Once there was a young fellow so ambitious that he wouldn't take time off from becoming rich and famous to go a-fishing. Work! Work! Work! And all the time he wanted to go a-fishing.

He became, in the natural course of events, an eminent man, a prominent citizen. And — when he was seventy years old he said to himself with a good deal of satisfaction that now he could go a-fishing.

But — he discovered that he no longer wished to go a-fishing.

Sadly he put away the rod and lines — and sadly he murmured to himself:

'Well, anyhow, I have been a Force for Progress and Civilization.'

And — perhaps it is kinder to let the poor old simp think that such things matter as much as going a-fishing.

And — that's how it all came about that we turned the key in the lock of our little home in the country, not so many years ago, and started off strange countries for to see: father, 'Mother,' and the big girl. True, there are a few preliminaries to be faced prior to embarking on a 'round-the-world trip. They are not quite as serious, however, as some may think. In view of the fact that man's allotted span of threescore years and ten is devoted mostly to giving hostages to fortune, there is no particular reason why he shouldn't avail himself of such an honorable custom in planning an indefinite holiday. Personally, I don't know of any better scheme than resigning a perfectly good job before one gets 'fired,' and leaving such a sense of relief with one's employers that they willingly present him with a handsome check — otherwise the eventful voyage might never have materialized. There are so many things one might do with a handsome check between jobs that it was no small problem to settle. And, granting that we resolved on a globe-girdling trip, just how much time should we give to it, etc.? Should we follow the man from Cook's and plan a hard-and-fast schedule, the expense of which could be fairly well approximated in advance and which would return us to our native land by a certain fixed date? Or, should we buy our tickets all the way 'round at the outset, just so we might be sure of getting back, and let the balance of the aforesaid handsome check work out its own salvation with due regard for the rapidity with which it might be depleted? We finally decided in favor of the latter plan, and it worked so satisfactorily that I cheerfully recommend it to any person contemplating a similar journey.

To be exact, the amount of money we determined to devote to our trip was ten thousand dollars. We figured, roughly, that such an amount would probably see us through a six months' absence. As a matter of fact, it sufficed for ten months, and that without 'scrimping' ourselves in any way. True, this was before the World War. It could hardly be done as reasonably to-day. I am persuaded from our experience, however, that a trip 'round the world is not necessarily anywhere near the expensive proposition it is generally supposed to be, even when one is traveling on a go-as-you-please basis. Ten thousand dollars for three people for ten months is modest enough in all conscience. The same trip to-day could be done for fifteen dollars per day if one confined himself to a strict programme, minus any side trips, including horse-drawn vehicles instead of motor-cars, which latter would in themselves increase one's daily average to twenty or twenty-five dollars.

Having been for many years enthusiastic believers in the idea of 'Seeing America First,' and realizing there was something more in that expression than a mere advertising slogan, we made up our minds to go cross-country and start from San Francisco on our 'first leg.' If one leaves his railway trip across the continent until the end of his journey, it's a dead-sure thing he will take whatever scenery there is to be had from the car window because of the probability of his being 'fed up' on scenery of all sorts and the inevitable pull on the heartstrings as he draws nearer his own hearthstone. And, while there is more to be seen from the car window in the United States than in any other country on the face of the earth, that's no reason why one should be contented with a 'half loaf' only to regret later on that he did not do the right thing when he had the opportunity. Accordingly, we planned for an extra week en route and re-visited the Petrified Forests of Arizona, the Grand Canyon of the Colorado, the Mariposa Grove of Big Trees, and the Yosemite Valley.

Considering that one meets with a goodly number of Occidental travelers in the Orient who may have more than a speaking acquaintance with the natural wonders of the United States, he can do much worse than indulge a bit of browsing around on his own native soil with a view to familiarizing himself with a choice few of its sublimities. And — what is more — he'll be glad he did it. Furthermore, it's an agreeable way to break a three-thousand-mile railway jaunt from the Atlantic to the Pacific coasts. In all the intensive sightseeing I have done during the past quarter of a century, both at home and abroad, I know of nothing more really wonderful and inspiring than the Giant Sequoias or Big Trees of California. Here we are ushered into the workshop of the Almighty Himself. It staggers the imagination to realize that these mammoth redwoods are the oldest living things in the world, that they have been standing there on the slopes of the Sierra for over three thousand years. The overwhelming magnificence of these godlike trees, which tower between three and four hundred feet in the air, is so tremendously impressive that the metaphor employed is not at all out of place. One almost expects to hear:

... the rushing garments of the Lord
Sweep through the silent air, ascending heavenward.

Yea, verily, 'A day in Thy courts is better than a thousand.'

In the brief space of time allotted 'him who in the love of Nature holds communion with her visible forms,' between train arrival and the departure of the steamer from San Francisco, there is one thing, at least, that he should see for the good of his soul: the unspeakable grandeur of the going-down-of-the-sun through the Golden Gate. A short run in a taxi to the heights of the city suffices for this glorious adventure which has no parallel on either the Pacific or the Atlantic coast-line. Neither will its equal be seen until you arrive in Manila Bay and watch with bated breath a similar celestial conflagration over the lofty heights of Mount Mariveles.

There are two trans-Pacific steamship lines plying between San Francisco and the Orient: the Pacific Mail and the Dollar Line. Both are excellent and include all the comforts of home. It just happened that the July sailing date of the former suited our plans better and we set sail on the *Mongolia*, commanded by Emery Rice, a young skipper of splendid capacity who was destined to give his life in his country's service in the World War which shortly followed. Having made our peace with the deck steward, we settled down in our steamer chairs to consider the responsibilities of leisure while yet the peaks of the Coast Range were in sight. So far as our beloved country was concerned, we had turned the key in the lock and thrown it away. I was still musing over that fool statement of old Aristotle that liberty was obedience to a self-made law when a dense fog closed around us like a pall and locked us in as completely as if we had been jailed. It was the most remarkable fog at sea that I have ever known in that it was the only one we were to encounter during our ten months' absence.

Running true to form, the weather that followed for the next two days was so cold that we were glad to don heavy clothes. Four days of the most entrancing, sunshiny weather imaginable followed during which the *Mongolia* swayed gently into the long, silent swell of the Pacific, more like a great bird upon the water than a huge fabric of steel under the impetus of steam. No such waves on that immense expanse of ocean as the traveler faces on the Atlantic — at least, not on that trip. On the sixth day it was a highly interesting, not to say exciting experience to see a cloud-bank ahead, apparently resting on the surface of the water, gradually become metamorphosed into land.

Hawaii — magic name, redolent of hibiscus and Bougainvillea, palm trees and the 'Pride of India.' It didn't occur to us until that hour that we hadn't sighted a single steam or sailing ship in the long stretch of twenty-one hundred miles from San Francisco — and we hadn't missed them either. 'How noiseless falls the foot of time!' It was the island of Oahu, on the western point of which stood famous Makapuu Head Lighthouse, one of the most powerful in the world. Diamond Head soon arises from the sea like a huge lizard stretching his head out from the mainland as if to guard the entrance to Honolulu Harbor. And now we can see the Stars and Stripes on the Government buildings, and a thrill runs through the assembled passengers on the deck as if they were setting eyes on the glorious emblem for the first time in many months instead of a few days. So mote it be, now and evermore.

As the big vessel warps into the pier, a brass band of forty native Hawaiians marches down from the plaza and greets her arrival with the stirring strains of 'The Star-Spangled Banner' and other patriotic airs. And — how those brown-skinned boys can play! This is one of the regular features of the arrival and departure of all steamers to and from the United States, and a mighty effective piece of work it is, too. Well, here we are with a stop-over of a little less than twenty-four hours. 'Tis ten o'clock and we may sail before midnight or we may pull out in the morning. No one can say — least of all the skipper. How shall we put in our time? Meanwhile, permit me to introduce the *Mongolia's* purser — Moses H. Hunt of blessed memory. May his eyes fall on this page after these fleeting years! Hunt was a genius, a real human being. Considerably over six feet in altitude, built like an athlete, tipping the scales at about two hundred and twenty-five pounds, with a drawl that would talk a bird out of a tree. And — oh, those pre-Volsteadian days! Hunt could mix a cocktail that would 'stir a fever in the blood of age.' And when at about five o'clock every afternoon his Chinese 'boy' would hunt me up, wherever I happened to be dispersed about the deck, and deliver the cryptic message, 'Number 1 man Hunt he say come topside plitty quick,' I stood not upon the order of my going, but went *pronto*, right straight into his little private office on the upper deck.

> Above the door was written bold
> The motto of the Crown:
> 'Who dallieth with a cocktail
> May not always drink it down.'

It was Hunt who related that most tragic story of the Kentuckian who dropped dead while holding a glass of Bourbon between his admiring eyes and the sunlight. 'Death by procrastination' was the coroner's verdict, which doubtless explained why Moses always had two glasses ready for me by the time I reached the door of his devoted little 'Speakeasy.' It was Charles Lamb, was it not, who sent the first drink down on a voyage of exploration; the second to proclaim the arrival of the third — and the fourth to announce the close proximity of the fifth?

> An' th' memory comes like a banshee
> Meself an' me wealth between —
> An' I long for a Mornin's Mornin'
> In Shanahan's ould shebeen.

Well, it was Hunt who had a motor-car waiting on the pier for us on the arrival of the steamer. This was his itinerary for the one brief day we had in Honolulu — 'Quiet Haven' — and I reckon it will answer for you: an eight-mile drive to the west over the crushed lava roads for a brief inspection of the United States Naval Station at

Pearl Harbor, containing ten square miles of navigable water, with thirty miles of deep water-front that is absolutely calm in all weather, and connected with the open sea by a deep and narrow channel. Thence six miles southeast of the center of the city to Diamond Head, the summit of which is the crater of an extinct volcano, in which the disappearing guns of Fort Ruger are emplaced. Few people know that this is one of the greatest forts in the world.

When one considers that the Hawaiian Islands, familiarly termed 'The Crossroads of the Pacific,' lie about midway between San Francisco and Japan, its importance as a first line of defense, in event of any offensive naval demonstration, will be immediately apparent. It requires no great stretch of the imagination to appreciate the advantages to the United States of a supply station, either in peace or war, halfway across an ocean five thousand miles in width. No, your Uncle Sam has not been 'asleep at the switch' in Hawaii, any more than he has in the Philippines:

> Where the old Trade's plyin' an' th' old flag flyin',
> They shall find him 'ware an' wakin' as they found him
>   long ago.

From Diamond Head we make our climb over excellent roads to the summit of the Punch Bowl, another extinct crater about five hundred feet high, from which a magnificent view may be had of the city and harbor below. There are about one hundred miles of splendid motor-roads in Oahu winding up hill and down dale through beautiful estates and tropical growth, most of which may be done in a day. Scenically speaking, the drive *par excellence* is that up beautiful Nuuanu Valley to the Pali, a sixteen-hundred-foot cliff overlooking the windward coast. The narrow coastal plain buttressed on one side by the precipitous mountain range which forms the backbone of the island and laved by an aquamarine blue sea on the other constitutes

one of the most spectacular views in the world of travel.
It was over this tremendous cliff that old King Kameha-
meha drove the army of the King of Oahu in 1795 after a
fierce fight in the Nuuanu Valley. That settled the King
business in Hawaii for all time.

Entirely apart from the wild beauty of the spot, one of
the interesting features of the Pali is the antics played by
the trade winds with the unsuspecting visitor. The motor-
car comes to a stop about one hundred feet back from the
cliff which is guarded on one side by the needle-like peak of
the Pali itself, against which the wind blows with great
velocity. It is only when the tourist reaches the angle at
which the wind is diverted from the slanting side of the
rock that he (not to mention she) is almost blown from his
feet — and what it does to tropical clothing of the feminine
gender is a trifle startling. This entertainment is regarded
by the local chauffeurs as an inalienable prerogative, in the
exercise of which they never seem to tire. By this time the
forenoon has passed and a dainty luncheon awaits us at the
Country Club upon the mountain-side, which is surrounded
by one of the niftiest golf courses ever.

The *pièce de résistance*, however, of a visit to Honolulu is
far-famed Waikiki Beach about six miles from the city.
An afternoon spent in those booming billows will furnish
memories for a lifetime. Perhaps some of my older readers
may hark back to the 'Geography' of their school days and
visualize a 'Scene in the Sandwich Islands,' consisting of a
crude illustration of an athletic Kanaka balancing himself
on a surf-board perched on the crest of a mighty comber
rushing shoreward at race-horse speed. It is a picture that
must be seen to be appreciated and Waikiki is the only
place to see it. For the flabby-muscled tourist who is un-
equal to the management of the surf-board, even *à la* 'belly-
whopper,' they provide a native-manned outrigger dugout-

canoe which will furnish all the excitement necessary.
With a bronze Apollo in the bow and another in the stern,
we paddle out beyond the bar and wait for a 'real one.'
Soon it comes racing in like a tidal wave. When about one
hundred and fifty feet distant, the two 'boys' bend to their
paddles with all their strength in order to hook on to the
monster at the precise moment when the speed of the canoe
approximates that of the wave. Result — the paddlers
rest while the dugout is carried in shore like a chip bal-
anced on the crest instead of being left behind, which latter
is exactly what happens to the amateur on the surf-board.
It is a stunt calling for more dexterity than any white man
has ever succeeded in acquiring and strangely suggestive
of that

> ... tide in the affairs of men
> Which, taken at the flood, leads on to fortune;
> Omitted, all the voyage of their life
> Is bound in shallows and in miseries.

On our way back to the city we stop in Kapiolani Park
for a visit to the Aquarium, second in importance only to
that of Naples. Here we find the most astounding aggregation of varicolored fish, exquisitely tinted and odd-shaped
freaks embodying all the colors in the spectrum. One interesting specimen bore the somewhat bucolic name of 'Hu-
muhumunukunukeapuaa' — a charming little fellow with
purple stripes around his body and a sky-blue, pink and
saffron-colored set of gills — and we hadn't had a thing
since we left the Country Club. The end of a perfect day
found us back in the city plaza just in time for the late
afternoon concert by the Royal Hawaiian Band — with
the kindly Hunt awaiting our translation 'topside' for a
libation to the ancient Hawaiian gods, than whom there
are no gentler this side of the Hesperides. That was, indeed, one day of harmonious agreement with that cheerful

old Nonconformist, Max Eastman, who states it as an in-
dubitable fact that 'The fundamental act of life is not
judgment, but choice. It is not what people have decided,
but what people *want* that is of original and divine importance' — and Hunt made it unanimous.

In the length and breadth of the Seven Seas there is no
such beautiful and touching ceremony as that which accompanies the departure of a liner from the port of Honolulu. What is there about that gentle-souled people, the
Hawaiians, doomed as they are to extinction, that so completely transcends our hustling, bustling success, our breed
of 'go-getters'? What spirit is it that brings a bevy of
pretty brown girls, a company of middle-aged, smiling
women, a score of romping children down to the dock with
their floral necklaces or *leis* to throw over the heads of departing passengers? The few coins they receive in return
constitute no answer to the query. Why should 'Greeting
and Farewell' mean more to a South-Sea Islander than to
an Occidental? Please don't hand me out any cut-and-
dried replies. Imagine, if you can, the hawsers thrown off
the pier, the great vessel slowly drawing out into the stream,
that incomparable band of native musicians playing 'Aloha
Oe' with a poignancy that would melt a heart of stone —
and the girls, women, and children throwing overboard
their wreaths of beautiful flowers to mingle with those
thrown over by the passengers, until the surface of the
water between the fast-receding ship and the pier is literally covered with them. 'Aloha Oe!' the last 'Aloha:
Greeting and Good-bye!' The surreptitious tears trickling
down the cheeks of many a voyager on the deck of the
Mongolia that morning proved conclusively that 'The
Colonel's lady and Judy O'Grady are sisters under the
skin.'

We may go back to Honolulu some day and take an

unlimited Inter-Island trip. We may go the limit in sight-seeing from Kilauea's fiendish crater to that Gethsemane of the Archipelago, Molokai. We may plan a holiday that will leave no historical or ethnological question to be answered from the date of Captain Cook's discovery of the islands in 1798 down to the present — but 'Aloha Oe' will never again sound as it did that morning we pulled out of Honolulu Harbor for Japan, no matter how effectively it may be rendered. And it is worthy of record that in the ten months that followed, we never heard anything, anywhere, in the way of music that went quite so deep. Yes, when it comes to 'our little brown brother,' we'll take ours from Hawaii and you may have the Filipino and his saffron-hued neighbor the Jap. Even old Hunt acknowledged that it always 'got' him a bit — and we had to go topside and talk it all over.

> 'Well,' murmured one, 'let whoso make or buy,
>   My Clay with long Oblivion is gone dry:
> But fill me with the old familiar Juice,
>   Methinks I might recover by and by.'

'Anyhow,' ejaculated Hunt, 'you know we never get any real fresh fruit until we touch Honolulu. We picked up some fine ripe pineapples. They taste pretty good when you dig out the inside, chop it up, and pack it back into the shell with just enough sherry to keep it from drying up on you and let it stand on ice overnight. 'Tain't half bad for breakfast, along with a ripe alligator pear.' And I smote him where he sat because the bugle was blowing for luncheon and there was no time for further argument.

CHAPTER II

UNDER NIPPON'S SKIES

And whoso will, from Pride released,
Contemning neither creed nor priest,
May feel the Soul of all the East
About him at Kamakura.

KIPLING

ELEVEN glorious days of sailing under Orient skies from Honolulu. Days of *dolce far niente*, the first of utter relaxation, with a complete indifference to wind and tide, during which old embers were rekindled, old memories walked unbidden into the picture, and it was good to be alive. The 'Land of the Rising Sun' was close at hand, and to-morrow would find the *Mongolia's* mud-hook hugging the bottom of ancient Yedo Bay off Yokohama. We were scheduled for Hongkong, and we didn't know whether we should proceed with the steamer or stop over. Furthermore — we didn't much care. The immemorial East already had laid its hand on us and we were taken captive even before we had set foot on shore.

The Filipino band aboardship had fulfilled every expectation. Venturesome passengers, with a *flair* for risking a bit of cold cash, had dropped tidy sums playing fan-tan with a Chinese member of the crew who acted as dealer up in the ship's fo'c'sle. The raucous-voiced, leathery idiot who took it upon himself to retail the daily wireless news to the occupants of the deck chairs was silenced at last. The big sail filled with sea-water, in which we had taken our daily plunge up forward, had been taken in. We had done our best to be courteous to the few folk we had met *en passant* — and there were some exceedingly nice travelers, too. But — when one goes on a pilgrimage to the Bagdad of youth's dream, the principal road to take, yea, the only road, lies between the covers of a good book — and we had not less than a dozen to contribute to the ship's library when we left.

'Twas late on a sultry and hazy afternoon when the vessel came to anchor. We were trying to make up our minds whether to go ashore for dinner or stay aboardship, when the haze suddenly cleared away as by magic and the snow-capped, symmetrical summit of Fujiyama, Japan's sacred mountain, swept into view as if a vast curtain had been drawn to one side simply to display the exquisite picture. It lasted for but a few moments, the haze once more settling down over the landscape like a fog, blotting out everything but the dour and unattractive sea-front of the city beyond. That wonderful mountain view, brief though it was, settled the matter of our next move then and there.

And here we had our first instance of the advantages of a go-as-you-please billet versus traveling in accordance with a hard-and-fast schedule. We packed up without delay and went ashore to one of the most comfortable and pleasant hotels it was our good fortune to find during our whole trip: The Grand. Pity 'tis that the terrible earthquake and fire of 1923 completely destroyed it, along with the few other attractions of that colorless city, Yokohama, leaving it as it is to-day, an unreconstructed mass of ruin, including the sea-wall, or bund, which has never been rebuilt. A rickshaw ride around the city before dark made it perfectly clear that we were not in the Japan of our expectation. Yokohama at that time resembled a cross between the Orient and the Occident that would have been rejected by both. Tawdry Theater Street, with its underworld atmosphere, wheezing talking-machines, and all-'round blowsiness, created an impression similar to that of certain sections of Paris: that it had been slung together for the especial delectation of those from 'furrin parts' having more money than brains.

The only decent section of the city lay along the seafront where resident Europeans had their homes, churches, hotels, clubs, and banks. The native city, so to speak, lay far back from the bay and was about as representative of Japan as the notorious 'Hell's Kitchen' district is of New York City. Being a seaport, however, with its hotels fronting on the broad waters of the bay, and conveniently connected by electric lines with near-by places of interest (which it still is), it was a good place to settle down — and, besides, Fuji was not far off, and we had determined on a pilgrimage to that famous mountain, not to mention Kamakura, on the seashore a few miles away. Had we to do it all over again, we would not materially change our plans.

Notwithstanding the ravages of the earthquake, the famous Tokaido Road, which was constructed in the eleventh century, connecting the ancient cities Yedo (the present-day Tokyo), Kyoto, and Osaka, a highway three hundred and fifty miles long, skirting the seacoast, still suffices for a motor trip to Miyanoshita and Lake Hakone if the traveler is willing to rough it a bit. This is also the route to Kamakura and Fujiyama, and it served during our trip as a rather bizarre forum for the display of certain startling Japanese characteristics, the memory of which still remains, indicating their peculiar attitude to the detested American. In every village along the road, little tots from four and five years upward, all of them wearing military caps, would run out from their homes and yell 'Banzai!' as the motor-car passed. And — as if this were not sufficiently indicative of their feeling, children of a somewhat larger growth, full-grown men in fact, would walk to the roadside in semi-nude condition and indulge in certain salutations more eloquent than elegant, the significance of which was not to be misunderstood for an instant.

If the Japanese did not like us then, they like us infinitely less now, after the action of our august Senate. However — just as long as we have good American dollars to leave with them, it is to be hoped that their hospitality will continue. We reached Miyanoshita in time for luncheon at the only hotel (and a mighty attractive one), situated atop of a sightly bluff about thirteen hundred feet above sea-level, giving onto an inspiring sweep of gorgeous mountain scenery in all directions. Those who have visited Miyanoshita will be genuinely sorry to learn that the earthquake shock precipitated a portion of the town over the edge of the bluff upon which it was situated, and destroyed part of the picturesque little hotel as well. Whether it will ever be rebuilt or not, no one seems to know. After luncheon we motored to Lake Hakone, an hour's run to one of the most beautiful spots in all Japan at that time. Fuji's peak was clear of clouds and beautifully mirrored in the calm waters of the lake at his feet. The Emperor's summer residence, together with the numerous homes of well-to-do foreigners and prominent Japanese, dainty tea-houses, and a good hotel made the spot most popular with the traveler. The earthquake has worked such havoc with the place, however, even to the diverting of the streams that supplied the lake which is now dry, that it is decidedly questionable if any effort will ever be made to restore it. Returning to Miyanoshita, we spent the night and motored leisurely back to Yokohama via Kamakura the next day.

One would hardly imagine, motoring into the little seaside village of Kamakura, fourteen miles from Yokohama, that it was once the capital of Eastern Japan, with a popu-

lation of a million, under the despotic rule of one Takasuké, a 'Tammany' constable, who arrogated to himself
the prerogatives of a weak-kneed Emperor and maintained
an *entourage* consisting of thirty-seven mistresses, two
thousand dancers, and five thousand fighting dogs. Surely
'thim were the good ould days,' until what resembled the
reform element of that early period — the fourteenth century — rose in its might, threw Takasuké out, and burned
the city to the ground. About the only thing that survived
was the gigantic bronze Buddha, the world-famous Daibutsu, which was cast and set up in the thirteenth century
and which constitutes the principal attraction of Kamakura to-day.

This is the largest bronze casting in existence and represents the Buddha sitting in state on the lotus. It is fifty
feet in height, with a circumference of ninety-eight feet,
and weighs nearly five hundred tons. Its eyes are of pure
gold, and on the forehad there is an embossed circlet fifteen inches in diameter, containing thirty pounds of silver.
On the head is a mass of what would appear to be curls,
but which, as a matter of fact, are eight hundred and thirty
bronze snails, each nine inches high, which, according to
legendary lore, crawled on the bald head of the original
Buddha to shelter it from the rays of the sun. It is one of
the most impressive statues I have ever seen.

The all-pervading dignity and mystical calm of that
intellectual, passionless face, the enduring majesty of
divine meditation in which is concentrated the whole
philosophy of Buddhistic doctrine, all haunt the memory.
This shrine is a place that the traveler can visit repeatedly
without surfeit. In fact, he does not get the full effect
from one visit. Entrance may be had into the interior of
the statue through a doorway in the right side of the lotus
pedestal. A ladder leads up to the shoulders where two

small windows may be found — though what purpose they are supposed to serve is not apparent. At the gateway will be found the following announcement:

Stranger, whosoever thou art and whatsoever be thy creed — when thou enterest this sanctuary, remember that thou treadest upon ground hallowed by the worship of ages. This is the Temple of Buddha and the Gate of the Eternal and should be entered with reverence.

Appropriate as is the notice, it would be less of an anti-climax if the native custodians of the shrine would remove the near-by sign prohibiting visitors from taking any photographs of the image, for the very apparent reason that the sales of the local product displayed upon the pedestal might thereby be curtailed. And again, one cannot help thinking that, despite the terrible disaster, there should be sufficient national pride somewhere between the imperial throne and the municipal government to rebuild the foundation of this priceless relic and put it on its feet, so to speak. The earthquake threw it clear out of plumb, since which time it has stood tilted forward and a bit to one side, creating an unholy impression that the 'Gate of the Eternal' was a trifle off its hinges. The attendants are still on the job, however, and the sale of photographs goes merrily on, notwithstanding their having been printed from a negative antedating the earthquake. The natives in and about Kamakura profess to believe that the present slant of the image is indicative of divine sorrow over the tragedy of the earthquake: 'Sweet are the uses of adversity!'

When I was in Yokohama there was a most interesting story current among the American and British residents relative to the visit of the late E. H. Harriman a year or two previous. It appeared, so the story ran, that that eminent railroad financier was so greatly impressed with the Daibutsu at Kamakura that he wished to secure a duplicate for his celebrated mountain ranch in Oregon, if he could be assured that it was a genuine antique. The canny Japanese members of his party, with an eye to the main chance, are alleged to have informed him that there were several in Japan, in out-of-the-way places, one of which undoubtedly could be secured for a consideration, say about fifty thousand dollars. Money being no object under such unusual circumstances, the details were soon arranged.

Several months later, a replica of the Daibutsu arrived in San Francisco in sections, all ready for transportation to the Harriman ranch. Whether the shipment was continued or whether some one noticed, when the sections were unloaded from the steamer, that they looked rather new, does not appear. At any rate, an investigation is said to have followed, in which it developed that the 'genuine antique' had been recently cast in a foundry in Osaka, whereupon it was promptly shipped back to that ancient city. The sequel to the story alleges that Mr. Harriman was compelled to enlist the good offices of the Department of State at Washington with the Japanese Government before he could get his money refunded. As the late Congressman Tim Campbell might say: 'What's a few hundred years' difference in the age of two perfectly respectable Daibutsus amount to between friends!'

We saw our first *torii* at Kamakura, at the entrance to the Hachiman Shrine, dedicated to the God of War. For the lack of a better term, the *torii* might be called Japan's trade-mark. It will be found guarding the approach to every temple and shrine throughout the kingdom. And, strange to say, I couldn't find a person in Japan, either native or foreigner, who could tell me just what it signified. Even my old friend Hamaguchi, the genial landlord of the Miyako Hotel in Kyoto, who is supposed to know everything, went 'shy' when I put the question to him. The

most any one could say was that it was believed to have
some sacred import, with the result that we always felt
guilty of *lèse-majesté* every time we passed under one because of our unfortunate Occidental origin.   It sort o'
seemed as if a genuflexion was in order — we weren't sure.
Not until I returned home and looked the subject up in the
encyclopædia did I discover the real significance of this
very commonplace Japanese symbol and I pass it on for
what it may be worth:

> Originally designed as a perch for fowls which sang to the
> deities at daybreak, the *torii* subsequently came to be errone-
> ously regarded as a gateway characteristic of the Shinto shrine.
> It consists of two thick trunks placed upright, their upper ends
> mortised into a horizontal log which projects beyond them at
> either side.   The structure derives some grace from its extreme
> simplicity.

I have felt much easier in my New England conscience since
I acquired that information.   The construction of these
symbols varies from wood to stone and cast iron.   The most
sightly one in all Japan is on the shore of the sacred island
of Miyajima (pronounced Mee-yah-jee-mah), of which
more later, when we arrive at that beautiful spot.

Following the example of various seaside resorts in the
United States, Kamakura established a bathing-beach
several years ago, of which I made good use that hot day in
July, during which a dozen husky Japanese fishermen were
drawing a huge seine ashore, laden with fish for the market.
It was a decidedly novel sight to watch them pick small
fish from the net as they hauled away, and eat them alive,
head and all, without even pausing to stun or kill them, bit-
ing off chunks and chewing them with a relish, while the
finny victim was still wriggling.   Truly, there's no accounting for taste even among Japanese fishermen.

Another interesting attraction of Kamakura is the shrine

of Kwannon, the Goddess of Pity, of which there are thirty-three throughout the kingdom. The Japanese worship her as the protectress of children and dumb animals. Before the earthquake, Kamakura was one of the most popular Holy Places in the country with the votaries of Kwannon, thousands of whom made annual pilgrimages to her temple, Hasé no Kwannon.

It's strange what deep impressions are made by little things. There is a most excellent electric-railway service between Yokohama and Tokyo, eighteen miles distant, and we decided to run up for one day's sight-seeing at a time, instead of separating ourselves from the creature comforts of the Grand Hotel and the sightly view from our room windows of the broad expanse of the bay. A train had just pulled in to the station as we reached it. As we waited for a few moments before the gates opened, the air seemed filled with a most peculiar musical hum, unlike anything we had ever heard, accompanied by certain distinct staccato notes of varying intensity, more suggestive of a xylophone than anything else, and blending into a tonal harmony most pleasing to the ear. A crowd of native Japanese who had just left the cars were coming down the long cement platform, and the musical sound which they gave out was the soft but resonant clip-clop of their *geta* or wooden sandals as they scuffed along their way to the street. It was a sound we were to hear many times in railway stations before we left the country, but it was far from commonplace that bright August morning in Yokohama.

There is an odd incongruity in the dress of the Japanese men-folk, a sort of combination of the East and the West, with a view to securing the maximum comforts of each. First the feet, with their close-fitting, native black socks or *tabi*, bifurcated, as it were, between the great toe and its nearest neighbor, so as to admit the strap by which they grip their *geta*. Next the characteristic kimono, with its flowing sleeves. Continuing the upward glance, one naturally expects to see an equally Oriental hat and bamboo umbrella as per the illustrations in the atlas of our school days. To the traveler's surprise, however, here's where the Occident intrudes itself in the shape of a thoroughly up-to-date straw hat, such as one would see on the streets of any city in the United States, and the mate to a Yankee silk umbrella or sunshade. The mystery was cleared up on our arrival in Tokyo, however, where we went through a mammoth department store which would compare favorably with any similar institution in New York or Chicago. Only the Japanese peasant sticks to the native hat, umbrella, and grass raincoat.

'Don't be surprised at anything you see,' was the last word a friend at the hotel handed us as we jumped into our rickshaws on our way to the railway station in Yokohama. We had occasion to remember that cryptic remark before we had been seated in the train five minutes. Directly opposite us was a prosperous-looking Japanese, accompanied by his wife. On entering the car, the first thing he did was to remove his kimono and undershirt, which latter he handed to his wife, who folded it carefully and laid it on the seat beside her. Just as we took for granted that he was 'going the limit,' he replaced his kimono, slipped off his *geta*, and squatted on his hunkers on the seat. Fishing a native newspaper out of his sleeve, he proceeded to bury himself in it while his wife obediently looked the other way and continued so to do for the balance of the trip. Not a word was spoken by either of them. It was a bit of a hot day and the gentleman was making himself comfortable — that's all there was to it. He was as oblivious of the presence of the three Americans opposite him as that of his wife — and that was 'going some.'

A sort of *table d'hôte* luncheon is provided at a station about halfway between Yokohama and Tokyo. It is passed through the open window by the vendors, including a pot of tea, a bottle of mineral water, or some other soft drink if preferred. We were curious to see how our stoical gentleman opposite would construe the dining amenities, and it was worth the price of admission to note the obsequious vigilance of the wife toward her lord and the high-and-mighty way in which he 'mopped it up.' Without a word he handed her a few coins. She bought two luncheons from the platform boy, handed one to her husband and laid her own on the seat, meanwhile turning her face away from him while he partook. When he had finished, she 'cleared the table' by dumping the scraps on the floor of the car while he resumed his newspaper. Then, picking up her own food, she stepped across the car and ate it while standing, with her back turned. Of course — if you don't fancy such customs on a railway train, you can look out of the window. The last straw, however, came just as the train pulled into Tokyo, when the dutiful wife picked up the folded undershirt and handed it to her liege lord with her head bowed. Stripping himself to the waist, as before, he put it on, and then, for the first time since the train left Yokohama, he got off his hunkers, slipped on his *geta* and left the car without a word, the submissive wife following meekly behind.

The habit of squatting on the hunkers is as old as humanity itself. It prevails universally throughout the Orient. Practically the only exceptions in Japan are the rickshaw coolies, the calves of whose legs are abnormally developed owing to their constant exercise. Your average Japanese, Chinese, Hindu coolie or Egyptian fellahin is a slimshanked, scissor-legged individual, who can squat all day long with his knees under his chin, even to the point of taking a nap. It was a novel experience to enter a bank, a railway station, or any other public institution where there were seats in abundance, to find a dozen natives squatting around on the floor waiting for whatever service was coming to them. Furthermore, those who know say it is the most restful position imaginable, which would seem to be borne out by the absence of chairs in the native homes throughout the Far East.

TOKYO

Taking it by and large, Tokyo, the capital of Japan, was anything but an attractive city prior to the earthquake. Any Oriental city minus sewers, with a population of two millions, suffering from an attack of Western progress and cheap modernization, would be apt to create a bizarre impression on the foreign visitor. The Ginza, the principal shopping street of that vast metropolis, looms in my memory as an unpaved highway of dust and dirt, over which were spread a myriad telegraph and telephone wires, intermixed with the feed wires of the city's trolley system, all strung on a crazy lot of poles careening in every direction and threatening to fall on the passer-by. The cars looked as if they had been imported from some city in the United States after having been in use for a score of years. The perspiring mob of natives which hung from the straps within, and stuck like flies to the running-boards without, as the ramshackle old fabrics lurched their way along a perilous roadbed, was more suggestive of the old Brooklyn Bridge 'rush hour' of a quarter-century ago than anything I witnessed during our long trip.

The Sumida River flows through the center of the city, besides which there are hundreds of canals, all of the consistency of thick soup, from which arose a stench that would stain furniture. And — if such a thing could be —

the architectural conglomeration of this great thorough-fare was even more of an offense to the eye than were the waterways to the nostrils. Side by side with the typical Japanese house of brown wood and *shoji*, or paper screens, stood two-storied buildings of brick, stucco, and corrugated-iron roofs, with plate-glass windows and possessing a common identity of mongrel vulgarity and ugliness. 'It's an ill wind,' etc. If the terrible earthquake and conflagration accomplished nothing else, they served a good purpose by sweeping those leprous-looking business blocks from the face of the earth.

When the traveler realizes that the city of Tokyo covers about sixty square miles, he can form some slight conception of the terrific havoc wrought by an earthquake which, in combination with the conflagration which followed, wiped out approximately half of it, including some one hundred and fifty thousand souls. Among the notable places destroyed were the ancient Temple of Kwannon, the Imperial Theater, the Government buildings, and the University of Tokyo, with its magnificent surroundings. Fortunately, the Imperial Palace was spared, owing to its having been surrounded by massive stone walls and a series of moats. The strictly native architecture of the Palace alone entitles it to a visit. A drive through picturesque Shiba Park, with its ancient temples and mausoleums of the later Shoguns, will richly repay all the time one can give to it. Here also is located the famous Maple Club Restaurant where the wealthy class of Japanese entertain lavishly. In Octagonal Hall, in the Temple of the Second Shogun, will be found the finest specimens of gold lacquer in existence, together with a splendid display of native carvings, sculpture, and paintings. Also Tokyo's mammoth bell, standing ten feet high and weighing fifteen tons. In Ueno Park, where the annual Cherry Blossom

Festival is held, will be found the Imperial Library of nearly three hundred and fifty thousand volumes; the Imperial Museum, Academy of Fine Arts, the largest lantern in the country, an ancient pagoda, and a very impressive bronze Buddha. A visit to the palatial home of Mr. Asano, Japan's multi-millionaire, will be found quite worth while.

There is one beautiful spot in this ancient city, which has been an influential factor in the formation of Japanese character since 1703. That it may remain untouched for all time will be the earnest prayer of every traveler who has stepped within its borders. I refer to the little cemetery adjoining the venerable Sengakuji or Spring Hill Temple, renowned from time immemorial as the resting place of the Forty-Seven Ronins whose romantic story will live as long as the soul of man is quickened by deeds of chivalry. Rome without the Coliseum would be no more of an anachronism than Japan without that little cemetery. In this hallowed spot the graves of these forty-seven warriors, encircling that of their lord for whom they sacrificed their lives, have been loyally tended by succeeding generations for two hundred and twenty-two years. The thrilling narrative goes 'way back into feudal times and typifies, as does nothing else in Japanese history, the Samurai's uncompromising and unswerving fidelity to his code. Listen, then, to the story of the Forty-Seven Ronins whose deeds have inspired the worship of the Japanese nation for nearly two and a quarter centuries.

In the province of Harima, early in the eighteenth century, there lived a daimyo, or territorial baron, Asano Takumi no Kami by name, who was Lord of the Castle at Ako. While at Yedo (ancient Tokyo) in attendance at the Shogun's palace, Asano was appointed to take charge of the reception and entertainment of an envoy of the Mikado — a most important ceremony. Being more of a warrior than a diplomat, Asano called to his aid another lord, Kotsuké no Suké, who was well versed in court etiquette, with an itching palm in the bargain. Resenting the limited size of Asano's fees, he grossly humiliated him in various ways while imparting the desired instruction. When, however, he went so far as insultingly to command his long-suffering pupil to lace his shoe, Asano, in a burst of anger, drew his dirk and slashed him in the face. Kotsuké would have been killed on the spot but for the interference of one of the Shogun's officers who rushed in and gave him a chance for escape. To degrade the royal palace by a private brawl was an offense to be wiped out only by death and confiscation. Asano was sentenced to immediate suicide by *harakiri* (disemboweling), which he performed that very night. His estate was confiscated, his family declared extinct, and all the members of his clan disbanded, becoming *ronins* or wanderers, literally men without a lord or a home. Forty-seven of them, under the leadership of Oishi Kuranosuké, Asano's principal retainer, determined to avenge their lord, and here is where the peculiar character of the ancient Japanese vendetta is shown.

To fail in avenging one's self on his enemy meant social ostracism. Contrariwise, to do so involved inevitable capital punishment. One of those peculiar contradictions, prescribed by custom, prohibited by law, despite which latter all of the forty-seven were ready to lay down their lives, if in so doing they might avenge their beloved master. Kotsuké, noted for his avarice, for which he was the most heartily despised man in the countryside, appreciated the situation and surrounded himself with a vastly increased body of retainers — he was taking no chances. Realizing that it was going to be a long, waiting game, the forty-seven, in order to give Kotsuké no cause for suspicion, decided to separate and await their opportunity for a united attack. Accordingly, they left Yedo and entered into various trades in other cities — the last thing a Samurai would ever dream of doing, a tradesman being infinitely beneath him in caste. And so they lulled Kotsuké into a false sense of security and bided their time. Even Oishi, their leader, in order to aid in carrying out the deception to its uttermost limit, discarded his wife and children, went to Kyoto and lived with a harlot, with whom he embarked upon a prolonged orgy of drunkenness and debauchery. Of course, all this information reached Kotsuké's ears through the reports of his spies. After two years' unbroken vigilance, he became, at last, fully convinced of his safety and let down his guard. Then things happened.

At midnight, on the 30th of January, 1703, during a heavy snowstorm, the forty-seven ronins attacked Kotsuké's house in a body, put his retainers to the sword, and dragged the pusillanimous wretch from an outhouse where he was hidden. Following the usual procedure, they gave the miserable man the chance to die by his own hand by committing *harakiri*, thus saving his face. Being too much of a coward to take his own life, there remained nothing for the ronins to do but decapitate him in accordance with their code. Having accomplished their mission, they took the head and marched to the Temple Sengakuji, where their lord had been buried two years previously, and laid it on his grave with appropriate ceremonies. Then followed the inevitable official sentence which they had anticipated for over two years, condemning all of them to perform *harakiri*. They were accordingly assigned to several daimyos, whose duty it was to see the sentence carried out, after which they were buried in the same cemetery with their lord, where their graves may be seen tc this day. In a little chapel beside the Sengakuji Temple are enshrined the sculptured effigies of the forty-seven men and their master.

There were several old men, one of them seventy-seven years, also two or three as young as sixteen. Near by will be found a diminutive well of pure spring water, over which is posted the following inscription:

> This is the well in which the head was washed.
> You must not wash your hands or your feet here.

In a little grove on the hillside is an enclosure maintained by voluntary contributions, around which are ranged forty-seven tombstones, with a monument in the center, each carrying its modest tribute of water and incense for the comfort of the departed spirit. Such are the loving ministrations which have been going on for two hundred and twenty-two years. As time moulders these eloquent mementoes of a day that is forever gone, they are renewed by following generations as an ever-living testimonial to the undying loyalty of the Forty-Seven Ronins to their lord.

YOSHIWARA

Nowhere in the civilized world is that most ancient of all professions, the courtesan, so gorgeously arrayed and so brazenly presented as in the notorious Yoshiwara. This most industrious and profitable department of Tokyo's municipal government has been carried on uninterruptedly, in its present location on the northern outskirts of the city, since the year 1656. Over no other whited sepulchre on the face of the earth has that ivy which 'climbs the crumbling walls to decorate decay' been trained with such egregious frankness or with greater financial success. For over two hundred and fifty years Japanese girls were regularly and legally sold into the vilest slavery imaginable, not only at the Yoshiwara, but in similar places in other large cities. And — their only hope of release was to save enough money to purchase their liberty from the brothel-keepers who had bought them. In 1900, however, as a result of the unceasing efforts of the Salvation Army, aided by one of the Tokyo daily papers, which had awakened to the necessity for at least a partial house-cleaning, a law was passed which enabled a girl to free herself of her shameful bondage by declaring her intention to the police authorities. There was an immediate exodus of four hundred inmates of the district, which number, before the year was passed, had increased to over eleven hundred, who left either with or without the consent of their owners.

Centuries of stoical self-repression, ancestor-worship, and cultivation of the military spirit are largely responsible for Japan's callous and indifferent attitude toward her women. Include in these racial characteristics the utter lack of any expression in the Japanese tongue corresponding to the word 'love,' the national custom of the parents in selecting their son's wife, and the ridiculous ease with which he can divorce her if he so desires — and we have an illuminating explanation of the incident in the train en route from Yokohama, the immemorial custom of the wife trailing along behind her husband on the street instead of walking at his side — not to mention governmental sanction of the Yoshiwara and participation in the financial profits derived from that unholy traffic, which includes between three and five thousand licensed courtesans in the segregated section of Tokyo alone. And — what is true of Tokyo is equally true of every large city in the country.

It would be difficult to imagine any place, at home or abroad, more dismal and disillusioning than Yoshiwara during the day. The æsthetic tendencies of the Japanese are the one thing that make a night visit tolerable, hence the title by which that section of Japan's capital is known throughout the Orient: 'The Nightless City.' It is distinctly one of the sights of Tokyo and touted accordingly by every native guide and police officer who is interested in entertaining the stranger within their gates.   Furthermore, it is considered good form to make a visit to the place. Of course, a man accompanied by a woman may possibly over-hear some remarks, in perfectly good English, from the habitués, that he would ordinarily prefer to avoid. That and the staring interest always excited by the foreigner is about all the attention he will attract.

The first feature that catches the eye as we approach the 'reservation' is a huge block of a building some hundreds of yards long and almost square, resembling a barracks more than anything else. Towering above the surrounding tea-houses like Gulliver among the Lilliputians, it looks as if it might accommodate the whole population of the place. Entering the enclosure between two massive iron gates guarded by two police officers, posted there to regulate traffic, one may park his car while exploring the interior. Once on the inside, under the brilliant illumination of the electric light, the spot is suggestive of that section of a circus where all the wild-animal cages are placed end to end on either side of a wide pathway so as to provide sufficient room for pedestrians going in opposite directions. The place is laid out on the lines of a small city, with un-paved streets about twenty-five feet in width, running at right angles. The squares are filled with rows of typical one-story tea-houses, known as *hikité chaya* — 'tea-houses which lead by the hand' — assignation houses in fact, where one with the money to pay for a bit of refreshment and some *geisha* music may enjoy a degree of privacy impossible in the big barracks.

Most of these tea-houses, however, are used for display windows. The front room on the ground floor is about twenty feet square and stands open to its full width on the street, with the addition of a row of vertical bars of the

THE FRAIL SISTERHOOD OF YOSHIWARA — ONE OF THE SOURCES OF TOKYO'S MUNICIPAL REVENUE

thickness of one's thumb, placed six inches apart and extending from the floor to the ceiling. Halfway back from the bars of this 'cage,' seated in a semicircle on the floor, are the inmates of the house: ten to fifteen highly rouged and daintily coiffured, diminutive Japanese girls from fifteen to twenty-five years of age, tastefully gowned in the most exquisitely fashioned and brilliantly colored kimonos imaginable. Yes — some of them are very attractive. In front of each girl stands a lacquered table about twelve inches square and six inches high, containing a small mirror and all the toilet requisites in the way of paints, powders, and pencils usually in demand by these frail daughters of pleasure. And there they sit, like a row of marionettes, rouging their cheeks, penciling their eyebrows, adjusting their elaborately built-up coiffures, or toying with a lipstick.

Their eyes light up with interest only when a possible patron stops in front of the cage for a critical observation. The great question, Will he come in or go next door? inspires each and every one of them to look her prettiest for the moment. Meanwhile a typical 'barker,' consisting of a husky Japanese, seated on the doorstep, explains in stentorian tones to the temporarily interested spectator, and to the passers-by as well, the superior quality of the wares of that particular house and the remarkably small financial outlay necessary for their acquirement, which latter is also displayed in big figures in the shop window. If the visitor happens to be an American, he may be assured that the vociferous announcer will spot him and address him most eloquently in his own language.

The remarkable feature of this display is that the inmates of each window are most attractively and uniformly gowned in accordance with a definite color scheme, which is not duplicated by any other window on that block. Gorgeous kimonos in all the hues of the rainbow — gold, red and blue predominating — brilliantly embroidered with the conventional dragon and exotic flowers. A wondrous exhibition, indeed, accompanied by every evidence of a master hand. The most exclusive houses, however, do not display their women publicly; in such the patron makes his selection from a series of photographs. And — at the far end of the street stands the most significant display of all: the hospital.

For three hundred years previous to the earthquake, one of the most popular diversions of the people — contemporaneous with Cherry-Blossom time — was the annual three-day ceremony of the procession of the courtesans: *Oiran Dochu* — a garish affair upon which the more intelligent class has frowned for some years and which will probably never be resumed. Yoshiwara is not a generic name as so many travelers imagine. It is the name of a little town on the Tokaido Road from which some of the most beautiful of these frail sisters came to take up their residence in Tokyo when the Shogun established his palace there in the seventeenth century, since which time the segregated district has been so designated.

CHAPTER III

NIKKO'S SUNNY SPLENDOR

But aye from ruined faiths and old
That droop and die, fall bruisèd seeds;
And when new flowers and faiths unfold,
They're lovelier flowers, they're kindlier creeds.
                                        DON MARQUIS

THERE is a saying upon which the world traveler in the Orient will occasionally stumble, to the effect that 'What the Taj Mahal is to India, Nikko is to Japan.' This statement is worthy of all emphasis despite its triteness, and is tacitly intended to serve notice upon the tourist that to visit either country without making a pilgrimage to those particular shrines would argue a most unfortunate lack of discrimination. One might just as well visit Rome with the expectation of being able subsequently to explain how he came to miss Saint Peter's.

The one outstanding characteristic that the Taj Mahal and Nikko have in common is that both represent the nth degree in the development of a radically different mortuary architecture by two widely dissimilar peoples of Mongolian origin. They also illustrate most profoundly the ennobling influence of woman on the one hand and a cynical lack of it on the other.

The tremendous strides made by modern Japan in every avenue of human activity have had a tendency to blind us to her great age. Nikko has been her chief religious center for hundreds of years preceding the Christian era. The most ancient writings indicate that from the very dawn of her history there have been temples in this vicinity. In fact, there are definite records of those which were built early in the eighth century. Nikko, the interpretation of which picturesque word is 'Sunny Splendor,' lies ninety miles by rail north of Tokyo, on the slopes of the Nikko-Zan, 'Mountains of the Sun's Brightness,' seventeen hundred feet above sea-level. It is, without question, the most beautiful spot in all Japan, and constitutes a brilliant example of that amazing capacity of the Japanese for blending decorative art with Nature in so winning and unobtrusive a fashion as completely to captivate the visitor.

The whole mountain-side is covered with ancient Shinto and Buddhistic temples, upon which the passing centuries have laid a gentle and mellowing hand. *Torii*, temples, lanterns, shrines, and pagodas punctuate the traveler's steps as he climbs higher and higher up the slope until, not far from the summit, he reaches the magnificent mausoleum of the first and greatest of the Shoguns or military governors — Iyeyasu, the founder of the Tokugawa Dynasty, who was buried with great regal pomp and circumstance in 1617; also that of his grandson, Iyemitsu, third Shogun, a trifle less impressive, which stands near by. After a day spent in this marvelous spot, one finds it comparatively easy to believe that it took six thousand of the most accomplished craftsmen and artists twelve years to complete the mausoleum of Iyeyasu alone, at a cost of over $10,000,000. Also, he will have become surfeited with temple glories for the remainder of his sojourn in Japan.

It is a matter of history that all the temples built by the Shoguns throughout the empire were paid for by the daimyos, or lords and barons of less degree, upon whom they levied heavy tribute, who in turn wrenched it from the peasantry. Thus was the wealth and power of the Shogunate maintained and the daimyos prevented from financing revolutions. Incidentally, it is an eloquent commentary upon the unspeakable 'nerve' of these old despots that they should have selected this sacred hill, Japan's Holy of Holies, as the final resting-place for their relatively unimportant ashes. From time immemorial it has been the custom of Oriental potentates and feudal lords to build costly temples to their various deities in atonement for their sins. So far as known, however, these two exceedingly retiring and modest individuals, Iyeyasu and Iyemitsu, are the only ones who managed to include their bones with the magnificent temples they built on the slopes of Nikko.

Doubtless old Iyeyasu and his grandson had determined to go Nikko one better by locating their tombs near the summit. It is quite possible that their final instructions as to the disposition of their earthly remains were based upon one of the immemorial, unwritten laws of the land: that which made it an offense punishable by death for any one to be caught looking down from an elevation of any kind upon a procession of royalty or the ruling clan which might be passing that way. So strictly was this despotic mandate carried out in olden times that a royal cortège ambling along the road was preceded by a number of spotters, whose particular job it was to see to it that whatever corresponded to the curtains and the window-shutters of that early period were decorously closed and the household occupants completely under cover, else that unfortunate householder had his headpiece dexterously removed on the spot. If any thoughtless peasant happened to top a hill, the hither side of which gave an unobstructed view upon the highroad, coincidentally with the passing of royalty, he was playing in hard luck and no mistake. As a matter of fact, even in these effete times, any Occidental visitor who, either from a lack of knowledge or disregard thereof, should violate this ancient point of etiquette by standing at an upper window or on any commanding elevation during the passing of an Imperial procession would give great offense and render himself liable to an exceedingly disagreeable experience.

When one appreciates the antiquity of Japan's Imperial Family, which (as native historians would have us believe) antedates the Christian era by several centuries, coupled with the old-time, universally accepted divine origin of the Emperor, that extreme religious reverence in which the nation has always held its sovereigns is quite understandable. From time out of mind, down to the present day, even the name of the reigning Emperor has not been known to the great majority of the people. Even among those to whom it was known, it was considered exceedingly bad form, if not irreligious, to mention it. For instance, the name by which the former ruler, Mutsuhito, was known to his subjects was *Meiji Tenno*, the latter word meaning 'Heavenly Emperor' and *Meiji* referring to the period of his reign. That modern civilization is still more or less of a veneer in Japan is indicated by the shocking action of the celebrated General Nogi, who, as recently as 1912, at the age of sixty-three, committed *harakiri* coincidentally with the death of Emperor Mutsuhito, in order that he might continue to serve his royal master in the spirit land. Following Japanese custom, General Nogi's elderly wife joined him in his frightful suicide by cutting her throat.

That 'divinity which doth hedge a king' does not seem to have been at all impaired by the fact that many Japanese rulers, even down to comparatively recent times, were the offspring of concubines. In other words, it was a wise prince who knew his own mother. This is another one of those eloquent instances where royal precedent, enjoying the sanction of centuries, throws additional light on the attitude of the present-day Japanese male toward his women-kind. Harking back to those early days, it would seem reasonable to impute to Messrs. Iyeyasu and Iyemitsu a thoroughly understandable determination to make it rather difficult for any ordinary mortal to 'look down' on them, even in death. And, by the same token, any visitor whose eyes may happen to light on this page will feel much more at home in the peaceful atmosphere and beautiful surroundings of the temples along the lower terraces, where the dappled sunlight breaks through the tops of the majestic cryptomerias, than he will in the partial gloom of the upper reaches. Nevertheless, he should make the climb.

Nikko, the town, consists principally of one long, rambling street lying at the base of the mountain, along which rushes the busy little river Daiya. Two excellent hotels, the Nikko and the Kanaya, afford all the comforts of home to the traveler, who can put in three or four days very profitably. At the far end of the town the sacred bridge — a brilliant, red-lacquered structure, eighty-three feet long by twenty-two wide — connects the famous avenue of cryptomeria trees, over forty miles long, with the approach up the mountain-side to the temples and the tombs. This bridge is for the exclusive use of the Emperor or other royal dignitaries on the exceedingly rare occasions they go up to Nikko to worship at those shrines. Along the riverbank for several hundred yards stand fifty-odd ancient stone statues, picturing Amida Buddha in the attitude of meditation, all discolored by the hand of Time and covered with lichen. On the base of each will be found numerous small stones representing prayers, deposited by pilgrims. As one gazes up the mountain-side, the stately cryptomerias, which border the pathway, tower one hundred and twenty-five feet above the ground, dwarfing the forest of firs and pines by which they are surrounded.

Nestling in the dark green foliage, on four successive terraces, as the visitor climbs, will be found the gorgeous memorial temples of Iyeyasu, in all their prodigal colorfulness of brilliant vermilion lacquer and mythological carvings in faint blues, grays, blacks, white, and gold, with a profusion of antiquated bronze and stone lanterns. It simply beggars the imagination to attempt their description. There is nothing to equal them in the country. On one will be found the original carving of the world-famous Three Monkeys, reproductions of which are on sale in every art store in Christendom, each one of which has his forepaws, respectively, over his eyes, ears, and mouth: a most eloquent sermon in pantomime from what might be termed the Knocker's text: 'See no evil. Hear no evil. Speak no evil.'

We enter the shrine through a mammoth granite *torii* which dates back four centuries, at the side of which stands a five-storied, lacquered pagoda, over one hundred feet in height, which was built in 1659, with the signs of the zodiac carved around its base. Near by stands the gate of the Two Kings, covered with carved figures of elephants, lions, tigers, unicorns, and dragons in a bewildering variety of colorful and decorative detail. Close at hand is the Hall of the Three Buddhas, consisting of three huge statues of Amida Buddha, twenty-seven feet high. A palatial stable for the sacred horse, an artistic marble and granite cistern for pilgrims' ablutions, and a tall cylindrical copper column surmounted by the lotus-flower and covered with mystic Buddhistic symbols to ward off evil influences, complete the list of funerary accessories, all of which were part and parcel of the royal ceremonies of interment in those early days of the seventeenth century. In addition there is the Shinto Abbot's quaint house and garden and a mammoth bronze bell, six feet high by four wide, which no one is permitted to touch except the priest, who sounds the hours at dawn and the close of day: all mute evidences of a religious devo-

NIKKO'S ANCIENT COLONNADE OF BUDDHAS

tion which has largely departed with the arrival of modernism. At one time there were three thousand priests officiating in the Nikko temples. Now there are less than fifty.

Above and beyond these resplendent displays will be found the final ascent, consisting of two hundred massive granite steps, which terminate at a tomb of austere simplicity within a stone wall. In the foreground is a low stone table, a small bronze pagoda, an incense burner, a pair of fierce-looking bronze dogs, and a bronze stork with a candlestick in its mouth. The archæologist may feel like sitting down with the implements of his trade about him and figuring out the symbolism of it all. The ordinary traveler, however, will note that the two hundred steps are damp and clammy, that the majestic cryptomerias towering above his head tend to shut out the sun, that moss and lichen are taking their toll of the trappings of death and that Nikko's 'Sunny Splendor' is suddenly become a figment of the imagination, so far as concerns the immediate surroundings. A fitting close for the stoical character of the Japanese Napoleon, Iyeyasu:

> The paths of glory lead but to the grave.

Acting on a sudden impulse, the source of which will inspire no speculation, one turns up his coat-collar, lights a cigar for a wee bit of uplift and says to himself, as he finds his way down the dank stairway: 'I hope to High Heaven, when the time comes for me to pass out, they'll *cache* my remains in the middle of a forty-acre field —

> '"Where the rain may rain upon it,
>   Where the sun may shine upon it,
>   Where the lamb hath lain upon it,
>   And the bee may dine upon it."'

However — it's not so bad when one gets back to his comfy

hotel with a real fire in a real grate (which is something one doesn't expect in Japan) and wishes he could be temporarily metamorphosed into a nice house-dog so he could curl up in front of it on the floor. Seated there in the gathering dusk, it was just the hour for a bit of introspection, when suddenly the air was filled with music. Deep, mellow, haunting tones, such as never were on sea or land, came rolling in and reëchoing through the halls of the house with a beauty and a sense of harmony indescribable. Utterly amazed I threw open the window and the celestial sound flowed in, exquisitely vibrant, like the waves of a vast symphony and exerting an overwhelming emotional appeal. 'Twas the Shinto priest up on the mountain-side, tolling out the knell of parting day. With a heavy billet of wood, hung like a battering-ram from a beam outside the bell, he gives two or three strokes only, a full minute apart, on that musical mass of bronze, and the harmony billows forth over the land 'like the benediction that follows after prayer.' The strangest part of it all was the long-sustained musical vibration which reëchoed through the hills apparently for minutes instead of seconds. This was no illusion. Japan being subject to earthquakes, these massive temple bells, wherever located, will always be found hung close to the ground and under a heavily hooded structure which impels the volume of sound downward. In Nikko the sloping mountain-side and the valley below are natural conductors. I think if I were the Almighty, I would stoop very low over Nikko-Zan, the 'Mountains of the Sun's Brightness,' both at morn and at evening. He for whom the morning stars sang together must surely have an appreciative ear. Also, I think I'd have a fairly decent mansion prepared, not only for the inspired artisan who cast that heavenly bell, but for the Shinto priest who was too wise a musician to over-play his hand.

After the inevitable surfeit of Nikko's temple glories, there remaineth a rest and an almost complete change of scene for him who can center his interest on what to me is Japan's greatest natural attraction: the stately crypto-meria trees, or Japanese cedar. These wonderful conifers are rivaled in size and beauty only by our gigantic Sequoias on the California Sierra. Towering in solemn majesty from one hundred to one hundred and twenty-five feet above the ground, with perfectly smooth, soft, brown-tinted trunks for two thirds of their height, the geometrical regularity of their dark green conical tops limned against the bright blue of the sky is tremendously impressive. They embody in very truth the all-pervasive religious atmosphere of the place, without which the gorgeous man-made temples at their feet would lose their entire significance. Most truly 'the groves were God's first temples,' in comparison with which even these marvelous fabrics are as sounding brass and tinkling cymbal. As the poet Knibbs so eloquently puts it:

We worship not what men have made: no thing so small is our
    desire.
The little words of men that die, the little thoughts of men that
    dream
Shall perish in their utterance: and build for these an altar fire?
Our creed is written in the sky, our song in the eternal stream.

It would almost seem that the Japanese craftsman, realiz-ing that his amazing capacity for mechanical detail had left him barren of that 'divine insanity of noble minds' upon which all true art rests, had been driven to seek an appropriate setting for his handiwork and found it under the cryptomerias on the slopes of Nikko. From that far-distant time down to the present, old Dame Nature has conspired with Amida Buddha to help the good work along to the genuine uplifting of every sincere pilgrim soul be he

Greek or Barbarian, bond or free, wise or unwise. So mote
it be!

The story of the Nikko shrines would not be complete
without the ancient tale of how these wonderful cryptomerias came to be planted. Reference has already been
made to the custom of the Shoguns of levying tribute upon
their dependent daimyos for the building of various temples throughout the land. It happened, when Iyeyasu's
rather expensive mausoleum was started, that certain
daimyos up in the mountainous districts, where graft was
scarce because of the poverty of the people, did their part
by sending down thousands of young cryptomeria trees,
with the necessary laborers to plant them. Tradition states
that they kept up the supply for twenty years. At any rate,
Nikko has a Cryptomeria Avenue forty miles long leading
from the town nearly halfway to Tokyo, not to mention the
thousands of trees on the mountain-side under which the
numerous temples have been built. This Cryptomeria
Avenue may be followed in a rickshaw for four miles from
Nikko to a sort of suburban station, where the departing
traveler may catch the train. And it is amply worth while.
The tree-tops meet one hundred and twenty-five feet overhead, forming a perfect bower which excludes the sun and
renders a ride or a walk an undiluted pleasure. And so, we
have a Japanese version of the Biblical aphorism: 'The
stone which the builders rejected is become the head of
the corner'; for the fabulous cost of Iyeyasu's mausoleum
multiplied ten times over could not produce that magnificent avenue of cryptomerias upon which Nikko's fame
throughout the world of beauty will rest for centuries to
come.

How a nation with such wonderful examples of Nature's
arboreal glories constantly before its eyes can devote itself
to the cultivation of that atrocious art of tree-dwarfing is a

mystery. Here in America we prune the superfluous shoots of a tree in order to strengthen its growth and send the life-giving sap into the branches. Conversely, the Japanese prune the roots of a young tree possessing the potentialities of a forest monarch and confine its development to a flower pot: an inhuman sort of practice closely akin to that of their Chinese cousins in dwarfing their women's feet. These dwarfed trees are tended like delicate children by expert gardeners in the rôle of valets, employed by the wealthy, who carry them in their arms for daily 'consti-tutionals' in the garden where they may get the air with-out being exposed to the elements. In fact, they are re-garded as family heirlooms and are handed down from gen-eration to generation, some attaining to two and three hun-dred years of age. And this brings to mind a mammoth cryptomeria enclosed by a balustrade on the first terrace of the Iyeyasu mausoleum, which is said to have been the 'household pet' of that somber old tyrant for many years preceding his death. Tradition has it that he left instruc-tions to plant the little dwarf at the entrance to his tomb, since which time — nearly three hundred years ago — it has attained to its present magnificent growth. It's a good story and it ought to be true, if for no other reason than to demonstrate the abnormality of practicing vivisection upon trees.

Everything lies in the point of view. Prior to the intro-duction of telegraphy in Japan in 1872, there wasn't a main highway throughout the country but was lined with those superb trees. Shortly afterwards, however, in their zeal for what they considered advanced civilization, the Japanese began cutting down the age-old cryptomerias because they interfered with the advantageous display of the more up-to-date telegraph pole. A roar went up from the foreign press which finally resulted in a halt being called by the authorities, but not until the greater part of the famous Tokaido Road had been stripped.

It is a bit difficult to imagine a situation either in art or Nature in which the part is greater than the whole. And yet — that is precisely the impression one gets of all Japanese activities, as instanced in their temples, their dwarfed trees, their miniature gardens. Everything is subordinated to infinite, meticulous detail, even to the carving of a grain of rice and the training of fleas. There seems to be no sensing of an *ensemble*. It is simply impossible to imagine a Taj Mahal, a Saint Peter's, or a Notre Dame Cathedral in the Land of the Rising Sun or a native mind capable of conceiving them. Doubtless, environment has a great deal to do with such a limited outlook. With 60,000,000 people spread over an area of less than 147,000 square miles, only twelve per cent of which is cultivable, the necessity for intensive application in every walk of life, accompanied by a correspondingly circumscribed spiritual horizon, would seem to be inevitable.

LAKE CHUZENJI

Over a mountain pass three thousand feet above sea-level, about eleven miles from Nikko, lies picturesque Lake Chuzenji, filling the crater of an extinct volcano: a most restful body of pure spring water seven miles long by three wide, with a depth of over five hundred feet. The trail runs along the bank of a brawling mountain stream and leads through most rugged and attractive scenery. Yes — this is a trip we must not miss. It can be done nicely in a day. The approved transportation is a tandem-rickshaw or two coolies — one to pull, the other to push — made necessary by a climb of over a thousand feet. You'll be ready to stop for luncheon at a typical tea-house where you can get some tea and cakes or a nice bit of broiled fish. On reaching the summit of the pass, the trail drops five hundred feet into a beautiful valley and passes Kegon Falls on the way. This fall has a most scenic setting with a drop of two hundred and fifty feet. For many years it seems to have exerted a baleful influence over certain Japanese young men with Nietszchean tendencies, several of whom commit suicide there every season by throwing themselves over the brink.

Rising from the level of the lake, Mount Nantai-Zan, with an altitude of eighty-five hundred feet, dominates the whole region. A number of shrines at the summit attract about twenty thousand pilgrims every summer. Along the trail one meets with frequent pack-trains of horses going to and from Nikko with supplies for the lake settlements and the copper mines back in the mountain district. The visitor will be amused to see the horses shod with straw shoes instead of the usual metal. Incidentally, that's a custom that holds good all over the country with beasts of burden: horses and bullocks alike. The next thing he will notice is that at least half of the rural natives in charge of these pack-trains are husky Japanese girls and it takes a quick eye to distinguish which from 'tother. The Lakeside Hotel provides excellent fare for the traveler and the trout-fishing is good. There have been folk visiting the lake who have gone so far as to say they would rather go trout-fishing than make a pilgrimage to some of the shrines at the summit of Nantai-Zan. Motor-boats, sail- and row-boats, not to mention the native sampan, are available for all aquatic needs, and one will always find plenty of good company amongst English-speaking cottagers if he would like to settle down in this lovely spot for a few weeks, there being quite a number who come up from Tokyo to get away from the hot weather.

CORMORANT FISHING

Shortly after my return home from my long trip, I was asked by an enthusiastic disciple of Izaak Walton, who was contemplating a holiday in Japan, if there was any trout-fishing in that country. There is, indeed, the most remarkable trout-fishing in Japan of any country in the world. It differs, somewhat, from the American method in that it is done at night and with cormorants instead of with a fly rod. Furthermore — like unto many other Japanese processes — it is a dead-sure thing. True, this detracts a bit from the delightful uncertainty of the sport as we know it here, but that is only an added incentive for the traveler to visit Gifu, on the Nagara River, and see how it is done. Gifu is a typical native town of about sixty thousand population, lying midway between Tokyo and Kyoto on the old Tokaido Road. Sometimes the railway train stops there, sometimes not. The city of Nagoya is not far distant, however, and all trains stop there. The first thing to challenge the wonder of the visitor is that these Nagara River fishermen are not in the business for either their health or for sport. They are market fishermen. Think of going to market for a nice mess of trout, ye experts with a two-and-a-half-ounce rod and a dry fly.

Never mountain stream was more crystal-clear than the deep, swift-flowing current of the Nagara as it winds its serpentine way through the narrow valley that shuts it in on either side. Your choice of two or three native hotels on the opposite side of the river from the town will see you nicely fixed for the afternoon. About 8 P.M. you will be escorted to your boat, a gable-roofed affair, with lanterns hung along the eaves, plenty of cushions and a diminutive brazier in the stern for cooking the trout that you are going to buy from the fishermen. It all sounds a bit hectic until

the real business of the evening begins. For — be it known
— all you are going to do is to sit on the side lines in com-
parative darkness and let them fish as can fish while you
look on.

While your native poler directs your boat to a good vantage-point, you hear a hollow sound coming from up the
river as of some one beating an empty keg with a bung-
starter. Suddenly a bright light flashes from a curve in the
stream above and a boat glides by with a fagot fire in an
open-work iron basket hung from an iron rod extending
from the bow, eight big cormorants perched on the gunwale
on either side, with four husky Japanese fishermen ready for
action. To each man is assigned his especial job as follows:
In the bow stands the master with twelve strings running
through the fingers of his left hand to as many birds, which
he handles with surpassing skill and rapidity. Next, stands
his assistant who handles four birds. Behind him comes
the fellow with the baton — a stout piece of bamboo, with
which he keeps up a constant tattoo on the gunwale, accompanied by shouts and cries to keep the birds up to their
work. It brought to mind that aphorism of David Har-
um's: 'It's a good thing for a dog to have fleas; it keeps him
from dwelling on the fact that he *is* a dog.' In the stern
stands the steersman with a big oar. Seven boats similarly
manned constitute a fleet and they fish every night from
May until October — the end of the season.

And such fishing! The blazing fagots in the iron basket attract the fish. The cormorants are dropped overboard and
the way they dart and dive hither and thither after their
prey is something to see. Here is where the remarkable
ability of the master comes in. It is his particular job to see
that the birds don't foul their lines, otherwise they won't
work. Each bird has a fiber ring around his neck which
prevents him from swallowing anything but the small, un-

marketable fish. The larger fish lodge in his pouch. He is drawn to the boat, lifted up and made to disgorge the fish, which drops into a bucket in the bottom of the boat. Once more he is placed in the water and the operation is repeated until the birds grow tired, or, having their appetite sated, refuse to work any longer. Each well-trained cormorant will catch in this way from four hundred to four hundred and fifty fish in a night. Multiply that by sixteen birds and you have an idea of the importance of the industry.

This cormorant fishing has been going on for untold centuries. The birds are caught and trained when young. If properly cared for they will live for twenty years. One most interesting and humorous feature of the proceeding is that each individual bird has his regular number and his regular perch on the gunwale. He is put into the water in accordance with his importance as a fisher, and that order is never changed, unless, perchance, some heedless bird goes out of his turn in the excitement, and then there is the devil to pay. They all stop fishing and begin squabbling among themselves until the whole bunch is taken back on the boat and the ' play ' starts all over again with nobody ' cheating.' After the night's work is done, the squadron is beached, each bird examined by the master to see if he has had enough to eat, in which event they are all placed on their separate perches facing outward where they enjoy themselves in a variety of ways until the next night when they are once more put to work.

CHAPTER IV

ANCIENT KYOTO

When you and I behind the veil are past.,
O but the long, long while the world shall last,
Which of our coming and departure heeds
As the Sev'n Seas should heed a pebble-cast.

OMAR

KYOTO — the serene, the city of repose, the most distinctive city in the country, the least spoiled by the infiltration of Western progress and withal the most friendly: for a thousand years previous to 1868 the residence of successive generations of Mikados. With a population approximating 700,000, characterized by modern business activities, it still retains its mediæval atmosphere together with national leadership in art, literature, and religion. Surrounded on three sides by mountains, supplied by crystal-pure water from Lake Biwa, a few miles away, it is blessed with such sanitation as prevails in no other city in Japan and constitutes a haven of rest for the traveler. Furthermore, it is headquarters for brocades and embroidery, also cloisonné, bronze, porcelain, and pottery. Indicative of the rivalry between Kyoto and Tokyo — the people of the former refer to those of the latter as 'ruffians,' while Tokyo returns the compliment with the epithet 'monkeys in brocade,' referring to Kyoto's preëminence in that field of manufacture. It makes no difference whether the traveler approaches Japan from the north or the south, he will be ready to settle down in Kyoto for a few days before proceeding farther. There are two excellent hotels in the city: The Miyako, up on the hillside on the outskirts, and The Kyoto down in the center of town. Both make a specialty of entertaining foreign guests. The view from the elevation of The Miyako is especially attractive.

Entirely apart from the sight-seeing feature of your stay in this ancient capital, you will want to do some shopping. And you'll find the cleverest lot of retail merchants in Kyoto that there are in Japan. They can spot the *nouveau riche* a mile away and what they do to him and to her is a great plenty. By that I do not mean to insinuate swindling tactics. I do mean to say that, in common with the practices of retail dealing throughout the Orient, neither your Japanese nor your Chinese merchant shows his finer goods at the outset. If he can sell you something 'made in Germany,' he will do it because he has a very keen sense of the eternal fitness of things and regards an easy sale more or less in the light of broadcasting his pearls.

And again — don't do your shopping in a motor-car; not that there is any particular disadvantage in it, but because you cannot begin to see certain parts of the city as satisfactorily in a motor-car as you can in a rickshaw, which latter is really the correct thing in leisurely Kyoto. They will try to convince you to the contrary at the hotels. Don't listen to them. Also, bear in mind that your courier, or guide, or chauffeur, or rickshaw coolie are always looking for 'theirs' wherever they may take you, and they generally manage to get it. I don't need to remind you that in such instances the shopper pays for it. Occasionally you'll come across the evidence of it in a rather unusual way that will cause you to smile, not only at the tactics, but at yourself as well. Suspecting, possibly, that the presence of your guide in the vicinity may have a bearing on the price of the goods, you finally decide to defer your purchases until another day. You will be most ceremoniously bowed out, with no effort at all at detention. Later in the day you may walk downtown unaccompanied, with the idea of making your purchase minus the presence of said guide. And it's quite possible that he may accidentally come in one door (or go out) while you approach from a different direction. You imagine you can almost hear him say to the merchant in the purest of Americanees, 'Where's mine?' No — you cannot lose him.

And then, there are certain merchants who have learned the value of having one price only. You'll find them out only by making the effort to get 'yours.' It's a most interesting adventure and plenty of fun to boot. Because if you can beat a Japanese merchant at his own game, you may hand yourself all kinds of compliments. But — don't crow too soon. He wasn't born yesterday. And they are all born traders, every last mother's son of 'em. They are the smoothest lot ever. Like as not you'll find that the clerk waiting on you spent several years in the United States getting intimately acquainted with the mental processes of just such individuals as yourself. Also, it's quite possible that you may discover over the shop door a name that you have seen on Fifth Avenue, only you were not sufficiently interested in things Japanese at that time to have been impressed. Well, there won't be much difference between the prices in Kyoto and those in New York unless you happen to know values, in which event you'll be shown something 'different' for the same money. That's precisely what you have been waiting for. And when Mr. Hokkaido finds that out, he will compliment you on your perspicacity and wide experience. But — you'll have to force his hand.

Meanwhile — if he happens to be a curio dealer — he will have escorted you upstairs to a perfect little gem of a room, seated you in the easy-chair, brought you cigarettes, and tea that resembles pea soup, along with the family autograph album in which the great (?) of all nations have inscribed their honorable names and you are invited to do likewise. The inference is unescapable, and many there are who enter in at that particular gate which is wide enough to include all your Red Gap relatives. No wise traveler will buy any curios from any but absolutely well-known and reputable dealers. Even at that he should insist on guarantees of their genuineness. Don't forget that Japan has been almost wholly denuded of her art treasures. It is little less than tragic to recall how the craze for Western progress not many years ago led to the scrapping of many a priceless relic which was supposed to be old-fashioned and which would bring fabulous prices to-day. Earthquakes and fire have done the rest. About the only real chance for a genuine antique in Japan to-day is when some poverty-stricken Buddhist or Shinto temple auctions off its relics. Remember Mr. Harriman and the Daibutsu at Kamakura.

The temptation to separate a man from his money is not confined to Japan, although I must acknowledge that they have a way with them over there that has a tendency to lull the traveler into a sense of security that would seduce the elect. You can acquire the necessary information at your hotel as to the reputable merchants. There are some excellent ones specializing in damascene work, gold lacquer, cloisonné, fine silks, and bronzes, and the best of them will concede a discount on a worth-while order. But — don't forget: they will not produce their first-class stuff at the outset. They know they have a market for all time and in all countries for the 'real thing.' They'll display their brummagem, meanwhile keeping an observant eye on the buyer. If he 'falls' for it — he'll never get a look-see at the worth-while products. And, while face-saving is not quite as prevalent in Japan as it is in China, you can, by sheer thoughtlessness and lack-lustre methods, unintentionally 'nurse' the native merchant along to a point of boosting the poorer material from which he will not recede. You'll simply have to leave and come back the next day at which time, as he views it, a new deal is in order having nothing to do with yesterday's experience — and you'll likely get what you want and at a fair price if you are a good buyer.

The native merchant is not altogether to blame for his way of looking at things. He figures that if you had any sense you would save your money instead of gallivanting all over creation spending it like a drunken sailor. Under the circumstances, it's not surprising that he considers himself better able to look after it than you and so he does his best to get it away from you and give you as little as possible in return. In addition, he doesn't think you know the difference between good stuff and poor, so why should he volunteer the former when you will be perfectly content with the latter? This is a purely Oriental point of view and, based on his experience with the tourist, we will have to concede he doubtless has good reason for holding to it. In short, it's a clear case of *caveat emptor* when you are shopping in the East.

After having finished with laying in a stock of kimonos and a profusion of other plunder that you will rarely look at after you get back home, it will be well to give a thought to what this very ancient capital of Japan has to offer in the way of sight-seeing. For, be it remembered that Kyoto's attractions outnumber those of all other Japanese cities put together. One dinner down in Theater Street and a bit of *geisha* entertainment will be about all you'll crave in that direction. And it is not cheap, blowsy, and tawdry as in Tokyo, or Yokohama before the earthquake. There is nothing to offend the most fastidious and you'll enjoy the experience — just once.

The Gosho Imperial Palace, which has been maintained in its present condition since 1856, occupies twenty-six acres and is situated in the center of a beautiful and very

ancient park of two hundred and twenty acres, filled with
magnificent, age-old trees. The attendant who escorts you
through the palace will call your attention to a creaking
board in the floor just outside the Emperor's suite which,
in those good old days, constituted His Majesty's guaran-
tee against a surprise. How typically Japanese!

Then there is the ancient Shogun castle, built by our old
friend Iyeyasu in 1602 as a treasure-house. You may be
sure he never depended on anything so *spirituelle* as a
creaking board — not he. Probably that is the reason
that it was carried on with an infinitely greater degree of
grandeur than the Mikado's Palace. Nevertheless, it was
in this very place that the last of the Shoguns was shorn of
his authority when the Japanese feudal system came to an
end back in 1868, and the Mikado was restored to power
after having been under cover, so to speak, for nearly seven
hundred years. Then the capital was moved to Tokyo. It
is worthy of note that the last of the Shoguns was one
Hitotsu-bashi by name who surprised his friends by refus-
ing to commit *harakiri* and thereby finish the job right.
Instead, he retired to the country, where he lived happily
ever afterward, thus saving his head by sacrificing his
'face.'

A motor ride of a dozen miles out to beautiful Lake Biwa,
the largest in Japan, is time well spent, including a brief
run to the little hamlet of Karasaki on its shores for a visit
to the sacred mammoth pine tree. This enormous tree is
believed to be over two thousand years old. It is situated on
a picturesque peninsula with low-lying branches covering
an area of three hundred feet under which stone piers have
been built to keep them off the ground. Without question
it is one of the most curious specimens of tree growth in the
world and well worth seeing. The return trip may be varied by a boat-run through a tunnel leading from the lake

under the mountain, which constitutes Kyoto's water supply — an ingenious bit of engineering.

Kyoto's Temples

Notwithstanding your surfeit of temple visiting at Nikko, there are three holy places in Kyoto that you should not miss: Inari, Kiyomizu-dera, and Chion-in, including the famous Higashi Hongwanji as a possible fourth. They can all be done in a short day and in a motor-car. If there should happen to be a pilgrimage in progress, so much the better. You'll learn more about the Japanese on that day than at any other time. And for this reason: Japan's pilgrimages are more or less of a social nature. There are thousands of associations throughout the land including the peasantry whose devotion is based largely on their superstitions and the age-old folk-lore which tends to keep them alive. These pious folk contribute the equivalent of a penny or two each per month to a general fund. When the time for a pilgrimage comes around, generally in the summer, a certain number are chosen by lot to represent the stay-at-homes on a journey to their particular shrine, the expenses of which are defrayed by the common fund. It is a most interesting sight to watch these devotees visiting a certain temple under the garrulous guidance of one who has 'been there before.'

The Japanese takes his religion much as he does his rice. 'All's grist that comes to the mill.' It may be a Shinto or a Buddhist shrine — it makes no difference which. If there is a bell hanging outside, they give it a pull to attract the attention of the god, toss a copper in the coin box at the entrance, say a little prayer, and go on their way laughing and joking in the most innocent fashion imaginable. If there should happen to be no bell, your pilgrim will clap his hands once or twice, as much as to say to the deity, 'I just wanted you to know I was here,' and proceeds as before. Most of the invocations are in Chinese and the average zealot has no idea what they mean. For those who make the ascent of Fujiyama, for instance — and there are thousands of them every year — the prayer runs thus: *Rokkon Shojo, O Yama Kaisei* — 'May our six senses be pure and the weather on the honorable mountain be fair.'

In certain Buddhist temples will be found 'revolving libraries' some of which are twenty feet high and contain all the Buddhist scriptures. And he who turns this wheel around once acquires the same degree of merit as if he had read them all: practically the same idea as the praying wheel of the Tibetans, with their everlasting *Om mani pudme hum* — 'The Jewel in the Lotus — Amen.' At other shrines certain prayers written on slips of rice paper may be bought from the priest for a small sum, which the devout worshiper chews into a spit-ball and throws at the image of the god hard enough for it to stick. It's quite a common sight to come across these sculptured deities at the entrances of temples, covered from head to foot with these salivary pellets, which answer the same purpose as the ringing of the bell or the clapping of the hands. They are supposed to serve notice on the god that the bestower was there, on the job, and did his duty, for which he should receive the proper credit. And he goes away believing that his individual prayer will be remembered and recorded in his favor.

Similar methods employed by the priests themselves consist in sitting before an image inside the temple and tapping a resonant, hollow box with a little mallet, by the hour, in order to secure and hold the god's attention. The first time I heard that tapping on approaching a temple in Kyoto one afternoon, it sounded more like a woodpecker on a hollow limb than anything else. I spent quite a little time looking over the trees in front in order to see, if possible, what a Japanese woodpecker looked like, before I finally discovered that the sound came from the interior of the temple itself.

Following an instinct as old as humanity itself, all temples throughout the Orient are built, wherever possible, in high places. The hills surrounding Kyoto lend themselves admirably to this impulse. The great Inari Temple is a most interesting instance in kind. Inari is the goddess of rice. She is by all odds the most popular of all the various Shinto deities. There isn't a hamlet throughout the length and breadth of the land but has its Inari temple. And her emblem is a fox. There isn't a kitchen in all Japan, either in the home of the millionaire, in the hotels, or the hut of the most lowly peasant without its altar to the fox. He's the one animal with whom the whole population, to use a slang phrase, wants to 'stand in.' Just how Inari came to choose him for an emblem, nobody seems to know, not even the oldest Shinto priest. But the fact remains that he figures largely in the national belief in demoniac possession and they take mighty good care not to give him any reason for hard feelings of any kind.

Pilgrims from all over the kingdom, old and young, rich and poor, high and low never miss a chance to visit Kyoto in order to worship at the great shrine of Inari. And there will be found as many Buddhists as Shintoists among them. Mr. Fox is a great leveler of creeds when it comes to the Japanese farmer. He likes to feel that Inari will not only keep the foxes from molesting anything on his little plot of ground, but that she will also use them as a sort of consecrated watch-dog to keep other marauders away. And herein we have an eloquent instance of that very human tendency to 'play both ends against the middle' in which the Japanese certainly has no monopoly. If you should happen to be in Kyoto in the spring, when the annual procession in honor of Inari takes place, you may have pointed out to you many local and military officials, along with the coolies, showing the universality of their regard for the goddess and wholesome respect for her foxy emblem.

The pathway to the temple leads up the hill apparently into dense woods. Thousands of *torii*, the uprights of which are painted a bright vermilion, the cross-beams in dull black, cover the trails which lead off over the hill-top in every direction. Follow these trails up and you will find that every one of them ends in a fox hole. The *torii* create the impression of an endless pergola. As you approach the temple itself, you will find it a very ordinary affair with its thatched roof, its tassels of hemp, its timbers bright with vermilion and gilt. Everywhere will be seen reproductions of foxes of all sizes in bronze, stone, and wood. And in the mouth of each will be found either a key to the heavenly 'go-down' or storehouse where there is supposed to be an inexhaustible supply of rice, a ball supposed to represent the world, or a scroll of the sacred Shinto writings. In short, the devotees of this faith leave no stone unturned to convince Mr. Fox that he is the 'whole thing.' And over each and every hole to which these innumerable processions of *torii* lead will be found a diminutive shrine carefully located amongst the rocks and moss, and almost completely hidden by numerous small red-painted *torii*.

So deeply is this fox principle bred into the people, especially in outlying districts, that there are certain folk who are supposed to 'own foxes.' That is to say, they are believed to have familiar spirits which are under their control, consisting of seventy-five or one hundred small, weasel-like foxes which accompany them everywhere, through which they can wreak all kind of bad doings on an enemy. Such people can never marry into anything but a 'fox-owning' family. Their good-will is much sought after, however, although no regular person would ever cross their threshold or have any dealings with them beyond borrowing a bit of money now and then at a goodly rate of interest, which the borrower is mighty careful to repay when the debt comes due. These fox-owners spend a goodly part of their time hunting for eligible mates in other families similarly situated. For a young man to marry the daughter of a supposed fox-owner would mean cutting himself off for all time from every member of his family. Fox-owning families are not openly known to be such. They are only suspected. It is a dangerous thing to ask a person if he is connected with one, the results of which might be a visitation in the form of fox or demoniac possession. When one thinks it all over, it is quite easy to account for Inari's popularity.

Next in favor with the great mass of Japanese is Kwannon, the Buddhist goddess of pity, who is supposed to look after the unhappy. It is to her that the Kiyomizu-dera temple is dedicated, and it is most decidedly worth a visit. Kiyomizu-dera, however, is something more than a mere shrine to that gentle goddess. Here come the sick in body and in soul, and especially children in arms, afflicted with a variety of distempers. If the infinite grace of the Almighty may be found anywhere in this sin-sick world, it should be on the heights of Kiyomizu-dera. If 'Arise, go in peace, thy faith hath made thee whole,' means anything anywhere, it should be in evidence in this devoted spot because there is enough faith manifested here — outwardly at least — every hour of the day, to move mountains. If you want to forget the personal pronoun for a few minutes, drive out to the foot of this heaven-kissing hill on the outskirts of the city and watch poor old humanity in action. You'll return to your hotel with a little different slant on life in general after making the climb up the hill to that aged, moss-grown, time-stained temple. You won't miss the dearth of architectural display and you will find an atmosphere, the reality of which will require no emphasis. A clear case of 'Silver and gold have I none; but such as I have give I thee.'

Fifteen minutes' ride in the motor terminates in a long, steep street given over to native porcelain shops, at the far end of which the paved path upward begins. Ancient stone lanterns on every side, past little shrines and chapels until you reach the spot where the original site was hewn out of the rock for the temple foundation. On all sides the tall, solemn pines add a dignity to the bunch of buildings lodged like a rookery on the steep slope of the hill. Here we find a roomy platform where the pilgrim may draw breath and watch the stream of natives that come and go. Incidentally, the climb is worth while if for no other reason than the view from the summit out over the city. The platform in front of the principal building seems to be a sort of rendezvous for old and young. The clatter of the *geta*, the tuneful echo of the temple gongs, the pleasant odor of incense in combination with the clink of the coins thrown into the box at the temple entrance, and the chatter of friends work a most genial transformation in the otherwise sober surroundings.

The principal attraction of this temple is a wooden statue of the god Binzuru — a squatting figure of an old man who, after a rather swift pace in his younger days (so the legend runs), concluded to devote the remainder of his life to steering the young idea in the right direction. He is supposed to possess remarkable healing ability, demonstrated on a sort of 'similia, similibus curantur' plan. That is to say, the believer rubs his hand over that portion of Binzuru's wooden anatomy which corresponds to the seat of his own ailment and then vigorously massages himself. It has its humorous aspects until some poor mother comes along with an ailing child or a babe in arms. Indicative of that abiding confidence in Binzuru's powers which has actuated countless multitudes of pilgrims for years on end, it might be remarked that his forehead and nose have disappeared, not to mention a much flattened abdomen and the total absence of his great toe. To the scoffing Occidental he is more interesting as an eloquent demonstration of the germ theory than anything else.

Kindly Kwannon's powers are not limited to bodily ailments alone. Near the temple entrance will be found a little shrine sacred to that deity who watches over the lovelorn. Just why the builders of this temple should have selected a frightful hobgoblin as Kwannon's assistant in delicate work of this character is beyond imagination. He has apparently taken refuge behind a rude wooden grating from which vantage-point he glares at the petitioner in a most fearsome fashion as she makes her prayer for a husband, generally after sundown when there is nobody around to hear or to see. And this is the way she does it: She buys from the priest a printed prayer to which she adds an oral one of her own addressed to the monstrosity behind the grating, accompanied by a couple of copper coins. Then she twists the paper prayer into a cord which she proceeds to tie into a knot in the grating, using only her thumb and little finger. As may be imagined, it's a stunt which simply could not be done without considerable practice. The fact that every square inch of the grating is so completely filled with these paper love-knots that one can hardly see through it, affords mute evidence of the universality of a doctrine in which both the Orient and the Occident find common ground.

One more shrine at Kiyomizu-dera, on the same terrace

with the temple, deserves the visitor's attention. 'Tis that
of the god Jizo whose especial care is the little children,
both in life and death. He is lodged in a wretched little
shack, in the shape of a bronze statue representing an old
bald-headed man with a most kindly countenance, seated
amid a multitude of crude clay figures, effigies of himself,
which have been left there as offerings by bereaved mothers. Of all the shrines in Japan this one of Jizo is the most
suggestive of the manger at Bethlehem and of Him who
said, 'Suffer little children to come unto me.' Those myriad stone and clay crudities by which he is surrounded
represent the tributes of untold thousands of mothers
among the very poor who have entrusted their babies, both
dead and alive, to Jizo's loving care. Tread softly, brother
— this is no ordinary shrine. All the wealth of Ormus or of
Ind would sink into insignificance beside that lowly shed
with its decaying timbers. For overhead is the blue sky
and underneath are the 'everlasting arms.'

Perhaps the most magnificent temple in Kyoto is Chion-
in, with its picturesque monastery and beautiful cherry
trees. It also is located on the hillside surrounded by ancient pine trees. An ornate, two-storied gate guards its approach. The principal attraction of this spot is the immense temple bell, weighing seventy-four tons, with a deep
and musical tone very much like the bell at Nikko. Unlike
Nikko, however, the visitor, if he be so inclined, may swing
the big billet of timber against it and hear a bit of music
therefrom. The Chion-in priests, like their brethren all
over the country, are very kindly and courteous in their
attitude toward the stranger.

Last, but not least, comes the great temple Higashi
Hongwanji — the most modern and massive place of worship in the city, and representing the purest type of Japanese Buddhism: the Ikko sect, which is the nearest ap-

proach to Christianity of any school. This building is two hundred and thirty feet long, with a main height of one hundred and twenty-six feet. The roof is upheld by ninety-six great pillars. This great shrine cost over three and a half millions of dollars and took sixteen years to complete. Practically all of the money was contributed by the common people. In the corridor will be found a most interesting memento of its construction, consisting of a cable of human hair which represents the gift of thirty thousand women and which was used for the very practical purpose of swinging some of the massive timbers into place. Also, most of the labor done over that sixteen-year period was donated by thousands of Japanese workmen and artisans, after their usual day's tasks were over. The interior decorations are gorgeous, and the ceremonies, accompanied by the ritualistic chant of the priests, 'Hail to the eternal splendor of Buddha,' are impressive to the last degree.

If the traveler does much going-about in Kyoto after nightfall, he will doubtless run across the professional massagers or shampooers, as they are more familiarly known. Massage is one of Japan's most ancient medical treatments. For many centuries the occupation has been limited to the blind, who not only were thus enabled to support their families, but to accumulate tidy fortunes besides. In earlier times they were under the control of an immense guild which issued licenses in accordance with the ability of the practitioner, some of which cost as high as one thousand dollars. The inroads of more modern medical practice have resulted in the gradual disintegration of the organization. Being blind, the *amma san*, or shampooer, makes his presence known by a melancholy bamboo whistle, as he taps his way through the streets o' nights, with the aid of a staff. He has had a bit of a hard time of it since motor-cars came into style, but he still clings to his prerogatives as a licensed operator and picks up a more or less precarious living.

Kyoto is a sort of headquarters for Japanese characteristics as well as for material commodities. It is always of keen interest to the visitor to learn in what particulars foreign folk differ from himself. The Japanese are very fond of hot baths — the average temperature being 110° Fahrenheit. They fairly revel in water that would parboil an Occidental. There are in the neighborhood of five hundred public baths in Kyoto, in which men, women, and children bathe simultaneously without the necessity for any privacy for either sex. As remarked by a witty visitor a few years ago: 'The nude is *seen* in Japan, but not looked at.' There is one little feature of these public baths that might feaze the average visitor: the water is not changed more than once a day. That isn't as bad as it sounds. The bather ladles cold water over himself before going into the hot tank and, inasmuch as bathing is a daily function, there are very few folk in need of an orthodox 'Saturday night' scrubbing.

Cremation is the approved way of disposing of the dead. There is so very little arable land in the country that none can be spared for cemeteries. In Kyoto there are twelve crematories all of which are kept continuously busy.

Japanese infants are not weaned until they are from three to five years old. This is one of the customs that makes the average Japanese mother prematurely old.

Every Japanese gentleman carries his own cuspidor in the shape of a section of bamboo with all the partitions punched through except one at the end. It is known as *Hai-fuki*. He carries this very useful implement in his belt. The ladies carry theirs in their corsage (if such a misleading term may be employed). The *Hai-fuki* is used in public as well as in the privacy of the home. It seems to be an indispensable adjunct to smoking, in which both sexes indulge. The Japanese pipe holds about two pinches of snuff-like tobacco. Three whiffs and it's empty.

Japanese babies are carried on the back, not in the arms.

Carpenters plane and saw *toward*, not away from, themselves as is our custom.

Books commence at the end and read backwards. And where we put the title, the Japanese puts the word *finis.* Likewise, all footnotes, so-called, will be found at the top of the page instead of at the foot.

In the momentous matter of dining, wine precedes the meal instead of being drunk with or after it. The effect of this custom can be better imagined than described. It accounts for the exceeding dullness of the average Japanese function. Everybody gets properly 'lit' before instead of afterward. Dessert, also, precedes the *entrées* and the roasts, and various other *pièces de résistance* (if they have such things in Japan).

Boats are hauled up on the beach stern first. That isn't a half-bad idea.

When Japanese leave a restaurant, they tip the proprietor, not the waiter. That is about all our lobster palaces in New York need to remove them beyond carping criticism of all kind.

In horse-back riding, the Japanese mounts from the right side. All harness buckles on the right side. When placed in the stable, the horse's head is where we would look for his tail. And instead of a manger, he feeds out of a tub that stands near the stable-door.

In building a house, the roof is constructed first. After they number the pieces, they take it apart and keep it until the balance of the building is finished. Then they put it on like a hat.

Japanese women blow their noses on a small sheet of soft paper which they afterwards roll up into a small ball and drop into their flowing sleeves.

Good breeding calls for the removal of the shoes, not the hat.

The women needle their thread instead of threading their needle.

Strangest of all, they dry themselves with a damp towel.

It is in marriage that the greatest difference is seen between Oriental and Occidental customs. The parents look after the matter up to the selection of a satisfactory partner for their child — boy or girl. Then the young couple are brought together through the offices of a middle-man who arranges for a meeting generally at his own home. After looking each other over, both have the privilege of objecting to a wedding, although no one ever heard of the young woman indulging her prerogative. There being no objection, an exchange of gifts follows after which neither can withdraw. In the great majority of cases the wife goes to live with her husband's family and becomes little better than a drudge. There is no such thing as a honeymoon, no bridesmaids, no love, as we understand the term. Custom prescribes that the husband may maintain a 'second establishment' if he can afford it. He makes no secret of the fact.

The Japanese case of 'mother-in-law' is about the worst in the world and reacts on the young wife only. If she doesn't obey, not only her husband but her mother-in-law as well, that is adequate grounds for divorce. Statistics show that every marriage in five ends thus. It is to be said, however, that divorces are rare in the upper classes. Here again we see the effect of custom; the upper-class Japanese sees no reason for divorce so long as he can keep as many mistresses as he desires. All he wants is for his wife effectually to efface herself. If she will do that and obey his mother, she can have a home as long as she likes. And she's not likely to object. All girls are married off without being consulted and they accept the situation as a matter of course as their mothers and grandmothers have done before them, from time immemorial. All things considered, marriage in Japan does not commend itself to Occidentals. There are those over there, however, who profess to believe that woman's emancipation will come within the present generation.

One of the worth-while experiences in Kyoto is a visit to the wrestling school which is conducted in an open pavilion not far from the central part of the city. It's an amazing thing to witness the tremendous strength and agility of these professional wrestlers who, with their mountains of fat, distended abdomens, and every evidence of over-eating and over-drinking, are the very antithesis of our trained athlete, here in the States. And it certainly goes to prove one thing: that there are other ways of building up muscular strength and developing one's wind than by abstemious living. The matches are fought out on a heavily matted platform on a level with the street and open on all sides, in much the same fashion as our pugilistic prize ring, minus the rope. A small fee admits one to a seat or he can stand on the outside and look in gratis. With the exception of a gayly colored breech-clout, the wrestler is naked. I should say that those I saw weighed considerably over two hundred pounds each. As an endurance test I have never seen anything in the way of athletics to be compared with it. Single matches are the usual thing. Sometimes, however, twenty-five or thirty men will take sides and select a champion to meet all comers. Under such circumstances the successful contestant must throw three antagonists in succession before he can win a prize. There isn't a split second's delay between the fall of a vanquished one and the rushing onslaught of his thoroughly fresh and anxiously waiting successor who hopes to down his adversary before he can recover his wind.

This style of wrestling has nothing in common with jujutsu, which is considered an art. As such it has been handed down in more or less of a secretive way from generation to generation by teachers who are supposed to be as much interested in its moral influence in character-building as in its physical aspects. Jujutsu is a part of the curriculum of aristocratic academies and an indispensable adjunct to the training of a Japanese police officer.

Before leaving Kyoto the traveler should visit the insect-dealer's shops down in the native quarter. There is where you will find the trained fleas and a lot of other insectivorous and interesting side-lights on what counts as amusement for the Japanese. Perhaps the most remarkable of them all is *Kusa Hibari* or the Grass-Lark. He is really a cricket and a wonderful songster. Don't expect to see anything that resembles our American cricket. *Kusa Hibari* is about the size of a mosquito with antennæ longer than his body, so hair-like that they may be seen only against the light. Your insect-dealer breeds these minute bits of ephemera year after year in a jar of clay. When they are full grown and ready for the market, he puts one each (always the male) in a little gauze-lined cage two and a half inches high by one and a half wide. And this little outfit sells for the equivalent of twelve cents. He must be fed every morning with a fresh bit of egg-plant or cucumber, which is pushed into his cage through a mite of a door just about large enough to admit the end of a lead pencil. Except when indulging in his one meal in the morning, he sleeps all day long. It is only when night comes that he

starts his remarkable little music-box which he keeps going
until dawn. The distinctive character of his song is its
weird, penetrating, bell-like sweetness that fills the room
with its resonance and suggests the rhythmic ringing of
tiny silvery bells.

Kusa Hibari's brief existence consists of a few weeks in
the Japanese midsummer. The first cold day will carry
him off. He partakes of that same strange tragedy that
enters into the life of the bee. When mated he stops singing and dies shortly afterward. His song, therefore, is
a love song inherited from countless generations, which
seems odd enough for such an atomic creature. Nevertheless, that is what keeps him going all summer long — singing for a mate, the mate that will never come. And that's
what the Japanese pays his twelve cents for — that song,
without any realization of its significance. What a mournful
working-out of Nature's laws, even in the case of a minute
insect whose very name, Grass-Lark, constitutes a practical
joke. He, who never saw a blade of grass in his life, who
wouldn't last overnight if he ever escaped from his cage,
who would be as much of an anomaly out in the fields as a
house-bred canary. Where did he learn his heart-breaking
little love song? He didn't learn it. He's just a part of
the great Scheme. He toils not, neither does he spin, but
he's worth his board and lodging for the summer months;
and so he plays his part, just as you and I do, brother —

> Ah, make the most of what we yet may spend,
> Before we too into the Dust descend;
>   Dust unto Dust, and under Dust, to lie,
> Sans Wine, sans Song, sans Singer, and sans End.

Having decided to go into China via Korea instead of to
Hongkong via Nagasaki, we took our departure from
Kyoto with no little regret, bound for the beautiful island

of Miyajima at the far end of the Inland Sea. The route
was ideal, giving us a chance for a train stop-over at ancient
Nara. Here we did the approved thing: fed the sacred deer
and ambled around a very unattractive Shinto temple
housing a Daibutsu as big as that at Kamakura, but infinitely less impressive. The ancient temple has been bolted
together as if in mighty effort to stave off senile decay.
Scenically speaking, Nara is very beautiful with its ancient
trees and abounding wistaria bloom. Picturesque walks, an
impressive avenue of stone lanterns, an imposing pagoda,
and another mammoth temple bell complete the list of attractions — and they are all worth while. If desired you
may take a side trip from Nara to the old, old town of
Yamada where Jimmu Tenno, Japan's first Mikado, is
buried. Or, you may do as we did: take the next train out,
passing through Osaka — Japan's Pittsburgh — and on to
Kobe for the night. There is comparatively little in these
big manufacturing cities to interest the traveler. So, you
will catch the first train in the morning for the exquisite
old garden of Korakuen at Okayama where an afternoon
may be well spent. This garden is said to be over four hundred years old and the great age of the trees and vines
would seem to bear it out. Domesticated cranes have been
trained to fit into the landscape with a highly artistic
effect. At the end of the day they are called in like chickens
and driven to their 'coop.' It is a charming and most unusual sight to watch these graceful birds dignifiedly strut-
ting along the shores of the lake at the call of the gardener.

Another train comes along in the late afternoon which
will drop you at the little town of Itozaki on the Inland Sea
where the mistress of the Hamakichi Hotel will entertain
you à la Japon for the night. It is a most interesting experience to sleep on the floor with half a dozen thick com-
fortables underneath and a curious little maidservant look-

GREAT TORII ON THE SACRED ISLAND OF MIYAJIMA

ing in every few minutes to discover if there is anything she can — *see*. A typical Japanese dinner at night and a hurried breakfast next morning — for the steamer is waiting out in the little bay for passengers who are bound over the Inland Sea. Just why they denominate as a sea a glassy body of water, smooth as a mill-pond, does not appear. An excited boatman will row you out, with just enough time to clamber aboard the steamer — a typical river craft with side wheels — and you're off for Miyajima. It is very much like a Hudson River day trip with considerable similarity in the scenery, and with odds in favor of the Hudson. Luncheon is served on board and you're glad enough when the steamer pulls into Miyajima late that afternoon. A very attractive hotel near the beach awaits your arrival and the tree-embowered spot looks mighty good. Yes — you certainly are ready for a rest, and it's a matter of supreme indifference to you whether or not there are any temples in the vicinity. You rather hope not. You don't want to see even a *torii*.

Beautiful Miyajima. Sacred and most exquisite island.

> 'Breathe — breathe the odorous sweetness that is ours,'
> Cry Frangipani flowers.
> 'Forget — forget — and know no more distress,
> But languorous idleness:
> Dream where dead leaves fall ever from green trees
> To float on sapphire seas —
> Dream and be one with these.'

Yes — this is the place over which you may rhapsodize without any fear of reprisal. Gorgeous old shade trees grow right down to the water's edge. The sun's glare, from which you have tried all day long to escape on the little steamboat, no more offends. Complete relaxation is yours as you stretch out on the veranda of the compact and tree-embowered hotel. Beautiful tame deer come and eat out of your hand as they wander here and there in the grounds and over the paths that lead to — (shall I say it?) the temple. But you don't care. You're not going to visit any more temples. You're just going to remain here for the rest of your life and rest. When the genial proprietor of the hotel comes and tells you that no one is permitted by the Japanese Government either to be born, to die, or to be buried on Miyajima, it doesn't seem to strike you as at all strange. Why *should* anybody be compelled to think either of life or death in such a place? With dreamy eyes your spirit lies 'under the walls of Paradise,' or words to that effect. Out in the little bay, about two hundred feet from the shore, stands the largest and most picturesque *torii* in all Japan. It is made of huge logs of camphor wood which were driven into the ground at low water, and it is worth all the attention it attracts which is quite a little. To-morrow you will go out in a rowboat and take a picture of it from the water — but not to-day, thanks. All you are going to do to-day is rest your body and invite your soul. You are not going to remain here very long and it's the last sight you will have of the Japan you will wish to remember in the after-years. When the dirt and tawdriness of Tokyo have slipped into the limbo of forgotten things and even the memories of ancient Kýoto are faded, Miyajima will rise in its beauty and enthrall the tired spirit with recollections that will not be denied. If travel won't do that for the asphalt-weary soul, then there's something wrong either with the itinerary or the soul. Whatever the future may hold, nothing will ever replace in the memory fair Miyajima at the far end of the Inland Sea.

CHAPTER V
KOREA — JAPAN'S UNHAPPY VASSAL

Pity thee? So I do. I pity the dumb beast at the altar,
But does the robed priest for his pity falter?
I'd rack thee though a thousand lives were perishing in thine;
What were ten thousand to a fame like mine!

WILLIS

THERE are some nations against which the cards are
stacked. Take your atlas down from the shelf and note the
geographical location of poor old Korea. The Russian Bear
on the north, China on the west, and Japan on the south.
Each and all wondering for years just how they might be
able to grab her off without exciting too much hue and cry
throughout the world. Korea — the 'Hermit Kingdom,'
with an antiquity so vast that the memory of man shrivels
up at the thought of it. And all she wanted was to be let
alone. That she managed to keep off the dogs for three
thousand years speaks not so much for her fighting qualities as it does for the fact that the other nations mentioned
were not much more enterprising than she. It's natural for
big nations to want to play big brother to a little nation.
The principal part of the game, however, calls for the little
fellow to do as he is told. Nippon realized for years the
menace of 'the bear that walks like a man' and knew that
Korea was all that stood in the way of Russian exploitation.
If Japan had not been strong enough to take her, Russia
most certainly would have done it. Then we should most
likely have had a fine bunch of Bolsheviks running the little
peninsula by this time. No one begrudges Korea to Japan.
That which makes us Occidentals feel badly for those
helpless folk is the way Japan has handled them. Korea

needed cleaning up. There is no doubt about that. Japan did a great job in that line.

But apparently she couldn't resist the opportunity for playing the part of the tyrant. She figured that she could do quite as well with vinegar as she could with honey. That's poor psychology when it comes to handling human beings. It's a long story of the rankest kind of injustice to a defenseless people which she had annexed and was exploiting with that ruthless efficiency for which she is noted: the kind of efficiency that travels hand in hand with unadulterated militarism, of which this old world is unspeakably sick. Japan knows but one way of doing things. That's the military way. She has done a fine piece of work in cleaning up Korea. And she hasn't a friend left in the country as a consequence. She is adept at dealing with material things. Spiritually and humanly speaking, she hasn't a cordial heartbeat in her whole body politic. Since her annexation (subjugation would be a better word) of Korea in 1910, upwards of a million and a half of natives have voluntarily exiled themselves to Siberia and Manchuria because they could not stand up under the unremitting pressure of the mailed fist. In that same period over four hundred thousand Japanese have settled in Korea with much greater advantages than they enjoyed at home and with the most heartlessly unfair discrimination against the native Korean who is treated as the scum of the earth.

Not without good reason has Japan been dubbed the 'Prussia of the East.' She has yet to learn that 'Peace hath her victories no less renowned than war,' and that she cannot permanently denationalize even as spineless and degenerate a people as the Koreans. Think of her banning the singing of 'Onward, Christian Soldiers,' in a Missionary Sunday School on the ground that it tended to develop a militaristic spirit among the natives! Think of abolishing

Korean newspapers, the Korean language, Korean schools, Korean religion and schoolbooks! Think of substituting for all these Japanese papers and periodicals, language, religion and schools managed by Japanese teachers with sabers dangling from their belts! Think of discouraging ambitious Korean students from seeking an entrance to the Tokyo University! And what's even worse: practically forbidding those who succeed to specialize in such studies as constitutional law, history, and economics. A Korean laborer receives less than half the wages of a Japanese of similar capacity. A Korean schoolboy is allotted eight years for primary and secondary education as against eleven years for a Japanese boy. If a Japanese is convicted of a misdemeanor, he is fined. A Korean convicted of a similar offense is flogged. If a Japanese happens to be killed by a Government-owned Seoul trolley car, his family receives one hundred dollars. If the same misfortune overtakes a Korean, his family gets fifty dollars. As a result of a peaceful and unarmed uprising of the Koreans in 1919, in an effort to create a public sentiment in favor of independence, between forty and fifty thousand of them were shot down like dogs.

And yet — and yet — when Japan took over the destinies of this wretched people she changed the name of the country from Korea to 'Chosen' (pronounced Sho-sen) which, being interpreted, meaneth 'The Land of the Morning Calm.' Was there ever a more delicious irony!

Well, don't let this sort of thing keep you away from 'Chosen.' The very thing that makes our gorge rise has contributed largely to making Korea a much more comfortable country to visit. One of these days Japan will wake up to the fact that militarism is rapidly going out of style and that extirpation isn't a game that commends itself to civilized nations. She has recently married off the half-witted Prince Yi—the last of the Korean royal family — to a Japanese princess. And then, just to show him a real good time, he has been made a lieutenant in the Japanese army. And still they say that the Japanese has no sense of humor.

It's a short night's steamer-run from the great Japanese port of Shimonoseki across the Tsushima Strait to Fusan. You step off the gangplank into the Korean Railways Station, your luggage follows promptly and you will be surprised to learn that the train leaves on schedule time. A standard-gauge railroad with thoroughly up-to-date equipment, even to sleepers and dining-cars, runs from one end of the peninsula to the other, connecting with the Trans-Siberian Railway at Harbin, Manchuria. While this is real service, we don't overlook the fact that it provides Japan with rapid transportation for troops, supplies, and manufactured goods into Siberia, Manchuria, and China. Too bad that Japan is so keenly interested in Asiatic penetration and so little in human nature and its flesh and blood concomitants!

Seoul (pronounced Sowl), Korea's ancient capital, is the only spot on the peninsula of any interest to the traveler. It lies in a picturesque valley, two hundred and seventy-five miles from Fusan, and is surrounded by a ruined wall fourteen miles in extent, built six hundred years ago — and not a little suggestive of the Great Wall of China. Including 65,000 Japanese, it has a population approximating 300,000. Long, wide streets are the rule, lined on both sides with interminable rows of cheap, thatched-roof shacks in which all business is done. The main thoroughfare is Chon-No, or Big Bell Street, so named on account of an immense bell, ten feet high, located thereon, which can be heard all over town and which for five hundred years has given the nightly signal for the closing of the eight city gates. The Chon-No runs straight east and west through the center of town, extending for miles and miles into the country. It has been the principal entrance and exit of the city for centuries. An unceasing flow of traffic prevails, consisting of every make of motor-car on the face of the earth, from the most expensive to the omnipresent flivver; huge bullocks laden with every kind of merchandise imaginable, from heavy building timber to fagots for fire-wood; undersized Korean horses, ridden by Japanese and led by native servants; husky porters burdened with terrific loads which they carry on their backs in a sort of harness peculiar to the country — all contesting with each other for right of way. Of all the cities visited on this long trip, Seoul with its Chon-No was the place that sent my memory trotting back to Fifth Avenue and Forty-Second Street, New York.

And everybody seemed to be happy. A multitude clothed in white — a cheap, native-woven grass-cloth, within the means of the poorest, not to mention some gayly colored silk outfits displayed by those who apparently possessed the means to cut a dash. It was a sight to remember — and an odor as well. For be it known that the Korean washes his grass-cloth suit of clothes with much greater frequency than he does his body. He seems to possess an inordinate pride in *looking* his best without reference to the aroma he leaves in his wake. In commenting on this fact to a resident, I was informed that the odoriferous folk came from the country, that they were not a city product. From what I saw of some outlying villages during a motor trip, I am quite willing to accept his statement as final. One would hardly believe it possible that human beings could live in such a frightful condition of filth. There is only one word in the English language that will express it: pig-sty.

More acreage in the outlying districts seems to be given up to the cultivation of a sort of native melon than anything else. Every field has a crude platform raised about ten or fifteen feet from the ground on which the farmer spends most of his time on the look-out for thieves.

After all is said and done, the most interesting feature of this ancient city is the native Korean himself. Solemn and owl-like, with a shaved head and mahogany-colored skin, over six feet in height, wearing big horned spectacles and a funny goat-like chin whisker and scraggly mustache, clothed in a long coat and rough white baggy trousers tied around the ankles with pieces of string. And — to crown all, his ridiculously small horsehair hat which he manages to keep on with the aid of a ribbon under his chin. It might be said, in passing, that he does not wear a hat for the same reason you and I do. He wears that 'Happy Hooligan' contraption to protect his official topknot which constitutes the same distinguishing mark of an adult Korean that a Chinaman's queue formerly did for him, with this difference: the topknot is the badge of his legal manhood, up to which period he is officially known as a 'half-man,' whereas the queue was an emblem of subjugation. The topknot resembles a sprig of asparagus growing out of a perfectly smooth ivory dome. He naturally takes good care of it, though just what protection a loosely woven horsehair hat affords is not apparent.

In addition to the 'Hooligan,' he always carries a conically shaped contrivance of oiled paper with which he covers the dinky bit of horsehair in rainy weather. If you can imagine this queer combination squatting down on his hunkers on the shady side of a tree and fishing out a thimble-sized pipe with a stem a yard long for a little solace, you would see a bit of comedy to be found nowhere else on the face of the earth. This gentleman is much given to gambling, bad liquor, and his neighbor's wife. Though just why this latter should be is a bit of a mystery. The Korean woman is even more grotesque than the man. All of them gross, animalized, and fat, with no more facial expression than a still-born calf and no more figure than a sack of wheat with a string tied 'round the middle. And to get within shooting distance of either would be all the evidence you would require that soap and water were at a premium in the 'Land of the Morning Calm.' He is devoid of kindly instincts either toward his own kind or animals. Altogether, Japan has a man's job on her hands to make a real citizen of him, which possibly explains why she has devoted herself to the material advancement of the country, leaving the Koreans to develop themselves largely under insuperable difficulties.

Architecturally the city of Seoul is nil. The ancient gates already mentioned, the deserted palaces, and a fairly good museum include the principal attractions. The one thing really worth while, which very few travelers ever visit, is the ancient tomb of the Korean kings about ten miles out of the city. It is entirely different from any other tomb I have ever seen. We were glad, indeed, that we went. An inexpensive flivver took us over the unspeakable roads to an embowered spot off on the hills, in charge of a native Korean who lived in a little cottage at the padlocked entrance. A silver key opened the gate, however, and we followed an ancient pathway up a hill, past an old wooden temple that resembled a gabled barn, behind which was the tomb. On the crest of the hill were two huge grassy mounds, in front of which were two massive blocks of polished granite. Surrounding the spot, which was probably one hundred and fifty feet in diameter, was a low limestone wall, on the inside of which were crudely sculptured figures of horses, sheep, dogs, etc., all of a size, all covered with

lichen, and all headed outwards from the grave, as if to
ward off intruders. In the front, which was open, stood two
huge effigies of royal attendants on either side, guarding the
entrance, as it were.

The *motif* is the oldest one known to man: those animals and officials are there for the purpose of accompany-
ing the disembodied spirit of their royal master and
ministering unto it during the long, long journey through
the nether world. Sun, sky, and verdure conspired to en-
shrine the spot with rural peace and all Nature smiled.
Here was one place that made me feel that I should like
to visit Seoul again some day. Just what emperor it was
that lay there, the keeper didn't know, or when he died, or
whether there were one or a half-dozen under the two turf-
covered mounds that were so highly suggestive of a haz-
ard on a golf course, and it made no difference anyway.
He was quite willing, however, for an additional coin to
sit for his photograph in the tomb of that 'Imperious
Cæsar, dead and turn'd to clay,' whose very name was
unknown to him.

There is a spot in this ancient city that will never be for-
got by the Koreans and which will be pointed out to visitors for years to come. It is a deserted garden in the rear of
the old North Palace where the Korean Queen was assassinated in 1895. She was a typical Oriental in her cruelty,
lust, and unlimited ambitions, and she stood in the way of
Japanese progress after *Dai Nippon* had done away with
all Chinese influence. And so, one night, between midnight
and morning, a gang of Japanese and Korean thugs, under
the direction of the Japanese Minister, dragged her out of
the palace and knifed her. The spot to-day is rank with
weeds and undergrowth, and the ancient wall, that originally enclosed it as part of the palace grounds, is crumb-

ling to ruin. This is a little incident that the more intelligent Japanese do not care to discuss. They lay the infamous job at the door of Viscount Miura who put it through while yet Korea was an independent nation and fifteen years previous to annexation. The Japanese government is supposed to have known nothing about it. If so, they never disciplined Minister Miura for his part in it.

Owing to the universality of the 'hot dog' sign which will be seen with almost as great frequency in the Orient as here at home, it might be well to caution the traveler that 'hot dog' in Seoul means precisely what it says. Dog meat is a staple article of food with the Koreans and native goat is sold as mutton. This is one way of serving notice that it will be a good thing under any and all circumstances to confine your eating to your hotel. If you anticipate being absent at meal-time, by all means take your luncheon with you. You'll enjoy it much more and you'll avoid any unfortunate after-effects. Also, avoid drinking from native wells.

In the public square in Seoul is a sightly stone monument badly cracked and chipped. Just what its significance was or is, I could not learn. The interesting thing about it is that many years ago a number of soldiers who had been sent over to discipline the Koreans, at a time when the Chinese Government was maintaining a sort of half-baked suzerainty, set fire to it. Tradition says they were very much surprised that the monument would not burn.

After two days in this queer old intrigue-ridden rookery, we resumed our journey north. The railway runs through a very picturesque, wild, and mountainous country with plenty of scenic variety. Crossing the famous Yalu River where the Japanese defeated the Russian army in 1905, we stopped for a few moments at that war-ridden town Antung, on the Manchurian side of the river. Late that night we arrived at another city which was celebrated for a Japanese victory: Mukden, where we put up at an excellent railway station hotel — The Yamato. A long railway ride the next day through Manchuria brought us to Port Arthur, or Dalny, as it is now called. Here we spent a day going over the melancholy remains of the most terrific battle-field ever known prior to the Great World War. No one would dream that there had ever been a town on that peninsula; that when Russia established herself there, she brought along with her commerce, travel, and society. Outside of France that is, beyond all doubt, the most shell-blown and mine-scarred monument to bloody war the world has ever known. It's a veritable Sodom and Gomorrah. No one but the Japanese War Department knows how many soldiers were sacrificed on that terrible hill-side. Picture it yourself: the whole terrain fortified from every conceivable angle with a view to repelling an attack from the sea which had to be made uphill against the Russian guns all trained downhill. And — in the end, those myriad lives were largely sacrificed in vain, as the fortress was finally taken by tunneling and mine-laying.

It may be you will come across a little book either in Tokyo, Kyoto, or Port Arthur, entitled 'Human Bullets,' written by a young Japanese officer who survived. If so, get it. The tactics were repeated by the German armies in France: the pouring-out of men like bullets from a machine gun: an attempt to overcome by sheer sacrifice of numbers, trusting that enough may get through to win a victory. A visit to such a Gehenna as this is bound to work a salutary effect on a civilian. Incidentally, it is worthy of note that the present Japanese fortification of Port Arthur gives that enterprising nation complete control of all China north of the Yangtze River and up to the Amur.

It is equally true that the fleet that holds the Pacific Ocean controls Port Arthur as well. Please take notice that Japan has not been 'asleep at the switch' since the Russo-Japanese War. What she might possibly lack on the sea, she makes up in her control of the Manchurian Railway which runs from Harbin on the Trans-Siberian Road, direct to Tientsin, and thence to Peking. Furthermore, no one realizes this fact any more thoroughly than China herself.

There is a steamship line plying between Port Arthur and Tientsin, China, across the Gulf of Pechili. That, after all, was what brought us on that roundabout trip from Japan. We hadn't lost any time and we had traveled through a vast territory of intensely interesting country that we should have missed had we followed our original plan and gone to Hongkong via Nagasaki.

It was a beautiful afternoon on which we pulled away from the dock at Dalny in a queer sort of undersized Japanese steamship and bid good-bye to Nipponese territory. The course lay past the southernmost point of the Liaotung Peninsula which Russia had 'leased' from the Chinese Government and which Japan had wrested from her at such a fearful sacrifice of human life. The memorial monument on the summit of 203-Metre Hill was silhouetted against the blue sky as we steamed by, while between us and the shore-line lay a picturesque Chinese junk becalmed on the glassy expanse of the gulf 'as idle as a painted ship upon a painted ocean.' And the famous names of a day that was dead came trooping through my mind: Togo, Nogi, Kuroki, Oyama, Kuropatkin, Makaroff, Rojestvensky, Verestchagin, blundering Alexeieff, and the wretched Stoessel — all gone to their final reckonings. 'Cui bono?' The memory brings to mind those lines of Stephen Benet's:

Stripped country, shrunken as a beggar's heart,
Inviolate landscape, hardened into steel.

No martyred patriot's bed this. Not a single victim on his native soil. Conquest and oblivion, that's all.

An odd visitation came our way during the night. There were quite a number of Chinese laborers spread out on the deck up in the bow, returning to Tientsin. When the morning broke, two of them were found dead — from natural causes. It was a most extraordinary proceeding to an Occidental mind to see their companions gather them up like so much merchandise, bend them double, and wrap them up in their quilts and then tie them securely with ropes so they could be carried: all done in the space of about two minutes. I happened to be on deck with my camera at the time and saw the last few moments of these hasty obsequies. No burial at sea for the Chinaman. They take him back and lay him away in his own home town where the code of ancestor-worship preserves his memory to posterity.

Owing to the great quantities of silt which both the Yellow and the Peiho Rivers have emptied into the Gulf of Pechili for countless centuries, it is possible for an ocean steamer to approach the land only at high tide, and not even then if heavily loaded; while ten to twelve miles offshore the discolored water discharged by these rivers can be seen pushing its way out into the sea. Our comparatively small steamer had no trouble, however, and at eleven o'clock we passed the two Chinese forts at Taku, guarding the mouth of the Peiho. One would hardly think that these insignificant-looking, low-lying fortifications, with their foundations sunk in solid embankments of mud and millet stalks, contained modern batteries. Deep ditches or moats guard the rear entrance to both, 'to keep the soldiers from straying away,' as the celebrated Viceroy Li Hung Chang once put it, with more truth than satire.

Tientsin is only twenty-five miles distant from the Taku landing if you use the railway. If you take the river route, the distance is sixty miles, from which you may gather the serpentine character of the Peiho. All luggage is transferred to the railway at Tongku, three or four miles up the river from Taku landing. It is a mighty fearsome experience to watch the proceeding, with tendencies toward heart failure and nervous prostration. A mob of yelling coolies officiate. A running noose of rope at the end of a hoisting cable is dropped down the hatchway. In a minute you see four or five trunks (your own included) coming slowly upwards while the carelessly looped noose which encircles them is slipping inch by inch toward the end of one of the trunks. And just as they are dangling over the ten feet of water between the vessel and the lighter below and another moment will see them all overboard, the whole outfit falls on the lighter's deck, quite safe from a watery grave. Yes — it was much more interesting to watch than the 'hogtying' of the dead coolies. When we reached the riverbank at Tongku, there were at least six coolies to each one of the three of us, doing their best to wrench our small bags out of our hands and carry them to the station, about fifty yards distant. Pandemonium and confusion worse confounded. There was nothing to do but yield — the discretion that is the better part of valor. We caught the next train for Peking where we arrived at 5 P.M. We had been warned in Kyoto that there was a revolution going on in China. When we saw every railway station guarded by soldiers, we believed it. Fortunately, however, the outbreak was confined to the country farther south, around Nanking and Hankow. We were undisturbed in the northern capital.

CHAPTER VI

CHINA — THE SURVIVAL OF THE UNFIT

> Our decks are rotting with the slime of ages,
> We kept no reck'ning and we laid no course;
> Our log-book's filled with mildew and blank pages,
> We drift beneath the ensign of remorse.
>
> JOHN ANDERSON, R.N.R.

IT's a perfectly safe thing to refer to Peking, China's capital, as the oldest city in the world. The likelihood of any one taking issue with the statement is quite limited. Its history can be traced back to the twelfth century before Christ. That's old enough to suit the most captious critic. The real interesting feature of this most ancient of all cities is the fact that it is still there, with a population approximating two millions. Still doing business at the same old stand and in accordance with the methods that prevailed prior to the Christian era. If such a thing as a slogan for Peking or for China at large could be imagined, it would probably run something like this: 'What was good enough for our ancestors is good enough for us.' The white man is as much of a 'foreign devil' to-day as he was when he forced his way into the Flowery Kingdom in 1860. And it's a fair statement that he will not be less so a century hence. Four hundred millions of people are a bit unwieldy. In China they are the very quintessence of inertia.

Assuming for the sake of argument that there's the slightest excuse for the use of such a word as 'regeneration' in connection with the Yellow Empire, all historians are agreed that such a condition can never be brought about from without, or through foreign intervention of any kind. The only hope is that there may be a sufficient number of young Chinese educated in foreign countries who will be willing to return home and sacrifice themselves in the almost hopeless job of awakening their sodden brethren, first of all to a real interest in life, rousing them out of that dumb stupidity against which even the gods are powerless. As the Reverend Dr. Arthur H. Smith, who spent a quarter of a century in missionary work in China, puts it, in his altogether admirable book 'Chinese Characteristics': 'It would be easy to raise in China an army of a million men — nay, of ten millions — tested by competitive examination as to their capacity to go to sleep across three wheelbarrows, with head downward like a spider, their mouths wide open, and a fly inside.'

Impossible as it may seem to the Occidental mind, it is a melancholy fact that the longer a man stays in China the less he feels he knows about the native character. Of all Orientals, the Chinese is the most remarkable combination of craftiness and stupidity, industry and laziness, indifference and hostility, honesty and crookedness, intelligence and superstition, filth and luxury. He is entirely lacking in 'soul,' pity, or altruism. He's the alien of aliens. He swings uncertainly between admiration for the teachings of Confucius and the lowest depths of depravity. Metaphorically speaking, and with a harmless attempt at generalization, this yellow gentleman has been conceived in sin, born in iniquity, built by contract, and rejected by the nations of the earth because he was not up to specifications. Incidentally, he's the most accomplished, dyed-in-the-wool grafter that ever lived, moved, or had his being on this mundane sphere. That condition holds good from the Emperor's throne that was, down through the various grades of public service to the most humble and scum-of-the-earth coolie in the lowest slums of Peking or Canton. And he glories in his shame. He cares not a tinker's damn for

your opinion and wishes you'd stay home. Take it from
me — he's worth going a long distance to see — and he
shines in Peking.

Fearing lest you may gather from my characterization of
our old friend John Chinaman that Peking would be a good
place to avoid — let me say that it is, beyond all peradven-
ture, the most colorful, picturesque, original, and highly interesting city in the Far East. There are two excellent
hotels: Hôtel des Wagon Lits and Grand Hôtel de Peking,
both on the American plan. The rates are not cheap by any
means, but you'd pay them ten times over in preference to
putting up at a native hostelry. And — expense is not a good
argument for staying away from either the hotel or the
country that you should visit on such a trip as this. Peking
was an afterthought in our itinerary. It turned out to be
the brightest one of the ten months' pilgrimage. For some
reason, the traveler planning a 'round-the-world trip rarely
thinks of including China, with the possible exception of
Hong Kong. And Hong Kong is not China by any manner
of means. When you get to Japan and begin looking the
ground over, you'll find that a little journey to Peking,
Shanghai, and Canton is a very simple thing, easy of access
and can be made with the same degree of comfort and luxury as if you were traveling in the United States. That
sounds rather large — but it's a fact. If we had it to do
over again, we should cut out any other country except
India in order to include China.

The first thing that catches the traveler's eye as he approaches this great city is its towering wall — thirty miles
in circumference and enclosing an area of twenty-five
square miles. It was built by Kublai Khan, the founder of
the Mongol Dynasty in China, in the thirteenth century.
Yes — it's quite a sizable metropolis. When you climb to
the top of the wall, within which the various legations are

OUTSIDE THE AN TING GATE — PEKING CITY WALL

enclosed, and see, for the first time that this vast hive of Oriental humanity is three cities within one, and that you have before you some of the most highly charged sight-seeing imaginable, you're properly glad that you included the Celestial Empire in your itinerary. And then — if you have been reading your history (which, of course, you have) you know that the celebrated Venetian globe-trotter, Marco Polo, was entertained in Peking by Kublai Khan, in the spring of the year 1280 — a trifle under six hundred and fifty years ago; that he came up the Peiho River from Tientsin, the same as you and I, and that he probably witnessed the construction of the very wall on which you are standing.

Kublai Khan was a real builder. He put those walls up to stay. They are fifty feet high, with a width of sixty feet at the base and forty at the top, the latter being paved as smooth as a sidewalk. Huge buttresses extending from the outer face of the wall itself are built at intervals of sixty yards, on top of which are guardhouses for soldiers. A crenellated parapet, running the complete circuit of the wall, affords a defense limited only by the number of fighting men it may take to man any section of it. The city has sixteen gates, each with a huge superstructure towering above the top of the wall, guarded by a semicircular extension and pierced with numerous loopholes. Barring the use of modern high-power siege guns, Peking is as well protected to-day as it was in the thirteenth century.

In order properly to orientate yourself, it will be necessary to climb the wall in the rear of the legations near the great Chien-Men gate for a general 'look-see,' as the natives put it in their pidgin English. To the north, the Tatar or Manchu City, commonly known as the 'Inner City,' takes the form of an immense square, in the center of which lies the Imperial City where the court officials and royal *entourage* have maintained their headquarters for nearly seven centuries. And — in the center of the Imperial City lies the Forbidden City, only it isn't *verboten* any more. Both of these smaller cities are walled. It was in the last-named retreat that the various 'Sons of Heaven' formerly concealed themselves from the prying eyes of common, ordinary human beings, both native and foreign. Here's where those who were suffered to look upon the royal personage as he sat upon his august Dragon Throne, spent most of their time on their hands and knees, bumping the tiled floor with their foreheads every few moments. Even as important a personage as old Li Hung Chang, the Viceroy, in his old age was kept on his hands and knees so long at one interview that he fainted.

Oh, they thought quite well of themselves, did those 'Sons of Heaven.' Yes — and when in the good old days they used to go once a year for the purpose of offering a sacrifice at the Altar of Heaven in the Chinese City, it was done under cover of darkness. Even the military escort which lined the route of two miles between the Forbidden City and the Altar, turned completely around and looked the other way as the sacred potentate approached. No ordinary human being might gaze on that august countenance, any divergence from which meant the loss of one's head including the queue. There was one person, however, with whom the Son of Heaven cut little figure: the Empress Dowager, colloquially known as the 'Old Buddha,' who disposed of the only fullgrown one in 1908. Having ruled the Empire as Regent with an iron hand for fifty years, meanwhile keeping a watchful eye on her nephew and stepson, Kwang Hsu, the only Son of Heaven then extant, from the day of his birth to the age of 38, she finally concluded that he wasn't strong enough to fill the Dragon Throne after she was gone. During her last illness, therefore, at the age of nearly fourscore, she issued an edict naming one of her favorites as Regent and his infant son as the Emperor-to-be. Then she left a nice little dose of poison in the hands of her favorite eunuch for the especial benefit of Kwang Hsu, with the idea of taking his soul along with her to the Nine Springs (the Chinese heaven) — and lay down and died. Remarkable to relate, however, the poison acted so quickly that poor Kwang Hsu passed out a day ahead of her.

Rather a remarkable character, this favorite eunuch, Pi Hsiao Li by name, whose emasculation was a genteel fiction created by the Palace for public consumption — a sop to the amenities, as it were. He was the son of a cobbler and known throughout the Empire as 'Cobbler's Wax Li.' Having attracted the attention of the Old Buddha, who was a veritable Catherine of Russia in her youth, he became a pseudo-Palace eunuch, from which lowly position he developed into the real power behind the Throne. At the time of the Boxer Rebellion he owned half the banks and pawnshops in Peking and was credited with a personal fortune of over $30,000,000.

Since the death of the Old Buddha China has posed as a Republic. That's about all it has amounted to: a pose. Former Viceroy Yuan Shih-kai, a favorite with the Old Buddha, ignoring the potential Son of Heaven, Hsuan Tung, who was only six years old when the Republic was declared, managed to have himself elected first President. That wasn't anywhere near as gratifying, however, as being a Son of Heaven himself. So — just as everything was settling down comfortably, the ambitious Yuan, having bribed the Chinese Senate and House of Representatives quite heavily, abolished the Republic overnight and had himself elected Emperor. More than anything else he wanted the chance to make one little prayer at the Altar of

Heaven, just like a real Emperor. And then — Dr. Sun Yat Sen, that annoying Hong Kong reformer who was always stirring things up in the southern provinces, hearing of the accession of Yuan to the throne, started a revolution in which all of Yuan's soldiers joined. And there he was: the Presidency gone, his enormous bribes gone, all Son-of-Heaven prospects gone, with the result that he died very shortly from a broken heart. He was the first Chinese on record who is alleged to have died from that particular ailment. There are those who are inconsiderate enough to say that China's very ancient persuader (a dose of poison) had more to do with it than heart trouble.

Since that time Peking has been without a real ruler and Sun Yat Sen ran things to suit himself down in the vicinity of Canton until the time of his death this last year. In a way, it's about an even break between comic opera and stark tragedy. It also casts an interesting light on the possibilities of China's regeneration. There are plenty of royalists who prophesy that Hsuan Tung, the former Emperor, who is now nearly twenty years of age and a real Son of Heaven, will find some way of bringing back the Dragon Throne. He's an English-educated, up-to-date young man, married, with an income of $4,000,000 annually and maintains a retinue of four thousand people in the royal palace at Peking, together with all the ancient traditions. That's what the Chinese think of royalty, despite their Republican tendencies. It's a most intriguing situation.

Turning about to the southward you face what is known as the 'Chinese City,' the walls of which were built by the Ming Emperor Yunglo in the sixteenth century. They are not as massive as Kublai Khan's work, however, being but thirty feet high, twenty-five feet wide at the base, and fifteen at the top. The wall on which you are standing (let us hope) is the original and constitutes the northern boundary of the Chinese City. To this very day there is no love lost between the Chinese of the south and their militaristic and dominant brethren of the north, the Tatars or Manchus, who have held the whip-hand for so many centuries. There are, nevertheless, those on both sides of the line who still look forward to the day when they will pool their issues long enough to drive out the hated 'foreign devil.' When one looks down upon well-paved streets, however, an up-to-date electric street-railway system, thousands of motor-cars racing up and down the highways, scores of modern shops of every description, and the towering radio masts rising above the Japanese Legation, it looks as if the white brother were there to stay, not to mention the altruistic Japanese. If more assurance is needed you have but to go out to the Nankow Pass through the Great Wall and take an aeroplane for the Ming Tombs and return. Just a trifle different from the chair trip under six-coolie power of a few years ago, although that is still available and — to my way of thinking — preferable.

It will take more than the demon of progress to reduce this most amazing caravansary to the dead level of the commonplace. The time may come when the queue and the ridiculous cotton shoe will perforce give way to Occidental trappings, but let us hope it won't be in your time or mine. 'Better a hundred years of Europe than a cycle of Cathay' — yes, but by all means let us have our glimpse of Peking while the camels from Mongolia, the flocks of sheep from the country without the walls, the droves of laden donkeys, the honking flivvers with their screaming yellow drivers, the painted Manchu girl in her rickshaw, with a fan to keep off the sun's rays, the omnipresent Peking cart, and the noisy funeral as well as the riotous wedding procession are all making frenzied efforts to negotiate the narrow passage of the An Ting Gate at one and the same time,

with you and me on the side taking it in with our cameras.
That's the only city on the face of the earth where such
sights may be seen, with a perfectly good hotel in the offing.
And — it's just as easy for a dear old lady who has passed
the allotted span to get there as it is for the sweet girl
graduate. Yes — and a mighty sight safer than the corner
of Fifth Avenue and Forty-Second Street. The street life
of Peking is something that is not scheduled in any guide-
book I ever saw. It surpasses in interest all the temples,
walls, and monuments in the Middle Kingdom. It will
drive the omnipresent personal pronoun into his hole and
make you thankful in the bargain.

In planning your time in this ancient capital, don't overlook one rather insignificant spot which nobody will think
to show you unless you request it: 'Tis the old unguarded
water gate through which a few British and Sikh soldiers
managed to worm their way during the last days of the
Boxer Rebellion in 1900. The desperate resistance which
the besieged legations within the walls had maintained for
two terrible months was fast coming to an end. Ammunition and provisions were about exhausted. Massacre was
in sight. It was the addition of these few brave Sikh fight-
ers that enabled the defenders to resist the one last attempt
made by the Boxer soldiery to rush them. The relief column of twenty thousand allied troops which had been ten
days fighting their way up from Tientsin arrived the next
day — August 14th — entered the city and raised the
siege.

What they did to Peking is better left to the imagination. Suffice it to say that the Old Buddha, after order-
ing the Emperor's favorite concubine (whom she disliked)
thrown into a well, deserted the city with a few faithful
attendants, including the weak-kneed Emperor himself,
whom she compelled to accompany her. They remained in

the ancient summer palace at Jehol until the trouble blew over. And when they returned to the Forbidden City, they found that it had been looted after the most approved methods of the Orient and Occident combined. There wasn't a jade teacup left in the kitchen. It was discovered afterward, however, that the Palace eunuchs had done quite well for themselves before the soldiers reached the spot. If you have time to read and the desire for an eye-witness account of this fearsome uprising, you'll find it in 'Indiscreet Letters from Peking,' by B. L. Putnam-Weale, a British correspondent. It's worthy a place in your luggage. And — don't be too hasty in your judgments, for the longer you travel in the Orient the more convincingly will it be borne in upon you that 'East is East, and West is West, and never the twain shall meet.' There's but one way in which the lion and the lamb lie down together here, and that's with the lamb on the inside. It really isn't necessary to reform the Chinese in order to do business with them. And if there's anything else that any Occidental nation wants in addition to the transacting of business, that's more or less of a personal matter and can wait.

The most highly wrought, deeply revered, and wonderful example of Chinese worship is the celebrated Temple and Altar of Heaven in the southeastern section of the Chinese or outer city. This marvelous shrine was rebuilt in the fifteenth century by the peerless and magnificent Yunglo, the last and the greatest of the Ming dynasty. Whatever there is of genuine religious feeling in the whole of China centers about this spot, which has been sacred to the personal worship of the Emperor himself ever since the days of Kublai Khan. Twice a year, the Emperor, as the Son of Heaven and the sole high priest of his people, went there to worship. The chief of these two gorgeous ceremonies was the sacrifice at the winter solstice, performed before sunrise on the morning of December 21st. The Emperor, who spent the night fasting, entirely alone, in a hall within the enclosure, made his appearance just at the break of dawn, surrounded by a gorgeous retinue and took his place on the altar facing the tablet of Shang-ti, the Supreme Being to whom only he acknowledged inferiority. On this occasion a two-year-old bullock, without spot or blemish, was sacrificed in a green porcelain furnace which stands near by. Surrounding the altar are large basket-shaped iron crates in which were deposited slips of paper containing a variety of writings, including the names of royal offenders whose lives had been forfeited during the past year. These were burnt — and the smoke arising was supposed to represent the Emperor's report to Heaven on his administration, etc.

The magnitude of this high altar may be gathered from the following: It consists of a triple circular terrace of white marble, two hundred and ten feet in diameter at the base, one hundred and fifty feet in the middle and ninety at the top. The circular stone upon which the Emperor knelt is in the exact center of the upper terrace. Surrounding that are nine concentric circles of other stones, representing that many heavens, the extreme limit of which is the horizon. Thus was our royal worshiper supposed to be in the very center of the universe: rather an impressive and important location. This is what Yuan Shih-kai hankered after. And it was that fond desire of his, more than anything else, that led to his undoing. The Chinese are a bit particular as to their Sons of Heaven. It's largely a matter of breeding instead of accession. No one knew that any better than Yuan himself. He took a long chance and couldn't get away with it. However — he paid the price. There are many Yuans.

Opposite this magnificent altar is the Temple of Heaven

with its brilliantly tinted, blue tiled roof. A sort of marble pergola connects the two. During the investment of Peking at the time of the Boxer outbreak in 1900, the Japanese troops were quartered in this sacred spot. They showed their appreciation of their surroundings by smashing the exquisite marble carvings on the three terraces. A most damnable piece of vandalism and a lasting disgrace as well to the Japanese soldiery. The most amazing feature of this altar, as well as every other temple throughout that vast city, is the almost criminal neglect which cries out on every hand. Grass and weeds will be found growing in the interstices of marble stairways, pergolas, and even in the joints of balustrades.

Not far from the Temple of Heaven is the Temple of Agriculture situated in an expansive park of several hundred acres. Here is where the Son of Heaven used to come once a year, accompanied by an immense retinue, and plough a piece of ground, thus propitiating the spirits of the earth and the air (not to mention his great ancestors), all of whom were credited with making the earth bring forth her fruits. At this ceremony the Emperor would remove his royal robes, assuming the garb of a peasant. In this humble decking-out he would lay his hand to an Imperial yellow plough, drawn by an ox led by one of his attendants. Meanwhile the royal *entourage* would follow in his footsteps scattering seed and singing hymns in praise of the gods of the harvest. All that has gone into the discard since China has become a Republic under the tyrannical sway of the Tuchuns or provincial military governors who, between them, control armies aggregating 1,200,000 men which they use for their own private purposes and to strengthen their own positions. Poor, doddering old Flowery Kingdom. Who can possibly figure her future?

There is a marked difference between the care bestowed

upon these temple surroundings and those of the Summer Palace where the Old Buddha used to spend most of her leisure hours. It would seem to be a total lack of public spirit or else the grafting of funds supposed to be used for those purposes. Just previous to the bi-yearly visit of the Emperor to the Temple of Heaven, the whole place was cleaned up and put in fine condition. Also, whenever any particular function was scheduled for any of the various temples in the city, the same cleaning-up process was observed. But — in the interim, there was not the slightest pretense of keeping these sightly places in order. Even on the summit of that towering dagoba in the Tatar city, beneath which are supposed to be buried two or three hairs from Buddha's beard and a sacrosanct finger-nail or two, flowers may be seen blooming. No one can tell how they got there. Also, it was news to me that Buddha had a beard. In contradistinction to such inexcusable carelessness, the Summer Palace had the appearance of being expertly 'manicured.' The grass closely cut, the walks immaculate, and the *tout ensemble* spotless. There was every evidence of the presence of the Old Buddha's spirit. No disposition on the keeper's part to lie down on his job even if she were dead. It certainly was an amazing contrast.

This lavishly beautiful Summer Palace is something the visitor should not overlook. It wasn't supposed to be good form to discuss the subject during the life of the Old Buddha, especially if there were any prospects of its reaching her ears. But — the fact is the crafty old lady financed it out of $50,000,000 which had been appropriated for a brand-new Chinese navy. Surprising how much at home a citizen of the 'land of the free and the home of the brave' feels when he hears such interesting little classics as that. However, the Chinese, despite their great poverty, are much like their British cousins — they dearly love a lord.

The Old Buddha was exceedingly popular because she was abler than any Emperor that ever sat on the throne and absolutely fearless. While superstitious in many ways, she wasn't misled by that Son-of-Heaven business. As long as she possessed all her faculties, despite the piling-up of the years, she didn't purpose stepping down from the Regency, where she was the real power. When, therefore, Kwang Hsu, the Emperor, rebelled against being kept in the background and started a conspiracy to dispose of the old lady in somewhat the same style she was accustomed to dispose of others, she just took him out to the Summer Palace and marooned him on a little island in the center of that beautiful lake. If it had not been for the world-wide scandal it would have created, she would have 'finished' him then. In fact that's what everybody expected. With a thousand eunuchs keeping an eye on things in general at the Summer Palace, it was comparatively easy to include Kwang Hsu. And so she let him live on until the time came for her own departure, and then she sent him on a day ahead. One of the principal attractions of this picturesque spot is the Jade Hill Pagoda which is most originally conceived and unlike any other in existence. The famous camel-back bridge, the exquisite bridge of seventeen arches, both of white marble, and the ornately carved marble summer house made to represent a floating houseboat, including the bronze pavilion — all are exceedingly worth while and will amply justify the eight-mile motor ride from your hotel.

There is comparatively little temple-visiting in Peking, but what there is is worth while. The Temple of Confucius, in the old University grounds, contains that ancient philosopher's ancestral tablet in a little alcove. In the Hall of Classics adjoining may be seen some very ancient carvings of the complete Confucian classics on three hundred stone steles or upright slabs mounted on the backs of colossal tortoises, indicative of long life. This art is peculiarly Chinese, and your time will be well spent with the camera. Also, there are a number of immense bells swung in the towers over the various city gates that are useful as well as ancient. Each has its own particular history or tradition.

The Astronomical Observatory is the most ancient of its kind in the world. It was built by Kublai Khan in 1279 A.D. Perhaps some of you who have been in Germany may recall having seen some very ancient bronze instruments mounted in the grounds of the Imperial Palace at Potsdam. They were a part of the loot which the Germans carried away from Kublai Khan's observatory in Peking in 1900 and presented to their appreciative Kaiser. One of the provisions of the Treaty of Versailles was that Germany should return them, which she has done. Incidentally, it's worthy of note that the first observatory in Europe was not erected until the sixteenth century.

You'll wish to see the Lama Temple, but you won't stay long. It really is a lama monastery founded about three hundred years ago and houses about one thousand of the most filthy and rascally lot of Mongol beggars to be found on the face of the earth. They call themselves priests, but as a matter of fact they are a bunch of scoundrels whom the authorities would throw out bag and baggage were it not that they are fearful of offending the Dalai Lama. The principal attraction is a huge image of the Buddha carved from a single tree and transported from Tibet.

Then there is the old Examination Hall with its three thousand little stalls where, in olden times, those who were candidates for public office came every three years for a three-day examination. It was something on the style of our Civil Service, only, in this instance, the applicants ranged all the way from youth to ninety years of age. Those little stalls you will see were the 'bed and board' of the candidates for the three-day period, during which they wrote essays on Confucian philosophy to demonstrate their fitness for public life. Here they were kept in solitary confinement until the examinations were over. Out of three thousand essays, the incorruptible (?) judges selected three hundred and sixty. From them they chose eighteen by the usual process of elimination. Out of those eighteen three were selected who were to be immortalized by the award of the highest degree of Doctor of Literature by the Son of Heaven himself. One would think that such a game might be played on the square. But no — human nature was about the same in those parlous days as it is now. It was quite possible, not only to bribe the judges, but the properly heeled candidate could buy an essay already prepared which he might copy and be sure of local immortality and a job to boot.

Twenty years ago these municipal examinations were the cause of a wholesale scandal in Peking which reached even to the Dragon Throne. The trouble was then, and is now, that not a one of these essayists looking for a Government job would deign to do any other kind of work. In addition, there are to-day in the neighborhood of fifty thousand successful candidates all over the Empire, who haven't the money to 'buy' an office now that they have passed their exams. And they won't work either. Some one has said these fellows are the original I.W.W.'s. One thing is sure — they are a very definite problem in Republican governmental plans.

To those who are interested in educational matters a visit to the Peking University will repay the time spent. It is a combination of all the Christian institutions in

Peking and vicinity, including one college for men, another for women, and a theological school. Every province in the Empire is represented on the roster. The faculty includes forty-one Europeans and thirty Chinese. Of five hundred alumni, forty-five are taking post-graduate courses in political economy and research work; one hundred and thirty-five are teachers, seventy-six ministers of the gospel, forty· physicians, thirty-six Y.M.C.A. secretaries, and twenty-two are in Government service. In addition to the above the Rockefeller Foundation built in 1922 the Union Medical College and Hospital, at a cost of $5,000,000. It's the finest scientific institution in all Asia. If any Oriental country has a wonderful opportunity to profit from the way the Occidental twig is bent, it's China. There is her only hope: the education of her youth. And Christianity is absolutely necessary to civic progress in this vast country. The governmental schools are indifferent to all religions and inclined to be antagonistic to Christianity. The dangers of atheism and communism are already apparent. Something more fundamental than a college diploma is needed to put young China on the right track.

Indicative of a typical Chinese method of disposing of a difficult political problem the following instance is about as eloquent and cold-blooded as could be imagined. The dining-room of the Hôtel des Wagon Lits is an immense affair divided into two sections by movable screens. One side is for the use of Europeans, the other for high-class Chinese who like to dine in style. One evening during our stay, there was what might be called a 'farewell dinner' given a local official. I should say there were in the neighborhood of twenty-five or thirty guests, and it was quite apparent they were all having a good time. On the way home, the guest of the evening was shot — all in accordance with a prearranged programme. Whether the gentleman most interested knew of it in advance, I never learned. He was scheduled to move on, and they simply wished to give him a good send-off. That, at least, was the way the story reached me. It didn't seem to excite any particular wonder, and I was given to understand that nothing would be done about it, as no one knew who fired the shot.

Those who plan to do some shopping will be interested in the following experience which, being a personal one, I can vouch for. It throws a most interesting light on the way a Chinese merchant's mind works, especially in his dealings with the 'foreign devil.' It is the custom of all hotels in the Orient to accord native merchants (for a consideration) the use of the hotel lobby for a display of their goods. At The Wagon Lits there were four Chinese dealers all in a row in a corner of the foyer, all with about the same line of stuff for sale: Mandarin coats, kakemonos, diminutive incense-burners, lacquer-work of all kinds, and ivory carvings. They were not allowed to solicit — simply to show what they had to those sufficiently interested to inspect and make inquiries. Bearing in mind what a figure 'face' cuts with the Chinese, let me say that if the merchant takes the initiative in recommending any one particular article to a possible buyer, in the hearing of a competitor, he must sell it, no matter at what price, in order to save his face. For that reason, he is quite careful not to overdo the matter of making a sale. He will show everything he has on display and quote prices with a blandness that scarcely comports with his knowledge that his competitor close by is listening to every word he says.

Now — in the Orient, nobody but an 'easy mark' ever pays the first price quoted on anything. Merchants who have the *entrée* to hotels are, as a general thing, fairly firm in their prices. Ten per cent is about all the would-be buyer can get off. I had been told by a friend who has traveled in China for many years that I could buy any worth-while article carrying a price subject to argument for about half the quoted figure. I was much interested in a Mandarin coat — a gorgeous bit of workmanship — for which the dealer wanted sixty dollars 'Mex' which is equivalent to thirty dollars gold. Finally the merchant said he would take ten per cent off, but my friend wouldn't let me buy. Up to that moment the merchant's 'face' had been well protected, as I had done practically all the talking. Ascertaining the address of his store in the Chinese City, I called on him the next morning before he came to the hotel, thinking that in dealing with him alone I might secure a real bargain. To my utter astonishment he showed me a coat infinitely inferior to the one I had admired at the hotel: price sixty dollars Mex, from which I could not budge him. After considerable argument he dug up the coat I wanted: price sixty-five dollars Mex. I laughed at him and left his shop.

In the hotel that afternoon I asked him to bring some of his goods up to the room, which is a common occurrence. He had the fine coat with him, and finally made me an offer of sixty dollars Mex, less twenty per cent, from which figure he would not recede. I asked him why he insisted on charging me more in his store than he was willing to sell for at the hotel. His answer was most illuminating: 'I want sell,' said he, 'I come hotel see you. You no buy. You come my shop next day. You want buy more than I want sell, so I raise price. When I come hotel, I want sell more than you want buy, so I put price down cheap.'

My friend said I would never get him below the twenty per cent discount as long as I continued to show any interest. The next day we passed by the dealer without paying any attention to him. This was the cue for his competitor, who stopped us with an invitation to look over his stuff. He showed me a beautiful coat which was practically a duplicate of the one I had been wrangling about with the other man. Here my friend interposed quickly and sneered at the garment saying he wouldn't have it for a gift. Then we busied ourselves looking at some manifestly inferior goods, and finally walked away. The dealer came after us with the fine coat on his arm, praising its quality, in which he was thoroughly justified. We were not even enough interested to ask him the price. Meanwhile, his competitor's countenance was a study. We walked away. The next day my friend bought the garment for ten dollars gold. In other words, having lured us away from the other dealer and then being led into declaring himself in favor of a coat which we had rejected, he would have lost face with his competitor if he had not made the sale, no matter whether it was a profitable one or not.

Any one attempting to do any shopping outside of the stores that cater entirely to tourist trade must be prepared to face a succession of anomalies which will stagger his sense of the eternal fitness of things. The saving of face and the frightful circumlocution of Chinese etiquette are little short of a religion with the native. Shrewd as he is, he would rather lose money than lose face and the Occidental directness of going to the bottom of a subject by the shortest possible route is anathema to him. He looks upon the foreigner as legitimate prey in every way. Unless you are prepared to be 'stuck,' don't go shopping in a native store without some one who understands the language. You haven't a chance for one tiny percentage of a square deal. You are interested in the quality and genuineness of certain goods and the price. He is not thinking of those factors at all. He is studying *you*, wondering how much you really know and what his prospects are for getting anywhere from twice or three times over what the article is worth. Only when he has satisfied himself on these points (and it does not take long) will he quote you a price on a really meritorious article. That's why the average merchant invariably unlimbers a lot of utterly valueless plunder before he will display the real thing. He's studying *you* with a view to selling you the imitation instead of the genuine — and this, without reference to price. In other words, unless you are wise you won't even get a look at the real stuff.

Furthermore, it's a breach of etiquette to go into a native store and even ask the price of an article unless you intend to buy. And — don't fool yourself that the merchant doesn't know the difference between the time-waster and the one who is a possible customer. If you will put up an argument as to the reasonableness of the price (whether you intend buying or not), you save your face and his too. If, however, you move on without any comment after having asked the price — that's tantamount to an insult and he's apt to ask you why you came in if you didn't intend to buy. That is his method of saving his face and letting you know that he's 'wise.' If a native buyer should be guilty of such a lapse, he would be greeted with the most eloquent line of Chinese profanity imaginable. Another thing: if you go into a store where there are several clerks and ask any one of them the price of any particular article, after having spent a little time looking around, you won't get any reply from him until he has questioned every other clerk as to whether they have quoted you a price on the same article. If, by any possibility, this rule should slip up in your case, and you were quoted different prices on the same article by different clerks — that would simply indicate that each one had sized *you* up differently.

The explanation of all this apparent waste of time is more fundamental than you would imagine. It is based on the

Chinese social system which runs as follows in the order given: Scholars, farmers, laborers, and merchants. You will note that the merchant is at the foot of the list. And here again we have another sidelight on the Chinese point of view. The merchant hasn't the brain of the scholar; he doesn't produce anything like an inventor or a farmer who cultivates the ground; he does not work like the carpenter or the manufacturer in making a necessary article for general use. He is just a trader, a medium of exchange. He doesn't increase the value or the utility of anything; he just sells things for more than he pays for them, and as such, he's an enemy of society, a sort of necessary evil. In other words, distribution of goods means nothing in the Chinese mind for the simple reason that he's in the habit of producing all his family necessities himself. When he has to go outside those exceedingly restricted limitations to the extent of patronizing the merchant, he regards it as a misfortune because he doesn't understand how anybody can possibly be justified in charging him a profit on one of the necessaries of life.

Given this view on the part of the four hundred millions of Chinese population and you can understand the merchant's reaction to it. Regarded as a pariah, he accepts the name and goes after the game. And the foreigner is his particular 'meat.' Furthermore, all's grist that comes to the mill and the end justifies the means. After you have mulled that over for a moment, you will appreciate just how it comes about that the tourist is prone to be fleeced as the sparks fly upward. Once more, remember Mr. Harriman and the Daibutsu.

These same business principles (?) hold good in Japan only to a more limited degree. With the Japanese, the Samurai formerly held the same exalted position as the scholar does with the Chinese. Here, again, we have another gulf

fixed, which explains the great difference between the two
nations that sprang from the same fountain head: With
the Chinese, the scholar, the man of peace, predominates.
With the Japanese, the Samurai or his logical successor,
the soldier, the man of war, predominates. And there you
are. You must not be horrified, therefore, when you read
of foxy Japan's ever-present, warlike intimidation of China
and steady encroachments on her territory. Neither must
you be surprised when you learn that about all China can do
is to put a howl to high heaven because she cannot defend
herself and she knows it. She has never cultivated the
fighting spirit. She suspects everything and everybody, including her own people. There is no such thing as mutual
confidence, even between neighbors, throughout the length
and breadth of that vast country. Fear, distrust, and
underground methods are the very breath of China's
nostrils, and she can no more help it than she can prevent
to-morrow's sun from rising.

There is no possible harmony of feeling or action between
the five major divisions of this vast stretch of country;
China proper in the southeast; Manchuria in the northeast;
Sinkiang in the northwest; Mongolia in the north, and
Tibet in the west, for the very simple reason that they do
not speak the same language nor have the same religious
beliefs. In fact, the present-day flag of the Chinese Republic carries five stripes signifying the five different races
which it encompasses: Chinese, Manchu, Mongol, Tibetan,
and Turki, all and each of whom utterly distrust and hate
the other. This, in a few words, is the explanation of
China's pitiful partitioning. Great Britain, France, and
Japan virtually control her. If it were not for the United
States standing off on the side with enough power and influence to insist upon the 'open door,' they would rend her
apart and throw dice for her cotton shoes. Do the Chinese

think any more of the United States on that account, you ask? The answer is NO. They would start another Boxer Rebellion to-morrow and clean every foreign devil out, hip and thigh, if they thought they could get away with it.

Beyond all question, the most remarkable characteristic of the Chinese nation as a whole is the universal habit or custom of 'squeeze,' or graft, as we have it here in the United States. This is really more important than it seems because the whole nation is honeycombed with it and always has been, from the Dragon Throne down to the most poverty-stricken coolie. There isn't any phase of activity, governmental, civil, mercantile, or private life, that is free of it. It is the one thing that Occidentals who have spent years in the country say is absolutely impossible to root out. The term 'squeeze' is so eloquent in itself that one would think the Chinese would find some other word less expressive of theft. It has, however, got to be purely a commercial term and refers to the pressure exerted by the fingers of any man through whose hands somebody else's money passes. A pressure that causes a certain percentage thereof to stick fast.

Governmentally speaking, the most bare-faced panhandlers in the nation for centuries have been the Palace eunuchs. Did the Viceroy of an important province wish an interview with the Emperor? It cost him more than a year's salary, yes — several years'. And he had to pay in advance. The chief eunuch handled the job and naturally kept 'his.' Where did the Viceroy get it? He gouged it out of the people in the way of taxation. Even the 'Old Buddha' snitched $50,000,000 to build her Summer Palace as you have already been told. It has its basis in that same bit of human nature that leads a restaurant keeper and a railway company to pay small wages to waiters and porters, with the expectation that they will 'squeeze' their living from the public.

If the European housekeeper in China does her own marketing, she soon discovers that her servants have followed her up and collected. She also learns that she has wasted her time because the servant can buy more economically than she, including his squeeze. If she posts herself on the market cost of various articles of food and checks up on her servant, she will find that she has been short-weighted. If she establishes her own scales and weighs everything herself, she will find on investigation that her servant returned a portion of the groceries after it was all over, for which the merchant gave him his squeeze. If she 'fires' her servant for squeezing, and hires another to take his place, she will find that the remaining servants in the house will club together and manage in some way to supply the discharged one with his squeeze until he gets another job — and meanwhile she 'holds the bag.' In other words, the Chinese regards his squeeze as his inalienable right and a foreigner who won't allow it simply cannot keep help.

The household servants have a code much like tramps have in our own country, consisting of certain cabalistic chalk marks on the gate which tell the story to all newcomers. It's a bred-in-the-bone custom to which every Chinese is a victim, gauged in accordance with his position in life. The higher up the scale one goes the greater the percentage. When it comes to a Government official they simply take it away from him without any fear of a comeback because they know that is precisely what he is doing with those who are courting his favor. In other words, to paraphrase Dean Swift:

> Big fleas have smaller fleas to bite 'em
> And so proceed ad infinitum.

A certain case came under my personal notice where a Britisher had made a definite contract with an exceedingly reputable Chinese firm on a strictly net basis, with the precise object of eliminating the squeeze feature. The contract had three years to run on a monthly payment plan, each one of which was met with scrupulous regularity. When the deal was completed and there was every reason to expect a renewal, the Chinese merchant asked for his squeeze, although not a word had been said during the three-year period. The Britisher referred him to the contract, and the merchant rejoined that he didn't think he (the Britisher) was in earnest when he proposed to leave squeeze out of consideration. And he had to make it good or get no renewal. The point of the incident is that the merchant pleaded absolute sincerity and declared that he regarded the net feature of the contract as the Britisher's method of saving his face in quoting a lower figure than there was any reason to expect. As the Britisher said to me: 'If you can beat this, go to it.'

When one recalls the checkered and spectacular career of the 'Old Buddha' and realizes that her squeeze amounted to $40,000,000 annually and that she left a private fortune of $80,000,000, one can scarcely blame the rest of the nation for desiring to accumulate a few pickings here and there. At any rate, that's a national characteristic that can only be done away with by a complete reorganization from top to bottom. And that's rather a large order for four hundred millions of people.

CHAPTER VII
CHINA'S GREAT WALL

And not in vain from age to age,
In forms of grandeur and of grace,
Is writ on more than History's page,
The progress of the human race —
The rise of mind and feeling, shown
In golden poems made of stone.
WILLIAM WINTER

IF there were nothing else in the vast expanse of China
to justify a visit, its Great Wall would amply suffice. How
many of the younger generation know, and how many of
the older have forgotten, that China's Great Wall is one of
the Seven Wonders of the World? Be you the most blasé
creature that ever left home, strange places for to see, this
tremendous stretch of ancient masonry, clothed in the romance of centuries, will strip your self-consciousness from
you like an old garment ready for the rag-bag and leave you
agape and glorying in your shame. You simply cannot
take it in at first. Its amazing age — 2137 years — and its
astounding length — 1700 miles — are just a bit too much
for the average mind to assimilate. You need to sit down
in view of it and think it over. Then it begins to dawn on
you that this primitive marvel constitutes a remarkably
illuminating index to the Chinese character. Old Shwangti,
China's first Emperor, who started this wall in the year
212 B.C., wasn't any more interested in the 'foreign devils'
at that time than is the China of to-day. He wanted to
keep them out. He wanted to be left alone and undisturbed. And so he built this great barrier, extending from
the shores of the Yellow Sea at Shanhaikwan westward
along the southern boundary of Mongolia to the eastern

CHINA'S GREAT WALL — ONE OF THE SEVEN WONDERS OF THE WORLD

frontier of Turkestan, where it joins the Hwang-ho River on the borders of the Great Gobi Desert. You probably recall a picture of it in the atlas of your school-days.

Minus any regard for the points of the compass or the configuration of the land, it winds irrationally up hill and down dale, over the tallest mountains — in places over four thousand feet above sea-level — and down into the deepest valleys. It suggests a political job with an unlimited appropriation. The height of the wall varies from twenty to thirty feet, with an average thickness of twenty-five. The runway on top is smoothly paved, with a pierced parapet on the outside, toward a possible invader, and a smooth coping on the inside. Every two hundred yards, for the full length of the wall, forty-foot towers are located for the accommodation of the soldiery. They not only did not *want* any visitors, but they determined not to have them if solid masonry and armies could keep them out. Well — we all know that they have not changed much in the twenty-one centuries that have flown. Their slogan to-day makes that perfectly clear: 'China for the Chinese.'

Without question this is the most stupendous piece of work that mankind ever undertook. It is said that half a million of men were engaged for ten years in completing it. One can well believe it. Running true to form — like so many municipal jobs — certain sections have been discovered 'way in back of beyond, in the mountainous districts, where the material used was so much mud and rubble. How natural it sounds in connection with public service! In those good old days they doubtless had their slang phrase corresponding to that with which we are so familiar: 'Get it while the going is good.'

One hundred miles out on the Peking–Kalgan Railway brings us to the celebrated Nankow Pass, where we spent one never-to-be-forgotten day on the Wall, at the very summit, where the soldiery of past centuries held back the Mongolian hordes that poured down that narrow defile with the hope of breaking through to the vast fertile plains of China. The Wall crosses the pass at right angles, beneath which is the age-old Pa-ta-ling Gate, only the gate has been gone for years. Huge bastions on either side show, however, what a definite barrier it must have been in its time. Even as we watched, a long string of camels filed through, laden with huge black baskets containing Mongolian grease which is sent to Europe for the manufacture of essential oils. The kling-klang of the bells sounded odd enough as the shaggy beasts padded their way under the arch in a trail not more than a couple of feet wide and as many deep where each camel had from time immemorial followed in the footsteps of the one in front instead of taking the more level track on either side.

It didn't seem possible that we were looking down upon a pathway that had been in constant use for over two thousand years. No garrison of soldiers now, no sentries, nothing but the rank growth of weeds and grass beneath the battlemented tower which we profaned with both luncheon and camera. The bare rocky mountain ranges stretching in every direction seem to be covered with a green moss, over which the gray masonry of the Wall creeps like some blind monster, with no particular objective, feeling its way in vast, impressive sweeps up the heights and down into the depths. 'Tis said by scientists that this colossal relic is the one man-made thing on the surface of our earth that could be distinguished by the inhabitants of Mars.

Another excellent view of the Great Wall may be had at Shanhaikwan about one hundred miles north of Tientsin. Here the Manchurian Railway passes through a breach in the Wall on its way down from Mukden to Peking. Originally the Wall extended to the edge of the seashore, ending in a huge tower founded on the reef that reaches out quite a distance into the water. Time and storm have taken their toll of this portion until now only a pile of débris remains to show how bravely the old fabric defended attack from the sea as well as the land. Shanhaikwan is situated about halfway between the sea and the hills which begin to rise sharply from the level of the plain. The old Wall follows the lay of the land straightaway up to the very crest of the range and then drops down out of sight only to reappear farther on and higher up. For many years some of the old Ming brass cannon were to be seen in the towers near the seashore. They doubtless are there yet, as they are a trifle bulky for the most aggressive souvenir hunter to carry.

Inasmuch as the famous Ming Tombs lie a bare ten miles from Nankow Pass, the proper thing to do is to cover both places on the same trip. This can be done by arranging for accommodations at a small but cleanly hotel at Nankow where one may spend the night after putting in one day at the Wall, starting for the Tombs early next morning.

There is no such thing as a road leading out to these fifteenth-century structures, which are fast going to ruin, more's the pity. There is a trail, however, which the coolies in the neighborhood know well. It leads off over the fields, across shallow streams, through native villages and farms — a mere footpath. The approved conveyance is a chair suspended from a couple of bamboo poles. Two husky coolies in front and as many behind constitute the necessary motive power. The only trouble with this mode of conveyance is the rhythmic trot of the coolies and the pendulum-like motion of the chair which has a tendency to lull the passenger to sleep. It's an altogether agreeable and novel experience and infinitely to be preferred to the *fin-de-siècle* aeroplane which is about as well fitted for those surroundings as a horse in a ballroom. The little hotel sends along an excellent lunch and the party returns in time for dinner and another night's sojourn.

There's a decided element of sadness in contemplating the criminal neglect of these ancient and historical monuments. Shortly before reaching the avenue of approach, we pass under a magnificent marble *pailou* containing five arches, which is most effectively silhouetted against the sky and marks the official entrance to the Tombs. These *pailous* are first cousins to the Japanese *torii* and serve the same purpose. This one just mentioned is the most magnificent of its kind in all China. It was built in the sixteenth century and stands at the first rise of a series of low foot-hills among which the Tombs are situated. Nothing but millet-fields in every direction: nothing to indicate what its purpose is, no buildings of any kind near. It looks as if it might have dropped from heaven and landed accidentally about a thousand miles from the place for which it was intended. Another rise and we see, half a mile distant, the bright imperial yellow of the tiles topping the thirteen royal sepulchers ensconced in an ancient grove of cedars against the hillside. The roadway is lined on both sides with a series of mammoth figures — elephants, unicorns, camels, lions, dogs, horses, and warriors, all facing each other over a crop of weeds which have overgrown the ancient paved highway.

Each one of these tombs is situated in a separate court, with an individual entrance. The one we are interested in is that of Yunglo who became Emperor in 1403. It was he who rebuilt the royal city of Peking in the fifteenth century and erected the southern or Chinese City wall. He was the most brilliant of all the Ming Dynasty and the only one whose name is remembered by latter-day generations. It just happened that there were no gate-keepers around on

the day we arrived, and, strange to say, the outer gate was
open. Entering through one of the massive, weather-
beaten doors, we found ourselves in a grass-grown court
which leads up to the terrace of the second gate-house.
This is surrounded by the most ornately carved white
marble balustrade imaginable. The intricacies of that
marvelous scroll-work would scarcely justify its exposure
to the weather. Encircled by several aged pines and cedars
a yellow-tiled and red-lacquered shrine stands on a broad
marble terrace surrounded by another exquisitely carved
marble balustrade. This shrine contains Yunglo's tablet —
a very simple bit of wood with gold lettering which is supposed to represent the departed spirit. In fact that is precisely what that tablet is, in the mind of the devout Confucian: Yunglo's very soul.

In the third and last courtyard stands an impressive
pailou and a tremendous bronze incense-burner at the
entrance to the tower that stands immediately over the
tumulus where have rested for many centuries the dust of
this remarkable Emperor. A sloping tunnel-like entrance
through the tower leads out on the terrace above where a
huge carved marble tablet or stele has been erected which,
for the lack of a better term, might be called Yunglo's
epitaph. It has been defaced by hundreds of autographs of
those vandals from all over the world to whom nothing is
sacred: Russian, Japanese, German, British, Scandinavian.
I was gratified to find none from the United States. And,
now — with all this ancient, imperial and barbaric display,
imagine the roofs falling in by reason of decay and vegeta-
ble growth so rank and heavy as to dislodge the tiles. Imagine these three courtyards with all their gorgeous trappings of royal dissolution going to rack and ruin and the
splendid marble platforms being thrust out of plumb by
grass growth between the slabs. Imagine the Peking

Government sending, once a year, as it does, the last lineal descendant of the Ming Emperors to worship at the tomb of his ancestors in a mess like that I have described; imagine him passing by those wonderfully carved marble balustrades without daring to put a hand on them for fear they will topple over. Not that he would be likely to care if they did. He's a part of the whole inexcusable, unpardonable, yes — criminal, neglect. It brought vividly to mind that tragic and most significant bit of invective from Solomon which present-day China might ponder with profit:

I went by the field of the slothful and by the vineyard of the man void of understanding; and lo — it was all grown over with thorns. And nettles had covered the face thereof. And the stone wall thereof was broken down.
Then I saw and considered it well. I looked upon it and received instruction. Yet a little sleep, a little slumber, a little folding of the hands to sleep. So shall thy poverty come as one that travelleth: and thy want as an armed man.

It's just a bit difficult to work up any great amount of sympathy for 'poor, down-trodden,' unspeakably lazy China, given over to graft, indolence, and superstition. She can worship at the tombs of her ancestors, but she's too confounded sodden, shiftless, and lethargic, and minus the necessary pride, to keep them from falling apart from sheer decay. 'China for the Chinese' forsooth! Mediocrity weighing mediocrity in the balance and incompetence applauding its brother! It's no wonder that the rapacious nations of Europe, not to mention her active neighbor Japan, have reached out from time to time and sliced off a large and juicy piece of territory for their own particular benefit. She has turned the other cheek so many times that she's learned to like it. When a nation has lost all self-respect, she cannot expect that the other nations of the earth will either leave her alone or play the good Samaritan when what's needed is a strait-jacket. This was the frame of mind in which I returned to Peking from our eventful visit to the Ming Tombs. And yet — if I were to start for China to-morrow, the lure of that Druid-like spot would draw me back.

One day at least should be spent without the walls of Peking, taking good care to return to the city before sundown at which time the gates are closed until sunup the next day. And there isn't influence enough in all the combined foreign government representatives in that great city to break this rule. Any one who has ever heard the clang with which a Peking gate closes, especially if he happens to be on the outside, will have some faint realization of what is meant by the 'outer darkness' of Scripture. Closing the gates is preceded by the ringing of one of the great bells, which can be heard for miles. The tolling starts a few minutes before the gates close so as to give every one fair warning. With the last boom of the bell, which goes echoing and reëchoing off over the hills, the iron-studded gates are slammed to with a crash that can be heard almost as far as the bell itself. And 'too-late' means that you turn back while yet there's sufficient light and try to find lodging in some native inn not too far away. It's far from pleasant to gaze upwards at a fifty-foot wall, with darkness coming on and face the fact that you're very much on the outside of it.

The vast plain without the walls is dotted here and there with deserted temples in the last stages of decay. Everything of value was long ago looted by the priests and sold to curio-dealers. The worshipers are gone, with all possible revenues, leaving the wretched degenerate priests, responsible to no one and dependent upon what they can pick up. The utter indifference of the Chinese Government to the destruction and the looting of these ancient monuments is one of the amazing things that faces the traveler on every hand. As a matter of fact, whatever there is of national reverence extends to just one thing: ancestry — and that's a religion of fear. There are a few places, however, with a sufficient trace of their former glory left to justify a visit.

First, I should say, the Yellow Temple, perhaps a mile from the An Ting Gate, which has been one of the most important headquarters of Buddhism since the sixteen-hundreds. In the court stands a magnificent marble dagoba erected to the memory of the Tibetan Tashi Lama who came to visit the Emperor Kienlung in 1780. He was supposed to have died of smallpox shortly afterward. This most exquisite creation, surrounded by four pagodas and a fretted *pailou*, stands on a marble terrace, as perfect as the day it was completed. Eight marvelously carved panels illustrating scenes from the life of the great lama, surround the base of the shaft, which is fretted and carved for nearly its complete height of thirty feet. And to think of a jewel like this being exposed to the weather! That's the most typically Chinese characteristic of all. And now for the story of how his wonderful memorial came to be erected, and you'll have another line on the Chinese make-up:

Son of Heaven Kienlung, notwithstanding his devout adherence to the Buddhist religion, is said to have grown weary of prostrating himself day after day before the Tashi Lama, his guest. And so he just quietly poisoned the holy man and caused the report to be sent out that he had died of smallpox. To save his face and make a thoroughly good job of the proceeding, he had the lama's remains returned to Lhassa in a golden casket. Then he enclosed the infected (?) clothing in an equally beautiful casket and deposited it under the dagoba just described. A short distance away in the same enclosure stand the remains of the Yellow

RUINS OF THE FAMOUS YELLOW TEMPLE ON THE
PEKING PLAIN

Temple itself: a mellow old ruin, most appealing in its deserted beauty, with grass and weeds flourishing all over the matchless porch, and on the caps of its noble columns and pilasters.

The Temple of the Great Bell deserves all the time you can give to it. This is another masterpiece of Yunglo's reign, said to be the largest hanging bell known. According to the records it weighs 120,000 pounds. It is the most artistic achievement in bell-casting in the world and contains 84,000 separate and distinct bas-relief engravings on both the exterior and interior surfaces: approximately eighteen feet in height, twelve feet in diameter, and nine inches thick at the rim. This magnificent bell was rung only at the annual festival or when, in case of drought, the royal mandate went forth to pray for rain. Then this bronze monster's voice could be heard all over Peking and the plains as well. It is said that the sound-waves created by the ringing of this mammoth tocsin would burst it. For that reason a small hole has been left at the top to allow for the necessary expansion.

Two or three miles out into the country from the An Ting Gate, located in the center of a field of millet, is one of the most remarkable pagodas in all China. The Chinese built these pagodas on the outskirts of cities as attractive places for evil spirits so that they might not be tempted to come in town and disturb folks. This particular pagoda is composed of thirteen stories and has eight marble panels around the pedestal, containing beautiful carvings representing scenes from the life of Buddha. It's an astounding anachronism to come across these wonderful sculptured monuments surrounded by a truck-farm. But — there's no accounting for the way the mind of a Chinese works. Just so long as pagodas accomplish what they were built for — to keep wicked spirits away — that's all that interests him.

To those of my readers who don't mind roughing it a bit I have a most interesting side trip to suggest. And this for the reason that I purpose making it myself if I ever go back to Peking, which I hope most fervently to do. Doubtless you will recall Samuel T. Coleridge's famous bit of verse — 'Kublai Khan.' Maybe you were told, as I was, that Coleridge wrote that poem after having recovered from an opium-smoking orgy; that 'Xanadu' existed only in his disordered imagination, and that the 'stately pleasure dome decreed' by Kublai was sheer dope. If that's the way you have been thinking all these years, both you and I owe Sam Coleridge a most abject apology. And — if you have to go to Peking to make it in due and ancient form, all the better for you. It really was Kublai Khan who had the dream. Whether it was a dope-dream or not has never been recorded. At any rate, he visioned in his sleep a wondrous pleasure dome away off in the hills beyond the city walls. When he awoke, he proceeded to make his dream come true. That's a way that real folk have, and mighty few of them are emperors at that.

Tradition has it that he went off on a long trek into Mongolia with a view to discovering a site that would match up with his dream. And he is supposed to have found it at Shangdu in the hills beyond Jehol, the Summer Palace of the Emperors for many centuries. Poetic license will transform Shangdu into Xanadu with little violation of dull fact. And Dr. Bushell, for many years connected with the British Consular Service in Peking, made numerous trips into the hills with a view to locating the site of this ancient palace which has lain hidden for untold generations, and mapping out a route to it. The Chinese Government would not permit any excavations to be made, however, and the site of Kublai Khan's royal hunting lodge still remains a secret of the jungle.

Shangdu lies seventy miles northeast of Peking and may be reached from Kalgan. The trail leads through the Kupeikou Gate of the Great Wall, not far from the Jehol Summer palace which in itself is highly worth while visiting. In Jehol there are several Buddhist monasteries similar to those found in Tibet and much more accessible. This will mean a real trip for him who can 'fork' a Chinese pony and carry his own bedding and grub, which the same is precisely what I hope to do before 'the silver cord be loosed.' I am told there is fairly good hunting en route. Fresh meat in the camp covers a multitude of sins. If Coleridge is to be believed, it shall be said of him who makes this journey that —

> He on honey-dew hath fed
> And drunk the milk of Paradise.

Let's go!

CHAPTER VIII

CANTON — THE HOME OF 'JOHN CHINAMAN'

Around the good world's wide expanse
    Are places great and small,
Whose names fair tingle with romance —
    And I would see them all:
There's Cairo, Fez and Ispahan,
    Shanghai and Singapore,
And Trebizonde and Cagayan,
    And Canton and Lahore.
                    BERTON BRALEY

AFTER ten days in Peking, we turned our steps away from that wonderful old capital with genuine regret. One could stay there six months and not exhaust its thousand and one kaleidoscopic attractions. We had intended to go to Shanghai by rail, but, hearing there was fighting going on at Nanking, we returned to Tientsin on an afternoon train, spent the night aboard the steamer, leaving early next morning for Tongku, where we coaled and waited for the tide to float us over the bar. Next day found us in the harbor at Chefoo from eleven to five. There is considerable native travel along the coast and the Chinese boarding-houses do a thriving business. It is a mighty interesting sight to watch their runners come aboard while the vessel is still under way. As we drew near to the anchorage and the big steamer slowed down a little, half a dozen sizable yawls pulled alongside, with four stalwart coolies at the oars. With the runner standing in the bow with a boathook, they put all their strength into the oars for a few moments, approximating as nearly as possible the speed of the vessel. Then the runner reaches up to the first deck railing with

THE MOST DISTINCTIVE PAGODA IN ALL CHINA —
LOCATED IN A MAIZE FIELD OUTSIDE THE WALLS
OF PEKING

his boathook, by the aid of which he scrambles up the side and lets the hook drop overboard where it is picked up by his companions. The first runner on board generally fills his house and the later competitors take what's left. Where two or three arrive simultaneously, the polyglot solicitation of business is more suggestive of a zoo than anything else. Touching at Wei-hai-wei at 9 P.M., we took on quite a number of passengers and then squared away for Shanghai. The Yellow Sea, being a shallow body of water, is none too comfortable, especially as the large vessels plying thereon are of light draft with a definite tendency to roll. It's comfortable enough in a deck chair, however, and the rest was very welcome. We arrived off Wusung after three days at sea and cast anchor at the confluence of the Yangtze and Whangpoo Rivers, taking a tender twelve miles up to Shanghai. As Sam Weller might have put it, Shanghai's reputation is 'warious.' Unless one deliberately drives over into the native quarter, he would never imagine himself in the Orient. And if he is fortunate enough to be invited to the Shanghai Club, which in all probability he will be, he will see a sight to be witnessed in no other place on the face of the earth: a bar one hundred and ten feet long, with the thirsty members standing from three to five deep between the hours of twelve and two. Thank Heaven, there's one place on earth where a man can imbibe a bit of refreshment without being overcome with the thought that he is his brother's keeper. And even if he is — it's all right in Shanghai which is an international city and practically every resident thereof except the Chinese is a member of the Shanghai Club and of the police department. Out of something over a million and a half population, there are about twenty thousand Europeans including fifteen hundred Americans. The fact that the town is 'wide open' doesn't seem to have interfered with its success commercially or with the ability of its average citizen to carry his liquor like a gentleman.

This is as good a place as any to state that during a ten months' absence on this world-girdling trip I never saw a European the worse for liquor. The disposition of certain kinds of people in public life, many of whom have never been beyond the borders of their own states, to sit back home and prescribe how the citizens of their country shall live their lives in foreign parts would be a joke if it were not so frequently tragical. Now — if you will turn to your encyclopædia you may find something like this:

Shanghai lies low. The summer months are excessively hot. Cholera occurs in the native city every summer. Malarial fever exists and dysentery is apt to become chronic in spring and autumn on account of the sudden changes in temperature and the moist-laden atmosphere — a fall of from twenty to thirty degrees taking place in a few hours. Smallpox is endemic in the Chinese city during the autumn and winter and enteric is common in the autumn. Europeans who adopt ordinary precautions, however, have nothing to fear from the climate.

What is true of Shanghai is equally true of practically every seaport in the Orient, and especially in Malaysia and the Philippine Archipelago. Many years of experience have demonstrated that grapejuice has no permanent demand in these frightfully enervating climates, and that alcohol, when taken in moderation, is practically a specific. Furthermore — every city where the white man has a foothold has its club, with initiation fees and dues within the capacity of the humblest clerk who has come out from home to locate in these far-off corners of the earth. I don't hesitate to go on record that these youngsters are more carefully guarded by their elders in these tropical countries than most of them would be at home. The Britisher is particularly careful of the 'cub,' for whom he feels a personal responsibility. Each one of them is practically compelled to join the club for the very excellent reason that white men in Oriental countries must keep closely in touch with each other. Climatic conditions are insidious and a weakling has no license to be in those parts, anyhow. If a youngster stays at the club too late at night or is noticed to have taken a bit too much, he is waited upon by one of the old-timers who cautions him with the remark that a man who cannot uphold the traditions of the Caucasian race in the Orient had better go back home. And — if he persists — that's precisely what happens to him. Especially is this plan carried out most ruthlessly with young men who develop a tendency to keep unwise company.

In every national legislative body are to be found the idiotic fundamentalists, whose greatest joy is to sit in judgment on the acts of their betters who are bearing heavy responsibilities as their country's spokesmen on the ragged edge of civilization. Men whose lots have been cast in strange places and who are playing their country's part in splendid fashion for a paltry income that is an unspeakable commentary on the home government. And sometimes the higher up they go, the more tragic it is: *vide* that brilliant, that gentle soul—Ambassador Walter H. Page and his untimely death. I ran across a most illuminating instance of short-sighted interference of this character when we were in the Philippines which shall have a little attention when you and I arrive there in the course of a few more pages.

Shanghai is a very much up-to-date city, with a beautiful bund or water-front along the Whangpoo River. Fine buildings abound, luxurious motor-cars, good homes, and all the accompaniments of wealth. The river activities which may be seen from the windows of the hotels — of which there are three, the Astor, Palace and Savoy — are a constant joy to the eye: junks, native sampans, sternwheelers operated by twenty-four coolies on a treadmill, lighters, launches, house-boats and private yachts — all coming and going night and day. The native city is about the least desirable — tawdry and evil-smelling, crowded to the gutter with an unbroken string of cotton-shod, pig-tailed yellow boys who take a never-ending interest in the foreigner.

There have been some of the most serious native outbreaks in Shanghai of any city in China. That's why every Occidental resident is a member of the police force and ready for action at any moment. The finer drives are Bubbling Well Road, the principal residence street; Rubicund Road, and several public gardens. Foochow Road might be called Shanghai's Broadway, with a number of good restaurants and an interesting night life. Since the establishment of the Radio Corporation of America's tremendous plant with the tallest towers ever designed, there has been a new lease of life, as it brings Shanghai in immediate touch with radio stations in various parts of Asia besides the five provinces of China. The principal shopping street is Nanking Road including both native and European stores. This is the place to get your silks, brocades, porcelain, jewelry, and ivory carving. You won't have as good a chance again, either in Hongkong or Manila.

We spent but three days in Shanghai, taking our departure on the Japanese S.S. *Shinyo Maru*, of the Toyo Kisen Kaisha Line of Steamers, for Hongkong, where we arrived two days later. Having rested well on the boat, the traveler may, if he likes, spend one night in a hotel leaving the bulk of his baggage there, starting off the next night for a seventy-eight-mile trip up the Pearl River to Canton. If you have not already purchased your *topi* or cork helmet, you'll find an excellent variety of this very necessary article at the English shops in Hong Kong. From here on --

until you are finished with Egypt — it will be unwise to go out into the tropical sun with an ordinary hat of any kind. Sunstroke in the Orient comes without warning and taking an unnecessary chance may spoil the balance of your trip.

In times past Pearl River was a favorite resort for Chinese pirates who didn't hesitate to attempt the capture of the night boat on several occasions. Present-day boats go heavily armed and have the native quarters fenced off with heavy steel gratings so that there is no danger from a surprise on board. Or — if preferred, one may make the short railway journey of eighty miles. Both trips are equally interesting. We took the river trip on account of docking the next morning in the very thick of the famous sampan or river-life population, estimated to be 400,000. There isn't a sight like it in the whole world. Generation after generation of the lowest and most villainous-looking Chinese are born and raised and die on these boats. The proper thing to do is to rise early and go out on the deck shortly after the boat passes Tiger Island. The river narrows as you approach Canton, and it seems to be so congested with these family sampans that you wonder for a while just how the steamer is going to get in to her dock. You will have the better part of a half-hour watching these river rats, male and female, from extreme age down to mothers starting their day's work with their infants slung on their backs.

Here and there a rakish junk towers above a myriad of small boats, with her high poop and a fishy eye painted on either side of the bow so that she may see where she is going — that being the belief of her crew from time immemorial. If there is a more hopelessly sodden, fiendishly wicked, utterly degenerate mob of inhuman faces anywhere than this Canton sampan population I have never heard of them. Note particularly the gaudy decorations of a so-called 'flower boat' for the particular delectation of those venturesome travelers who like to view the river-life at closer quarters and who actually take their lives in their hands in following their peculiar bent. Their tawdry hangings, foul lanterns, and acrid odors surround them with a sort of individual mephitic smudge which might have emanated from the depths of the Pit. And when night falls, they look like an uneasy lot of will o' the wisps, flitting here and there over the foul surface of the river, to the accompaniment of some of those astounding native musical instruments that induce a fearsome nightmare for several days afterward. As cargo-carriers the sampans seem to have an unlimited capacity: huge baskets of vegetables, pigs, ducks, and boxes of tea. The woman does most of the steering and about all of the work. The rudder consists of a long oar which she handles with great dexterity, balancing herself on a spring board that seems to lend an added grace to the job in hand. These people earn a precarious living by ferrying passengers across the river and by taking in night lodgers, if you can imagine such a thing. To see these boats tie up to the bank ten and fifteen deep for the space of four or five miles on both sides of the river, at the end of the day, is a sight to remember. Each sampan has its little lamp, and the evening meal is quickly served while darkness covers the scene.

Having been told that Canton is a city of two million population, you expect to see some sort of distinctive architecture. It really is difficult to imagine that the vast expanse of low-lying rookeries stretching away to the skyline is a city. As the steamer passes along the river-front, one looks in vain for any streets. You can see where there are breaks in the line of houses, but you wouldn't call them even alleys as they appear to the eye. The shacks that are built along the riverside sag drunkenly on their piles and look as though they might topple over at a touch. Your Chinese guide meets you at the dock and takes you to the

Victoria Hotel, located on what is known as the Sha-mien or European reservation. It is separated from the city by a narrow, noisome canal or wide ditch into which the river flows and which, at high tide, is filled with sampans. At low tide it is filled with the most indescribable aggregation of filth imaginable. A small bridge connecting both banks is for the exclusive use of the European population. You will notice as you approach the hotel that massive, bullet-proof square steel armor plates guard each window and door facing the canal — eloquent souvenirs of a native attack some years ago since when the hotel management has taken no chances. There is nothing to alarm the visitor in this situation. It is precisely as I put it: anybody who has ever been subjected to a native outbreak in any part of the Orient decides, then and there, never to take any more chances. The point is that no Occidental ever knows just how the Oriental mind is working from year to year. Eternal vigilance is the word where there is any possibility of a misunderstanding.

There is only one way to see Canton and that is in a sedan chair. The streets are so narrow that a horse-drawn vehicle could not get through even if there were roads or horses, which there are not. There are slimy, large-sized slab paving-stones lying askew which the bare feet of countless thousands of native Chinese have worn smooth in the course of passing centuries. No European would even care to take the chance of walking. If he didn't fall into a mass of filth at the first turn, he would probably put his foot on a paving stone which had its foundation in muck, thereby ruining a perfectly good suit of clothes. The sedan-carriers cry their way through the city, warning the crowds to make way. They have to stop at each corner and swing round slowly for fear of running either end of the swinging chair into the shop of some native merchant. Streets with a width of from six to ten feet, where not more than two persons can walk abreast with any comfort, are not conducive to speed. The ramshackle houses seem almost to meet overhead, thereby shutting out what light might ordinarily seep through. Balconies and swinging signs of every description also aid in killing what little sunshine there is so that a snap-shot with your camera is practically out of the question. There is no public square anywhere, no breathing place, nothing but these swarms of evil-smelling men padding it silently here and there either barefoot or shod with the characteristic noiseless cotton shoe, and showing by their glances that they don't appreciate your presence at all. These are the Southern Chinese who in past years found their way to the United States as day laborers on railroad construction or running a laundry. They don't look like, act like, or talk like their Peking brethren, with whom they are about as much in sympathy or understanding as they are with the traveler from abroad. If anything, they are more ignorant and more truculent than the Northern product.

In short, Canton is one vast Ghetto of two-story houses. You are ready to believe there are two millions in that terrible place. You wouldn't question it if you were told there were five millions. And this vast hive of humanity is enclosed within a weed- and grass-grown city wall about six miles in circumference. On the north the wall rises to the summit of a hill which practically limits its extent, which is the city burying-ground. On the other sides the city is surrounded by one of the most offensive ditches in all Christendom which is filled by the rising tide of the river and left most horribly putrescent when the tide recedes. Now — just recall that Peking has practically the same population spread over a territory enclosed by thirty miles of walls as against ten miles at Canton, including the suburbs. And yet the city is said to be a healthy one. There are twelve gates, which are policed all day and closed at night.

The standard bill of fare for the native Cantonese consists of horse-flesh, dogs, cats, rats, hawks, owls, leprous-looking fish, silkworm grubs, green and brown worms from the rice-fields, and edible birds'-nests. And you may as well know it first as last, the various lines of animals mentioned are not always killed for the market. Many of them die a natural death from a variety of ailments. In fact, the Chinese have been known to eat poisoned meat without any ill effects. If you are sufficiently interested to ask your guide to take you where these market delicacies are displayed, he will do so; if not, you had better instruct him to the contrary or you may accidentally run into them as I did.

And when I tell you that not one ounce of any edible animal is wasted, except, possibly, the hair, I am not indulging the slightest exaggeration. Even the bones are pulverized and used both for food and medicine. And this holds good in Peking as well as in Southern China. I am quite frank to say, however, that if we had gone to Canton first, we never should have gone to Peking or any other Chinese city. If you'll take a little suggestion — go to Peking first, and then do as you like as to Canton. You'll want to go back to Peking. One visit to Canton will more than suffice the average American, with the beds at the Victoria a slight improvement on the Chinese peasant's *kang* or brick settee on which the whole family lives and moves and has its being except when it's on the clay floor. Inasmuch as I have never tried the *kang*, I can speak only for the Victoria beds which I hesitate to do by reason of a limited vocabulary.

There are several spots in Canton that you might visit,

now that you are here. The beautiful porcelain pagoda which was restored a few years ago is really worth while. The five-floored pagoda on a hill just outside one of the city gates may be worth a look. The old Execution Ground is a memorable spot now given up to the making of cheap pottery. When I was there, the former 'Lord High Executioner,' who was then quite an old man, was bewailing the unlucky change in the law which had substituted shooting for the time-honored method of decapitation (which paid him a fee of one dollar Mex per head). Picking up a weather-beaten skull of some poor devil who had thoughtlessly gone away and left it, he offered, in pidgin English, to pose for me with the charming little memento in his hand, for a bit of *cumsha*. I consented. I noticed, however, that he seemed to have considerable trouble keeping his eyes off the empty skull and centering them on the camera, which, the guide explained, was owing to his recognition of an old friend who was one of the last to come under his kindly ministrations. 'Alas — poor Yorick!'

It may be remarked that Canton is headquarters for jade. I stepped into an up-to-date-looking shop where several very likely-looking pieces were displayed in the window. I asked the price of one dark colored bit that was worth at the outside twenty-five dollars. The Cantonese clerk looked me straight in the eye and replied in the most flawless English, 'Seventy-five dollars.' I asked him if I really looked like that. He laughed most amiably, but did not offer to reduce the price, and it is hardly necessary to say that I didn't buy. At any rate, it indicates the class of transient trade that slips up from Hongkong now and again looking for jade. A word to the wise.

Perhaps the most interesting spot in Canton is the City of the Dead — a sort of mausoleum where the bodies of well-to-do Chinese are kept sometimes for years before a satisfactory burial-place can be found by the surviving members of the family. This strange situation is the outcome of the national belief in geomancy, one of the oldest superstitions in the world. In China it goes under the name of *Fung-Shui* which teaches the constant presence of spirits of the earth and the air — both good and bad — and their equally constant influence upon both the living and the dead.

Fung-Shui has done more to block China's progress as a nation than any of her ancient notions. It has particular reference to locality, with a constant propitiation of the spirits in one's immediate neighborhood so as not only to ward off trouble, but to attract good influences. Therefore the possibility of the spirit of the dead being discontented with its tomb or general surroundings, in which event it would be apt to exert malign influences upon the whole neighborhood. Great care is taken in the selection of a grave. It reminds one of the game of golf: there are so many things one mustn't do that he forgets all about the things he should do. A hill extending in the wrong direction, the angle of a road, the location of certain trees, and possibly the direction in which a near-by stream may flow — all figure in *Fung-Shui*, when it comes to selecting a final resting-place for the bones of their ancestors.

Now — when you consider that ancestor-worship is the highest type of Chinese religious belief, you can see where *Fung-Shui* leads into the most endless and hopelessly involved superstitious speculations. Especially is this the case when there is a difference of opinion amongst the members of the surviving family as to where the grave of their father should be located. In their belief, it means the difference between honor, riches, and posterity for those who are left and some dire affliction, to the third and fourth generation. One coffin remained in the pleasant waiting-room of the City of the Dead for nearly eight years before the family could reach a unanimous decision. Meanwhile they were paying twenty-five dollars per month for the temporary resting-place of their beloved dad. In view of the fact that all Chinese coffins are hermetically sealed, this is not as serious a sanitary problem as it otherwise might be.

This is really a very pleasant place — the City of the Dead. It is located out near the walls on a side hill where population is not congested. The sun shines on it and creates quite a cheery appearance. The interior of the place is divided into little compartments with sufficient room for a chair where the survivor may come and commune with the spirit of the departed and share a cup of tea with him. In fact a fresh cup of tea is placed there on the little mortuary table every day for the benefit of him who has gone on before. If he doesn't drink it, the attendants drink it for him. Likewise a diminutive altar for worship, artificial flowers, and commemorative scripts of the virtues of the dead man.

These evil spirits, for which the native Chinese are constantly on the lookout, are supposed to fly in a straight line. They are unable to dodge around a corner or 'zoom' in any way. That has its advantages. All the worried householder has to do is to construct a screen outside the doors of the house, the screen being of greater area than the door itself, so the spirit cannot by any means enter. It would appear that he bumped headlong into the screen instead. It is for a similar reason that the corners of most Chinese and Japanese temples and other important buildings turn upward and are ornamented with sharp points, put there for the express purpose of helping this straight-line flier to impale himself. *Fung-Shui* enters into almost every aspect of daily life. It affects building, mining, the construction of railroads, bridges, etc. In fact it has reduced the minds of otherwise intelligent and normal men to the most fanatical cowardice. A few years ago one of the attachés of the American Legation wished to construct a chimney on the native house he was occupying, so as to have a little fire during the very cold Peking winter. A prominent Chinese near by objected most strenuously, believing that such an unusual and heathenish proceeding would permanently derange the *Fung-Shui* of the whole neighborhood. The American had to go without his chimney. The Old Buddha was kept nearly a year before a final resting-place was found for her remains. When the matter was all settled and the interment had taken place, a committee of important native officials memorialized the Throne to the effect that an important coal mine located forty miles distant from the Regent's tomb should be permanently shut down lest it disturb the *Fung-Shui* of the spot and her bones be troubled.

One night sufficed for our stay in Canton. The next morning we took the steamer for an eighty-mile trip down the Pearl River to the Portuguese settlement of Macao. This was the first bit of Chinese territory ever ceded to another nation — done in 1557. It furnished a first-class excuse for Great Britain, France, Germany, and Japan, who followed suit in the ensuing years on a variety of pretexts — principally force — until the complete partitioning of the vast Empire of China would have been an accomplished fact if it had not been for the insistence of the United States upon the 'open-door.' Macao is a sordid sort of Oriental Monte Carlo. Here a man can spend all the time he wishes in Chinese gambling-joints, smoke all the opium he likes, and drink himself to death if he desires. It is supposed to be a very devilish place for the traveler who sometimes covertly runs up for a night from Hongkong and takes the lid off. Chinese gambling-houses are planned in a very interesting way for the entertainment of the foreigner. The tables are located on the first floor, immediately under a railed opening on the floor above, around which foreigners cluster and send their bets down in a little basket on the end of a cord. The money is placed as per usual in the game of fan-tan and the winnings sent back upstairs in the same little basket. If there are no winnings, no further attention is paid to the foreigner until he puts down another bet via the basket.

Macao is beautifully situated on a curving peninsula about three hundred feet above the level of the river. A very picturesque crescent-shaped bay indents the land, on which numerous junks traffic to and fro — most of them pirates. Outside of the principal product of the city — opium — the favored occupation is smuggling. Two or three fair hotels face the bay — The Macao being as good as any. Three points of interest are worth while: the famous grotto of the Portuguese exiled poet Camoens who found leisure to sing the achievements of his ungrateful country; the rather rococo sunken gardens of the principal Chinese resident who has made a great fortune out of opium; and the cross-surmounted ruins of the Jesuit Church of Saint Paul, built in 1594, destroyed by fire in 1835, which inspired that beautiful hymn 'In the Cross of Christ I glory,' written by Sir John Bowring, British Governor of Hongkong in 1854. All that is left of this ancient edifice is the front wall at the top of an immense flight of steps overlooking the bay. The cross at the peak of the façade is most suggestive of the line of the hymn: 'Towering o'er the wrecks of time.'

Returning to Hongkong, we were glad to settle down in the Hongkong Hotel and rest for a few days. Except in the

native quarter there is little about Hongkong to suggest
the Orient. If you look up your history or your encyclopædia, you will find that Hongkong was 'acquired' from
China by Great Britain in 1843 under the terms of the
Treaty of Nanking. A few words concerning this treaty
may not be out of place, indicating, as it does, Great Britain's present interest in the most nefarious traffic in the
world: opium. In the first place, it was the British East
India Company that introduced India-raised opium into
China in the early eighteen-hundreds, both in secret and
open violation of her laws. The Chinese Empire, realizing
what a dreadful scourge opium was, was doing her best to
keep it away from her vast population. These troubles
reached a climax in 1840 when Commissioner Lin was sent
to Canton by the Emperor with the most sweeping instructions to put an end to the opium traffic. On his arrival he found twenty-two British ships in the Pearl River
below Canton loaded with nearly $10,000,000 worth of
opium. Being there in open defiance of the law, they were
subject to confiscation. Their surrender was demanded
from the British Government Agent, Captain Elliott, who
complied and pledged himself and the British Government
that no more opium should be brought into the port. The
opium was confiscated and destroyed on the spot by Commissioner Lin. Now listen to what happened:

The British Government dispatched a naval and military force to China. The Chusan Islands off the delta of
the Yangtze River were attacked and captured. Nanking, the former capital of the Empire, was besieged, and
China forced at the point of the bayonet to enter into a
treaty with Great Britain which called for the payment of
$21,000,000 divided as follows: $6,000,000 for the opium
surrendered; $3,000,000 for a variety of other claims, and
$12,000,000 for the cost of the war, all of which was ac-

companied by the unconditional cession of the island of Hongkong. This defeat of China in her effort to kill off the opium traffic in 1840 resulted in the starting of poppy cultivation on Chinese soil, in addition to the steadily increasing British importations from India, until the number of opium smokers in China in the early part of the twentieth century footed up to between twenty-five and thirty millions. Pretty good business for Great Britain who had secured the legalizing of the traffic in 1858. It was not until 1906 that the Chinese Government was strong enough to promulgate an edict directing that the growth, sale, and consumption of opium in the Empire should cease in ten years. An appeal was made to the British Indian Government to help out by reducing their exportations, which they did to the extent of 5100 chests in 1908. In the same year the opium dens in Hongkong were closed as they had been in Peking and Canton two years previously. These are the conditions which color China's natural aversion to Occidentals of all sorts. The likelihood of the opium traffic ever being rooted out is exceedingly slender. Just as long as opium remains a British Government monopoly in Hongkong — the most important port on the China Sea — Great Britain will continue to be responsible for the continuance of one of the most degrading vices in the world — with China as her principal exhibit.

Hongkong is truly a beautiful city. Great Britain has done wonders there. There is no question of her being a veritable bulwark of defense, controlling as she does the Straits of Formosa on the north and of Malacca on the south, thus keeping open the great highway of trade between China and India. The harbor has an area of fifteen square miles with sufficient depth to accommodate any number of large ocean steamships. The Peak, a good-sized mountain overlooking the bay and rising from sea-level for nearly two thousand feet, is well fortified. The view from the summit is passing beautiful. A fine military road circuits the entire island, affording a charming motor ride of twenty-two miles. A funicular runs from the business part of the town at sea-level to the summit, where many of the Europeans have their summer homes. The population of the city, including Kowloon, across the bay, is about 625,000, including 15,000 Europeans, the balance Chinese. Splendid shops are the rule and a fine lot of hotels which are patronized pretty much all the year 'round: the Hongkong, Astor, Grand, King Edward, Carleton, and Peak. A fine water system and the absence of mosquitoes make it an ideal home for the white man. With the extension of the new railway from Canton to important northern Chinese cities including such points as Calcutta, Singapore, and Bangkok — Hongkong bids fair to become the great Asiatic commercial center. And — no traveler but is glad to see Great Britain in the saddle in such a strategic point. Her splendid colonial history is an inspiration to the rest of the world. Now — if she will only shake off the opium fumes from her record and wipe the slate clean for future generations, we will sing her praises more enthusiastically than ever.

CHAPTER IX

THE LURE OF THE PHILIPPINES

Below the Line the tall, slim palms are waving
  As gentle trade-winds blow in from the sea.
Below the Line the murm'ring waves are laving
  Upon a firm, white beach so dear to me.
The gulls wheel o'er the smiling, sparkling water,
  And white-clad forms upon the sand recline —
My tropic islands call and I am going
  Somewhere — somewhere below the Line.

WILLIAM DANIEL

MANILA is a short two days' run of six hundred and thirty miles from Hongkong through the China Sea. When your steamer rounds into Manila Bay and passes Corregidor Island, with the glorious old Stars and Stripes whipping in the trade wind from the fortification on its summit, you feel like a real human being. And then you find yourself running to the skipper and asking him to let you off for a few minutes — you promise not to stay long — just so you can climb up the heights and bury your face in 'Old Glory' and shed a few tears. That being a trifle out of order, you look around and wonder if there isn't some 'damphool' who would like to take issue with you as to the precise importance of the United States in the general world scheme.

Oh — you'll make it wide enough for him to include any side-issue that happens to float in between the splinters of that rounded block that surmounts his shoulders. You'll give him any odds that happen to occur to his milk-and-water mentality and consent to having one hand tied behind you in the bargain. And what you'll do to him would be like stealing acorns from a blind pig — it'll be so easy. Then — pausing for a moment lest possibly you may be trying to cover too much territory — those laconic words of a day long past come hurtling through your mind: 'You may fire when ready, Gridley,' and it's all off again. And — let's see, who was it we were fighting then? Oh, yes — the Spaniards, sure. And a German admiral butted in, too. Well — bring 'em all on. With that old Red, White, and Blue bit of bunting floating up there, you could lick your weight in wildcats. All you want is a chance. Then you'll take a furtive glance around to see if any one was watching when you pulled your handkerchief out of your pocket and pretended to polish your glasses, and you may note several others similarly engaged. Oh, brother — if you won't do all those things in the space of a very few minutes, after having been out of sight of that blessed emblem for four months, then all I can say is, this book isn't meant for you.

And — now you are passing Cavité, where Aguinaldo has been enjoying his *otium cum dignitate* on a profitable plantation for nearly a quarter of a century since he saw the 'light.' No one knows better than he that the Philippines have in the United States Government the best friend they ever had or ever will have and — he's 'wise.' You've heard a lot of the down-trodden 'little brown brother' piffle, and you are wondering if there has been any truth in all the propaganda that has come to your notice since the Honorable Francis Burton Harrison 'got the gate.' About that time your steamer is docking beside a concrete pier that compares favorably with anything in New York Harbor, and your glance takes in the expansive, grass-carpeted Luneta, or parade ground, a stone's throw from the sea-wall. If a ship's officer should walk up and tell you that twenty-five years ago that whole Manila water-front, so-called, was a cholera-breeding bog, that there wasn't any such thing as a sea-wall, or a pier, or sufficient depth of water to allow an ocean steamer to anchor within two miles of the shore; that the city's sewage ran through open ditches in the streets, that smallpox was prevalent and leprous beggars on the street were common, you may take it from me that he would be giving you the facts. If he should go further and tell you that the advent of the United States Government control had meant the construction of a city water supply and reservoir, paved streets, sewers, electric railways and public buildings, one of the finest hospitals in the world, twenty-five hundred miles of macadamized roads throughout the islands, the establishment of public schools and education of half a million children in the English language and sanitary living by one thousand American teachers; a Supreme Court, a Postal Savings Bank, a million-dollar ice plant, the rebuilding of nearly five hundred miles of almost useless railways and the construction of as many more, the stamping-out of cholera and smallpox and the building of a leper colony on Culion Island, segregating over five thousand of those unfortunates — and all without one dollar of expense to the United States Government, every dollar being raised by local taxation — you may take his statement as representing one hundred per cent truth. That fine hotel, overlooking the Luneta, 'The Manila,' where you will stop, is United States Government-owned and conducted with an excellence of service that compares favorably with any first-class hotel in the United States. Opposite, across the Luneta, is the splendid Army and Navy Club and The Elks. Five miles out in the hills, and connected with the city by electric railway, is Fort McKinley, where are quartered about two thousand troops. Between these three places, the hotel, the club, and the fort, the American population — over five thousand out of a total of three hundred thousand — manage to maintain an interesting social life. They are the most hospitable people in the Far East and any decent citizen of the United States will find a warm welcome awaiting him just as soon as he makes himself known. That has been the history of Manila ever since the Taft Commission of 1900 put it on the map as an eloquent example of America's qualifications for colonial government.

No American with a spark of patriotism in his soul should visit the Philippines without making it his business to learn their history as a colonial possession of the United States. I can say this now in retrospect. I did not appreciate it until I arrived there. That's precisely the reason I am writing in this strain. Know, then, that we went to Manila for one week's sojourn, fully expecting to be on our way to Singapore by that time. Owing to most unexpected and fortuitous circumstances, for which I have never ceased to be grateful, we were brought in touch with the late Congressman Clarence B. Miller, of Minnesota, who had just arrived on behalf of the Minority Committee, during the Wilson Administration, for the purpose of probing to the bottom the reasons, if any, for the hue and cry then being raised throughout the United States for Philippine Independence. We were invited to join his party. As may be imagined, it was a rare opportunity to see things and be brought in touch with conditions that would have been otherwise utterly impossible. We accepted with alacrity and were with him for four weeks during his tour of the archipelago, including public gatherings in civilized towns, and pow-wows with native chiefs of pagan tribes. Of all the poor, ignorant, and misled people on the face of the earth, the Filipinos are most to be pitied. They have been exploited by conscienceless, half-breed leaders and led as lambs to the slaughter by the most unscrupulous and self-seeking '*politicos*' that ever battened at the public crib *and got away with it.*

Think of independence for nearly eleven millions of people spread over fourteen different islands and divided into forty-three different tribal groups speaking eighty-seven or more different dialects none of which are known to the others! Recall the fact that, while head-hunting has largely been done away with through the vigilance of United States Government officials, it is, nevertheless, one of the obstacles which prevent various tribes from trespassing on each other's territory. Imagine over ninety-two per cent of those eleven millions being pure-blooded Malay with about as much capacity for enlightened self-government as a lot of children — several of whose chiefs told Congressman Miller that their understanding of independence was that it was something to be given free to all by the United States Government which, if planted with their crops, would greatly increase the harvest. This is the stuff that has been handed out by political advocates of independence with the idea of enlisting the support of pagan tribes. Over against this ninety-two per cent of people who still have a large percentage of savagery in their personal systems, we may place the seven and one half per cent of *mestizos* or half-breeds, consisting of a mixture of Spanish and Chinese blood with the Malay, possessing all the satanic capacity for exploiting their less-gifted brethren that has been for untold generations characteristic of those two nationalities, and absolutely lacking in everything that savors of public interest or civilized growth.

It is a significant commentary on the problem of self-government that, out of the eleven millions of Philippine population, only two men, Messrs. Manuel Quézon, President of the Philippine Senate, and Senator Sergio Osmeña, respectively Spanish and Chinese *mestizos*, have ever succeeded in attaining to any particular political preferment beyond the average of the *caciqués*, or political bosses.

Also, that ninety-five per cent of all the commercial business in the archipelago is in the hands of foreigners. These two men have been the moving spirits of the Philippine Independence Mission with an annual appropriation of $500,000 supposed to be devoted solely to that object here in the States, during the eight years covered by the administration of Governor-General Francis Burton Harrison, now living in Scotland. Perhaps the most interesting phase of that splendid appropriation for independence propaganda was that the Mission was absolved from the necessity for accounting for the way in which the money was spent. That the naïve members of the Independence Mission were gifted with rather an extraordinary sense of the eternal fitness of things in this respect may be gathered from the following schedule which was published in the 'Manila Times' in reference to the Mission's allowances during its various trips to the United States:

MANUEL QUÉZON, President of the Senate —
    For clothes — $900 monthly, plus $90 per day during
        stay in United States.
    Total $3600 monthly.

MANUEL ROXAS, Speaker of the House —
    For clothes — $900 monthly, plus $90 per day during
        stay in United States.
    Total $3600 monthly.

SERGIO OSMEÑA, Senator —
    For clothes — $900 monthly, plus $45 per day during
        stay in United States.
    Total $2250 monthly.

CLARE M. RECTO, Minority Leader of the House —
    For clothes — $900 monthly, plus $45 per day during
        stay in United States.
    Total $2250 monthly.

The great trouble with us here at home is our compara-tive ignorance of these vitally important conditions in our commercially valuable and highly strategic territory in the Far East. And it seems to be impossible to interest our Senators and Congressmen in anything so far away from home. To them, the Philippines are a political proposition — nothing more. Outside of commercial channels, we have been a bit slow, as a people, in arriving at a proper appreci-ation of our responsibilities as a world power. We cannot turn our backs on them with any degree of self-respect, the opinions of some of our statesmen (?) in Washington to the contrary notwithstanding.

The first thing that will catch the eye of the visitor to Manila, as he drives down town in a *calésa*, or one-hoss shay, will be the carabao or water-buffalo — the Filipino's indispensable beast of burden. His speed is about two miles an hour, which is unnecessarily rapid for the average native. His horns have been known to measure from six to eight feet from tip to tip. He is called the water-buffalo for a most excellent reason: he must have his bath at least once a day or his hide dries and cracks and he goes crazy. Hence the number of carabao wallows you will see in the suburbs and along the country roads. Nothing pleases him quite so much as a mud-bath, lacking which — no work. He's a born Bolshevik, with the difference of the bath. Furthermore — he doesn't like white folk and has been known to resent with his horns any attempt to make a household pet of him. On the other hand, a Filipino tot of five years can lead him around by the nose.

The next thing to attract attention will be the *cochero's* (driver's) method of urging a trifle more speed out of his horse. He has a dialect which will appeal to you. The all-important term for the horse is *sigué*, pronounced 'segay'

ONE OF THE GATES IN THE ANCIENT CITY WALL OF
MANILA AND A NATIVE 'TAXI'

by the *cognoscenti* and 'siggy' by the driver, the same being
a close relative of our familiar term 'giddap.' And when
the horse won't 'siggy' *pianissimo*, he raises his voice to
high heaven and you wish you had taken the motor-car.
Frequently even that crashing *crescendo* is unavailing, and
then he has a nice little way of leaning over the dashboard
(and it's well-named) and, gathering his noble animal's tail
in his two hands, he does his best to twist it off. You owe it
to yourself to take at least one ride in the *calésa* — it's
quite a bit cheaper and infinitely more entertaining than a
commonplace motor. But — don't make the mistake of
sitting beside the *cochero* — that isn't good form. He's
worthy a more detailed description than I can give in prose,
so I'm going to let my good friend Nobert Lyons, at one
time editor of the 'Manila Times,' do it in rhyme. You will
note he puts it in the form of a query, supposed to be addressed to you after you have returned from the ride:

> Did he sport a nether garment
>   Of a weird chromatic hue
> And a dinky old sombrero?
>   And perhaps he didn't chew
> Betel-nut and plug-tobacco?
>   Ever see the mixture ooze
> From his classic coral liplets,
>   Flavored by the rankest booze?

I might add that it's strictly *au fait* for the *cochero* to go
barefoot, and some of them have an educated great-toe
which ranges at right angles from the foot and is supposed
to be more or less prehensile.

On your way across the Luneta you will pass the bronze
statue of José Rizal, the Filipino martyr who was executed
by the Spaniards for publishing a book exposing the evil
character of their government and the immoral life of the
friars. His trial was a farce. The monument marks the
spot where the Spanish shooting squad did its work, De-

cember 30, 1896. It is not generally known that Rizal's remains are buried beneath the monument under several tons
of bronze and concrete, where, it is hoped by those who are
familiar with the story, they will rest in peace until the end
of time. Rizal, being a genuine martyr, became the only
national hero the Filipinos ever had. And, with their child-
like way of looking at things, they simply had to make the
most of it. The result was that his remains were on the
move for sixteen years, fluctuating between the little town
of his birth, Calainha, where they were alternately claimed
by his family and a local secret society of which he was a
member, and the Paco Cemetery in Manila, where they
were kept in a niche in that famous above-ground burial-
place which still bears his initials. Finally, as a result of the
constant hustling about to which these poor bones were
subjected, they were enclosed in a small portable chest, in
which manner they figured in various patriotic parades.

In recognition of his martyrdom, the Philippine Government set aside December 30th as a public holiday, which in
later years has been seized upon by that redoubtable opportunist Quézon as a good time for an impassioned speech in
favor of independence amidst the huzzas of the *taos*, or
farmers, who come into Manila from the country roundabout for the occasion. When the monument was ready
for erection, Vice-Governor-General Newton W. Gilbert
saw an opportunity for the final disposition of Rizal's
bones, to which the family and the secret society consented.
The little chest, therefore, was tenderly deposited in the
concrete beneath the monument where it will remain undisturbed for some time to come. At any rate, it won't figure
in any more patriotic parades nor provide Señor Quézon
with further opportunities for a lifelike imitation of Marc
Antony.

Manila is an ideal city in which to wander about and observe the life of the people. The city occupies an area of about twenty square miles of low ground and is divided into two sections by the Pasig River which empties into the bay at that point. The ancient city, or 'Intramuros,' as it is called, lies on the southern bank of the river and fronts on the bay to the west for nearly a mile. It is enclosed by a wall over two miles long, with a maximum height of twenty-five feet, built by the Spaniards in 1590. Prior to the American occupation it was flanked by a moat on the land side, which was bridged by six drawbridges located at as many gates which were closed every night. The moat is now filled with earth and is devoted to tennis courts, golf links, baseball grounds, etc. In one corner stands Fort Santiago, which was built as a part of the ancient walls for the purpose of defending the city at the mouth of the river. The remainder of the old city is taken up by the really fine old Byzantine Cathedral of the Immaculate Conception built in 1581, the Dominican University of Santo Tomas (1601), various churches, convents, and Government buildings. A modern city has been built up outside the walls, consisting of the union of several towns which have been converted into municipal districts. Two modern steel cantilever bridges and the ancient Bridge of Spain, a stone structure which has been in use over three hundred years, cross the Pasig. The latter, devoted to light traffic only, leads directly into the main business and shopping section of the city — the Escolta, which might be called Manila's Broadway, and the Rosario, noted for its Chinese shops. Most of the American population will be found in Ermita, Malate, Pasay, or San Miguel where there are beautiful drives and fine residences, especially along the banks of the Pasig River, among them being 'Malacañan,' the official residence of the Governor-General. Outside the fire limits the greater part of the population live in nipa-palm thatched huts of bamboo frame, where the streets consist mostly of *esteros* or navigable tidewater streams which flow in from the bay.

The one cemetery in the city is the Paco, outside of the walls, where there are seventeen hundred niches for coffins in two concentric walls: this owing to the fact that the marshy character of the ground makes interment impossible. These niches, like the cemeteries in New Orleans and Havana, are rented for periods of several years. If the rentals are not renewed, the remains are removed and destroyed.

A visit to Bilibid Prison is worth while. From a central platform overlooking the surroundings of the institution may be seen the serving of meals to prisoners who, on the stroke of a bell, arrive and depart from established canteens with their food — the whole proceeding, covering the service of approximately three thousand prisoners, being in the nature of a drill which is completed in twenty minutes. Incidentally, they have an unusually fine band of fifty pieces which takes great pride in its proficiency. Bilibid is one of the most successfully conducted penal institutions in the world and carries on extensive manufacture of rattan furniture, silverware, carriages, and laundry. It is really one of Manila's finest exhibits. A day's sail up the Pasig River to Laguna de Bay will prove interesting, not only for the finer residences to be seen along the banks in the vicinity of the city, but for the native life and customs to be witnessed farther upstream. Pasig River life, near the mouth, in conjunction with shipping, is picturesque. A goodly part of the loading and unloading of cargoes is done by natives with their nipa-thatched *cascos* or lighters, from steamers anchored out in the bay. The Manila Meteorological Observatory is one of the best equipped in the East. Under the efficient direction of Father Algué, who might be called a typhoon specialist, it has prevented losses to shipping and other enterprises which in former years mounted into millions of dollars.

It probably won't be in accordance with your bringing-up, but — if you're in Manila over Sunday you'll have to go to a cock-fight. That's the national sport — the one thing that Uncle Sam has not been able to cure. There are several cock-pits in the suburbs that will accommodate in the neighborhood of five thousand persons each — and they're always filled all day long of a Sunday. Consider-able money changes hands, and the expertness of the 'banker' who stands in the ring with the contestants and their birds is something to see. Rolls of bills are thrown from the seats above and around the pit, landing on a blanket on the ground. No one ever heard of the gentle-man's getting his bets mixed or to fail to return the win-nings to each and every bettor figured to the last *centavo*, without pausing a fraction of a second to figure them out. He is really quite as interesting as the birds. Cock-fighting is what keeps 'poor Juan' poor, indeed. He'll bet, every Sunday, every *peso* he earns during the week, and his wife is mostly with him when Sunday comes.

The Manila Aquarium is one of the finest in the world. Those tropical waters contain an immense variety of the most brilliant, multi-colored fish of all shapes and shades. There are twenty-seven tanks, including some very large ones for the sharks that are common to those latitudes.

By the time you have spent a week in Manila, I venture the statement that you will be sufficiently interested to wish to take a steamer trip into the southern islands. There are a number of inter-island steamship companies whose vessels make every port in the archipelago. One place at least you should visit if at all possible: Zamboanga on the island of Mindanao. I'll have more to say about this and the other tropical spots in this great archipelago of ours in the following chapter.

CHAPTER X

CRUISING AMONG THE ISLANDS

I hear the call of the wanderlust,
And God knows why, but go I must;
Until my bones are drifting dust
    I'll follow the sea-gull's cry.
The bow-wash song to the dog-watch bell,
The kick o' the wheel and the chantey's spell
Get hold of a man in spite o' Hell,
    And a better man than I.

KENDALL BANNING

It was a particularly gracious act on the part of the late General J. Franklin Bell, U.S.A., stationed in the Philippines during Congressman Miller's visit, to place his dispatch boat *El Aguila* at Mr. Miller's disposal for a cruise in the southern islands in order that he might trace the ramifications of the *Independencia* virus as distributed by Señor Quézon and his associates of the Independence Mission. At the eventful banquet given to Governor-General Harrison on his arrival by the business men of Manila, General Bell sat on the platform and made a graceful speech of welcome on behalf of the army. It was not until both he, Congressman Miller, and myself were seated in his motor on our way back to our hotel that he ventured to express his surprise at Mr. Harrison's remarkable address and that he should have so unreservedly ascribed his appointment to the influence of Señor Quézon. Said he: 'I fear Mr. Harrison has started something that will make him considerable trouble before he has been here very long. It is unfortunate that he should not have waited until he got his bearings before committing himself in a manner that he is bound to regret.' In other words, it was quite apparent that General Bell took it for granted that Harrison had simply overstepped the limits of political common sense. Being familiar with Señor Quézon's tactics, however, it was with considerably more than official courtesy that he assigned *El Aguila* and her crew to Congressman Miller and his party. *El Aguila*, by the way, was formerly the private yacht of the late Mark Hanna and was sold by him to the United States Government for the sum of one dollar at the outbreak of the war with Spain. Her former habitat was Lake Erie. She was a splendidly equipped and thoroughgoing sea-boat. Lest there be any misunderstanding, I would like to make it clear that our voyage was made at our own expense. Beyond the fact that *El Aguila* was always in commission, no expense whatever, so far as her civilian passengers were concerned, was borne by the Government.

One beautiful morning in October we steamed out through Manila Bay, past Corregidor Island and Mount Mariveles on our long trip which was to keep us at sea for nearly five weeks. Colonel Wallace C. Taylor, of the Philippine Constabulary, had us in charge — a fine fellow. We visited various ports of fifteen different islands: Samar, Leyte, Panay, Oriental and Occidental Negros, Cebu, Bohol, Mindanao; Jolo, in the Sulu Group; Siasi, Tawi Tawi, Cagayan Sulu, Palawan, Culion, Masbate and Romblon, including an afternoon and evening at Sandakan, British North Borneo. It was the experience of a lifetime to note the splendid conditions that had followed the raising of the American flag throughout this vast archipelago: a clear case of American decency, patriotism, enterprise, unselfish devotion to, and a keen understanding of, the native and his limited capacity, over and over again: the greatest inspiration to a citizen of the United States that could be imagined. Several ports there were where but one white man was stationed — and he a khaki-clad 'buddy,' right as a trivet, his uniform spotless, exercising paternal control over a band of semi-civilized natives who had been taught what that wonderful flag waving above his own particular shack stood for and were trying in their own halting, limited fashion to swing into line with it. Scores of schools where sanitation and the English language were being taught by wide-awake American teachers, accompanied here and there by schools for industrial training for those who were equal to the effort. Nobody but a deaf, dumb, and blind man could have failed to be impressed by the progress that was apparent on every hand. And then to listen to the local 'orators' — full-grown, native stool-pigeons of Qué- zon and his lieutenants — barefoot, clad in overalls and a *camisa* or shirt worn outside the trousers — men who could not speak the English language, but whose children had learned it in those very schools — get up and rant by the hour, in dialect, of the great blessings of independence, in- variably finishing with the statement that they did not need the American soldiers or school teachers any more, they could care for themselves and educate their own chil- dren, etc., etc., *ad nauseam*, all of which was translated by an official interpreter. Everywhere we went we heard the same argument without any variation, proving con- clusively that they had been thoroughly primed and prompted, even to precise words and expressions, as to what they should say. There was frequent evidence of their 'speeches' having been committed to memory. A child could have appreciated the cut-and-dried character of the performance. And yet they say Señor Quézon is an astute politician!

In some respects it was an abominable experience, al- though mighty illuminating. It made me wish then, it makes me wish now, that some enlightened American poet might arise that could extract sufficient divine fire from some remote altar of our national pride to raise the Philippines from the slough of political opportunism to an approximation of Kipling's 'The English Flag.' If you haven't read that incomparable appeal to all the patriotic decency there is in man, let not another sun go down until you have absorbed its matchless glory into your very soul. And — whenever you come across the word 'English,' just substitute the word 'American.' You can never tell — it may strike a vibrant chord that will sweep into the discard that smug complacency and self-satisfaction with which so many of us are cursed. Who knows —? You might do a little investigating on your own account, just for a change, instead of continuing to 'let George do it.' And then possibly you might sit down and write that particular brand of Senator or Congressman with whom you are blessed or cursed, as the case may be, that if he votes to turn the Philippines over to a coterie of self-serving political grafters in order that they may continue to exploit their semicivilized and pagan brethren in the name of Independence, he will have you to reckon with at the next election.

Permit me to repeat what I said in the previous chapter; It isn't that our wiseacres in Washington have any particular opinion one way or the other concerning the Philippines. It scarcely assumes the importance of a purely party question. It is that the Philippines are so far away, so remote, that they really don't know anything about them and are too busy with their own log-rolling and fence-mending to care to learn. Either that or the princely generosity and Lucullan entertainments of the Philippine Independence Mission have made more friends and supporters in Washington for that Oriental outfit of propagandists than some of us have suspected. Much may be accomplished with $500,000 per year provided by Filipino taxpayers outside of the accumulation of an exotic wardrobe. And now let

Kipling, in 'The English Flag' give you a glimpse of what
the American flag has done in the Philippines:

The South Wind sighed: 'From the Virgins my mid-sea course
        was ta'en
Over a thousand islands lost in an idle main,
Where the sea-egg flames on the coral and the long-backed break-
        ers croon
Their endless ocean legends to the lazy, locked lagoon.

'Strayed amid lonely islets, mazed amid outer keys,
I waked the palms to laughter — I tossed the scud in the breeze.
Never was isle so little, never was sea so lone,
But over the scud and the palm-trees an [American] flag was flown.

Friend o' mine — that's the view you'll get if you go
a-cruising in the Philippines, and a bit of a different slant
as well on the reason for Old Glory staying where she is than
you ever had before. You won't relish the idea of seeing
the prideful results of twenty-five years under that flag
sacrificed by a bunch of chair-warming Senators and Congressmen on the altar of their own narrow-chested stupidity
and lack of public spirit. You'll acquire a new conception
of what it means to 'give that which is holy unto the dogs,'
and you'll agree with me that the givers should accompany
the gift.

But listen — you won't get very much excited over
these things sitting here at home. That's precisely what's
the matter with these Washington barnacles. They have
clung to the old ship so long, fearing they might lose their
jobs, that they have lost all desire to venture outside the
borders of their own States except on mileage. Why, the
very fact that these 'velvet-glancing' *mestizos* have traveled from Manila to Washington and return several times
on money that has been wrung from the Filipino tax-payer,
has given them a certain advantage over our elephantine
intellects at the national capital. If a few of these disciples
of the 'pork-barrel' would do as Congressman Miller did

— go out there and learn a few things at first hand, they might return with an idea or two sired by something they saw en route. But no — their sole ambition is to make a political issue of the Philippines, not one that involves an appeal to statesmanship or any cerebral activity.

In these tropical waters it is customary for those who have grown 'tired of four walls and a ceiling' to sleep on deck. A cross-legged, canvas cot with a sheet as a concession to the amenities is all-sufficient and the rhythm of the propeller does the rest. After you have watched by the hour the phosphorescent waters break into lambent flame all about the vessel until it almost seems that the hull is about to catch fire, you may lie down with the impression that the star-studded, ebony sky overhead is almost within arm's length, so intensely brilliant are the constellations.

Navigation in the Philippine Archipelago is not to be taken lightly. The total number of islands is 3141, many of which are less than an acre in extent, all volcanic in character, with a coast-line of over 11,000 miles, fringed with coral reefs and indented by innumerable bays. The larger islands are traversed by mountain ranges from 2500 to 7500 feet in height and are connected with each other by submarine mountain ranges which extend from the archipelago itself to Celebes and Borneo. With the exception of Manila, there isn't a port where steamers can approach nearer than a half to a quarter of a mile — they all anchor offshore. Shallow channels connect the interior waters with those of the Pacific Ocean and the China Sea. Darkness comes swiftly. Almost simultaneously with sunset the stars appear. Half-speed at night is the customary thing, and one frequently awakes amid a stillness so profound and a sea of such glassy smoothness that if it were not for the beat of the screw he would hardly know that the vessel was moving.

Early morning found us anchored off the little town of Pasacao, in the Camarines. The water was so shallow that even the launch could not approach within a hundred feet of the beach. Accordingly a number of the natives walked out with sedan chairs in which we were carried ashore and seven miles overland through limitless savannas of *cogon* grass higher than a man's head. We brought up in the little town of Pamplona where a river boat was waiting to take us to Nueva Caceres where Mr. Miller had a typical meeting with the townsfolk and listened patiently to the childish reasoning of Quézon's pupils. Afterward there was a visit to the Bishop's Palace, the seminary, and the public schools, with a parade by the children. A *bailé*, or reception and dance, in the evening finished off the day's work and we spent the night very comfortably, farmed out, as it were, to the homes of resident Americans. Motor-cars were waiting in the morning for a beautiful drive to the village of Legazpi in the Province of Albay on the eastern shore of the island. Here we made a circuit of Mount Mayon, an active volcano and one of the most perfect cones in the world. In that long ride of sixty miles there wasn't an angle of that magnificent peak, towering eight thousand feet above the level of the sea, which showed the slightest departure from a symmetry so perfect as to completely entrance the beholder. Japan's Fujiyama is not to be compared with it. The ancient town of Legazpi was entirely wiped out in 1814 by an eruption which cost twelve hundred lives, since which year the volcano has been quiescent, although there is a more or less frequent discharge of smoke. The explanation of its symmetry is found in the character of its slopes which consist entirely of a deep deposit of ashes which have never hardened and which make it a most difficult peak to climb. After a meeting with the *Independistas* we went aboard *El Aguila* which had been waiting our arrival.

Two days' perfect sailing through cerulean seas brought us into the beautiful harbor of Iligan Bay on the northern coast of the great island of Mindanao — the largest of all the southern islands and peopled by Moros. The Moro is a Mohammedan fighting man against whom Spain had waged an unsuccessful war of conquest for over three hundred and fifty years. When he goes into battle, his wives go with him. As a general thing he fights until wiped out. He didn't know what to think of the United States soldiers, who finally conquered him, because they did not follow up their victories with extermination. He despises the Filipino, first, because he is of smaller stature and doesn't possess the fighting qualities that he (the Moro) does, second, because he knows the Filipino is afraid of him. It was not until after the Moros had been subdued by Pershing's soldiers in the early nineteen-hundreds that any Filipino would take the chance of showing his face in the Moro Province or in the Sulu Archipelago. And not even then until the Moros, having been assured by then Provincial Governor Leonard Wood of the protection of the United States troops, turned in their rifles. These were the conditions that Harrison found, and his first act was to reverse all that Wood and Pershing had done by displacing American civil Governors and United States soldiery throughout the province and substituting the Moros' ancient enemies, the Filipinos, both in civil and military departments. Then Quézon and his emissaries came down and herded a lot of them together and induced them to sign petitions for independence. These he exhibited later as indicating the success of the Filipino Government with its former adversaries when, as a matter of fact, it was a case of a fully armed Filipino constabulary bulldozing a disarmed enemy into the exercise of that discretion supposed to be the better part of valor. Quézon subsequently went so far as to address a number of *datus* or head-men in his usual bombastic fashion, stating that the United States Government had already been done away with, and that it was only a question of time when all the Americans would be driven out — and then the Moros might look for trouble. The result of this tirade was that the datus went out and pulled down the Philippine flag wherever they found it, leaving the Stars and Stripes to wave by itself. These are all matters of record up at Camp Keithley, Lake Lanao, where Quézon's meeting with the datus took place.

It was for Lake Lanao, in fact, that we were bound when *El Aguila* dropped her anchor in Iligan Bay. Adjoining the little town of Iligan was Camp Overton, U.S.A., the commanding officer of which had a couple of cars ready for us, and in a few minutes we were on our way over an excellent road for an eighteen-mile ride up into the hills to Camp Keithley. This camp is most beautifully situated on the shore of the lake, two thousand feet above sea-level in the very heart of the Moro district. On our way we stopped at an outpost located near the foot of one of the most picturesque waterfalls I have ever seen. From an escarpment fully two hundred feet above the level of the roadway, it poured in full volume over the edge of a precipice apparently into the tops of a grove of mammoth trees which hid the base of the cataract from sight. The Spaniards named it after one of their favorite saints: Maria Cristina.

Keithley is the only regular Army camp in the Philippines or the United States which has been named for a private. Private Keithley, having been ambushed by Moro warriors about a mile from camp during the Spanish War, was mortally wounded, but managed to crawl on his hands and knees for that mile and give the alarm which saved the camp from massacre — and then fell over dead. Across the outlet to the lake, not far from the commandant's quarters,

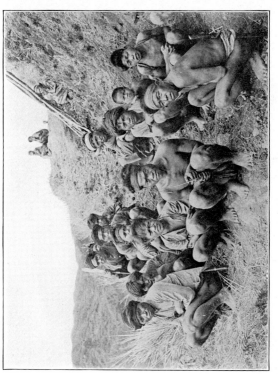

PHILIPPINE ASPIRANTS FOR INDEPENDENCE

is the Moro village of Dansalan, the datu of which had called in his lieutenants for miles around to sit down in solemn conclave with Congressman Miller, as the representative of the President of the United States, to tell him what they thought of independence. The conference took place in front of the chief datu's house — a tall, sharp-gabled, two-story building, richly carved in arabesques, brightly painted in reds and blues, and from the peak of which waved a beautiful American flag. In very simple fashion and speaking in his own tongue, which was translated by Major Gilhouser, resident Governor, the datu pointed to the Stars and Stripes and said that was the flag the Lake Lanao Moros lived under and they wanted no other independence but that which the American flag gave them. Among the datu's retainers were two who had made a pilgrimage to Mecca and earned the title 'Haji.' They spoke with equal earnestness of their loyalty and agreement with their leader. These were the same Moro chieftains that Quézon addressed a few months later who went out and pulled down the Philippine flag as a result. The datus were gorgeously clad in vari-colored silks, and each carried an ivory-hilted, gold- and silver-inlaid wavy *kris*, more as an emblem of their authority than anything else. They were a highly picturesque gathering. A little way off to one side in the middle of a field were three Moros — an elderly father and two sons — threshing grain with their feet, treading it out in a most primitive fashion. We spent the day looking over the chief datu's jeweled knives and ornately engraved armor which was in constant use in earlier days, but which are now regarded more in the light of family heirlooms than anything else. I tried to purchase a piece and was met with a curt refusal. These datu chiefs are high-born men — aristocrats to the core. Each has an ancient lineage, his own priest and his own territory, with anywhere from ten to fifteen subordinate district datus who report to their chief at regular intervals.

Lake Lanao is a spot of great natural beauty, surrounded by mountain peaks and vast forests. Marahin Island in the center is used for a general market-place by the Moros who congregate there once a week for trading. They come by scores in their canoes from the various villages along the shore. On the island is a typical Moro storehouse, with the usual ornate carving and the omnipresent, American-made corrugated-iron roof — a combination of past and present, creating a most incongruous appearance. We spent an hour amongst these natives, did a little buying, saw a large variety of cheaply dyed textiles of a distinctly modern weave and were just a trifle surprised to find the legend 'Made in Germany' on an attached label. What interesting lessons one learns when far from home! We didn't see anything that resembled American manufacture in the display, much less any labels or trade-marks of home origin. It was interesting to learn, however, that the boat in which we were sailing around was a monument to American ingenuity and resourcefulness. It had formerly been a Spanish gunboat which the Spaniards had scuttled when the Americans took possession. Our men raised it and put it in shape and it is still in service. Leaving the island market-place, instead of returning to Keithley, we proceeded to the far side of the lake for a brief stop at Camp Vickers — one of the loneliest spots I ever saw and in charge of a small guard. Here we found half a dozen Government mules on which we finished our journey across that peninsular-like portion of the island to Malabang on Illana Bay. After being entertained at dinner at the officers' mess, we embarked in a launch for an evening's sail to the Ludlow Barracks on the bluff overlooking the sea at Parang where *El Aguila* came to meet us the next day.

Our muleback trip across the island is worthy of special mention. The trail led through a tropical forest hedged in on both sides with jungle growth, towering trees, bamboos, orchids, and giant ferns. The Philippines are noted for their gorgeous bird life and we certainly had our share of it that eventful day, not to mention the numerous monkeys in the tree-tops which kept up a continuous chatter of protest at our presence. This trail was known as 'Lovers' Lane' in Pershing's time because there were so many Moro ambushes with corresponding fatalities to our men, until one day 'Black Jack' determined on a clean-up. And, from all I could gather, that ended the ambushes in Lovers' Lane, and started the Lake Lanao Moros on the road to good citizenship. If you have ever seen a display of the various knives used in native Philippine warfare, you will appreciate what the possibilities of an ambush were. The term *bolo* covers a variety of heavy steel knives sufficient for all purposes. Three there are which were most constantly in use in those good old days before the American pacification was completed: the wavy, double-edged *kris*, two feet long, ground to the sharpness of a razor, generally carried in the belt and used either for a slashing stroke at close quarters or for stabbing; the *barong*, a heavy curved-edge 'butcher's cleaver,' twenty inches long and a quarter of an inch thick on the back of the blade, also carried in the belt, used either for domestic purposes or fighting; and last, the *campilan*, or two-handed sword, over three feet long, an eighth of an inch thick at the back of the blade for half its length, the edge and point being ground almost as fine as a razor. It is in the handling of this latter-named toy that the Moro excels. His plan was to sally forth in a party of five or six, which divided and concealed itself on either side of a trail where a soldier was apt to pass. Then, as the victim approached, one contingent would rush out

and engage him face to face while the other would creep up
from behind and, with a diagonal stroke with the campilan,
delicately divide him in half from the neck to the waist-
line on the opposite side. That form of ambush got to be so
familiar that, whenever soldiers went for any distance from
camp, they practically walked back to back so as to anticipate an attack from either before or behind. When, however, the Moro really learned what kind of a man the American soldier was and particularly what kind of men Wood
and Pershing were, he discontinued that kind of warfare
and has played a decent, loyal game ever since, which is
considerably more than can be said for some of his more
enlightened Filipino brethren in the vicinity of Manila.

Continuing our journey on *El Aguila*, our next stopping-
place was the Cotabato River in the southern part of Mindanao. Owing to the shallow water, we anchored well out
as usual and were transferred to a stern-wheel steamer of
light draught which took us ashore. Here we had quite a
session with old Datu Piang, a Chino-Moro *mestizo* as wily
as a fox. For years he successfully defied the Spanish, even
to the point of capturing one of their brass cannon which he
had set up as an ornament to his 'front yard.' He had several of his head-men with him who had come in from the
country roundabout to have a pow-wow with Congressman
Miller on the subject of independence. Among them were
Datu Gimbongan, a negroid Malay with an expansive
waist-line. Then there was old Datu Ynock who had been
quite a fighter and lady-killer in his day. He had one ear
hanging by a shred of skin of which he seemed quite proud
— the story being that it had been cut off in a fight and he
clapped it back hurriedly and tied it fast. Ynock was said
to have been a self-appointed 'protector' of all the women
captured during his warfare with the Filipinos, for which
they requited him by compelling him to work on the roads

in the chain-gang, when the tables were turned. Ynock had made a pilgrimage to Mecca, and was very proud of his title 'Haji' and of a Scottish tartan which he managed to pick up somewhere and wore draped from his neck to his ankles.

The conference duplicated that held at Lake Lanao — all the Cotabato Moros being happy under the United States Government and violently opposed to Filipino control. It was a gay sight to see these various datus arrive at the river landing-place in their thatched barges, each accompanied by his official betel-nut box-bearer. The more important the official, the larger and heavier and more gorgeously engraved brass betel-nut box he sported. And it was weighty enough for a bearer to carry on his shoulder. Having finished with the ceremonial portion of the visit, the party went up the river to Fort Pikit where we remained overnight. The Cotabato, with its vast flat, marshy jungle country stretching away for miles on either side, is ideal territory for the guerrilla warfare the Moros practice, being criss-crossed with trails which a white man could never negotiate. Old Piang was very proud of the fact that he had a son in the Constabulary, a handsome youngster of about twenty-one who looked well in his khaki and puttees. Here we saw for the first time native women pounding grain into flour with long, hardwood pestles, in a mortar made from a hollowed-out section of a tree. It was primitive indeed.

We steamed away from Cotabato in the teeth of an impending storm, which fortunately passed over, and came to anchor in the Gulf of Davao the next day about noon after a rough night's passage through the Celebes Sea. A little wind kicks up quite a sea in these shallow waters and in the typhoon season inter-island traffic is correspondingly hazardous. About the only thing that will outride a heavy storm, unless there be plenty of sea-room, is the native *vinta*, or outrigger canoe, which carries a square sail in the handling of which the Moros are most expert. Our party was received most graciously by both the civil governor and the *presidenté* or native mayor of the town, who vied with each other in entertaining us. In the evening we were invited to a *bailé*, or reception, at the home of the *presidenté*, at which everybody danced the native *rigadon* which is much like the lancers of our earlier day. The native population of Davao being principally Filipino, at the gathering held by Mr. Miller next day, repeated the same old rigamarole that I have already described in favor of the blessings of independence. We were all getting a bit fed-up on this independence propaganda, although we had to admire the shrewdness of Quézon in having his political henchmen ready for us wherever we put into port. Nothing like $500,000 per year to keep up one's interest in a political issue.

During the afternoon we took a trip via the steam launch to Tagun, a settlement a few miles up the coast where we found one of those lonesome Constabulary officers, Lieutenant Cochran, the only white man in the district — in charge of seventeen different Moro tribes and making a splendid job of it too. He called the various chiefs together for a conference with Mr. Miller and once more we got the Moro side of independence — they wanted none of it and still less of the Filipinos. Their attitude toward Lieutenant Cochran was most apparent in a complete confidence in his sympathetic fair-dealing. He told us, nevertheless, that he never slept without his revolver under his pillow. 'These pagans are liable to break out almost any time in a new place,' said he, 'and while I have the unquestioning trust of these chiefs to-day, one never knows what the morrow may bring forth.' One of the reasons for our trip to Tagun was to pick up Lieutenant Cochran to act as interpreter during our conference with the Bagobos which was to take place the next day. This is a particularly shy pagan mountain tribe in the southern part of Mindanao which rarely comes down to the sea or maintains any commerce with white men. Incidentally, the Bagobos have a dialect of their own which Lieutenant Cochran spoke fluently. And so we took him back to *El Aguila* with us, trailing his launch behind. There was no disguising the keen joy he felt over an opportunity to 'mix it' with a party of real, honest-to-God Americans, in which, to indulge a bit of slang, he had 'nothing on us.'

One would be hard-boiled, indeed, who could fall into an experience of that kind without a greater regard for the Anglo-Saxon than, perhaps, he might ever have had. An event of that character is scarcely likely to increase the visitor's self-esteem. It doesn't help at all to say, with a degree of *laissez faire:* 'That's his job.' You can't do that without wondering a bit what you would do if the job was yours. Yes — travel in out-of-the-way places is a good thing for a citizen who is used to traveling on asphalt at home. It tends to reduce his ego quite a bit.

Returning from Tagun, we passed a little cove on the shore of which was located a fruit-bat or flying-fox colony. It was a large tree, completely denuded of leaves from the branches of which probably fifty of these creatures were hanging head downward in bat fashion. Being nocturnal in their habits, they were sleeping. We tried to work our way inshore sufficiently close to take a photograph, but the water was entirely too shallow and we had to give it up. These creatures abound in the southern islands and are voracious devourers of figs and bananas. They attain the size of a small cat with a wing-spread of from three to five feet, and when they fly about at night your olfactories tell you of their close proximity.

Another animal common to the Philippines of which we saw several is the iguana. He's more wicked-looking than anything else, and creates anything but a pleasant appearance in his green hide, posing statuesquely in the middle of the road as if disputing the motor's right of way. This fellow attains a length of five feet. He's a great tree-climber as well as a swimmer. Instead of being dangerous or aggressive, however, he's dull-witted, and really hasn't sense enough to get out of the way. Incidentally, the natives are very fond of both the eggs and the meat of the iguana which is said to be excellent eating. While we are on the subject of lizards, it might be remarked that the little gecko is a sort of a house pet and will be found everywhere, not even excepting your hotel room. With their sticky little feet they scurry up the walls and across the ceiling with a flit and a dash that are quite intriguing. Sometimes they lose their foothold, however, and drop to the bare, hardwood floor with a resounding plop that is a trifle disconcerting because you confidently expect to sweep up the remains, only to see the little creature scurry off as if nothing had happened. No — I have never known one to drop on the bed. But then — most hotel beds throughout tropical countries are covered with canopies and the rooms are provided with electric fans as well, which are equally necessary to restful slumber.

Another incident of this visit to Davao comes to mind as I think back over the years — a human document, so to speak, which had its pathetic side. Sufficient water has flowed under the bridge to pardon the narrative. One of the residents — who shall be nameless — was an elderly man who had served as Captain in the American army of occupation fourteen years before and had settled in Davao with his wife and boy after the cessation of hostilities. He had gone into raising cocoanuts and had amassed considerable of a fortune. They threw open their home in a most hospitable manner to *El Aguila's* party and served a delightful luncheon: a clear case of 'hands across the sea.'

During the brief hour we spent with them our host buttonholed Mr. Miller and myself and deprecatingly suggested that we avoid saying anything to encourage his good wife if she started any discussion as to going back home. 'We have been here many years,' he went on to say, 'and I have about twenty-five thousand cocoanut trees, which net me more money than I can possibly spend. Our son is in college in the States and my dear wife doesn't see any good reason why we shouldn't give up this place and go back home. She doesn't appreciate that we are getting along in years and that all the friends we had before we came out here are either dead or have moved away. I know if we went back to the States now, we should be both lonesome and unhappy. It's far better that we stay here.' There was a touch of the dramatic in the homely recital which was not without its effect on us both. It eventuated precisely as Captain —— had said. His good wife did open up the question with a vengeance and we played our hypocritical parts to the best of our ability. It called to mind a conversation I had had with an old Britisher on the veranda of the Yacht Club in Yokohama who boasted that he had been in Japan forty years without a visit to old England. 'Why should I go back there,' said he, 'only to find out that all my old friends are dead? I'm better off out here. One can't have his cake and keep it.' And that's the tragedy of the Anglo-Saxon in the Far East. He makes his bed and has to lie in it. Man pays. He pays for being born, for living, for dying. Everything has its price. 'Each ounce of dross costs its ounce of gold.' What was it the Psalmist said about his preference for the 'Dorkie-bird' to the tents of wickedness?

CHAPTER XI

IN THE SULU SEA

All around the world they lie,
  On all the forty seas,
And the chorus of their call goes by
  On every vagrant breeze;
Sleepy little beach towns,
  A-sprawl for miles and miles,
Or dirty river-reach towns
  On delta mud and piles.

Tawi Tawi, Zamboanga,
  Cebu and Principe,
Sandakan, Malabang,
  Jolo-by-the-sea —
Oh, the finest hymn-book printed
  Is an old geography.

LEO HAYS

STEAMING away from Davao shortly after sunrise next morning, we came to anchor opposite the village of Dalaion at seven-thirty. And what a sight was that on shore! Dalaion is the center of an extensive hemp-raising district. The natives bring the hemp down from their fields up in the hills and sell it to a resident agent who stores it in a big nipa-shack until the arrival of the steamer which takes it to Manila at stated intervals. But — it was not the hemp shack that glued our staring eyes to the shore. It was a band of Bagobos — the most gorgeously togged-out aggregation of distinguished-looking pagans the traveler ever laid eyes on. They had come down from the heights of Mount Apo to greet the messenger of the President of the United States, as they understood Mr. Miller to be. There were some ten or fifteen datus with as many more youths, slim as young girls, with rather fine features betokening a different ancestry from anything we had seen — and handsome as young Greek gods: long black hair, tied in a flowing knot and decorated with a gayly colored kerchief of native cloth; decked out with ivory ear-disks, about half as big again as a silver dollar, which were inserted into an enlarged slit in the lobe of the ears; tight-fitting, knee-length trousers made of specially treated and exquisitely dyed hemp fiber, with a short, close-fitting, beaded jacket to match; broad garters of bead-work, tied and dyed to harmonize with the rest of the outfit, and bare feet. And strange to say, it didn't seem to be overdone. Never in all our travels had we seen such a brilliant display of sartorial grandeur. We were taking all this in with our binoculars almost before *El Aguila* let go her anchor. A few moments later, and we were in the launch which grounded about two hundred feet from shore, and we had the unexpected pleasure of having those gaylyclad youths come out with sedan chairs and carry us to the beach. Meanwhile the weirdest string music imaginable filled the air accompanied by the tom-toms and copper gongs, which were far from unpleasant.

A few steps from the beach, hidden by the jungle growth, ranged around the little plaza in front of the hemp warehouse, we came upon our orchestra consisting of a dozen Bagobo women, costumed as brilliantly as their men, who had started the festivities in a most auspicious manner. Half of them were seated on the ground behind ornately carved racks upon which their copper gongs were strung like a huge xylophone. These they beat alternately with the hide-covered drums or tom-toms presided over by other feminine artists. The stringed instruments consisted of long sections of hollow bamboo stalks about four inches in diameter, the outer surface of which had been cut into thin narrow strips, fastened at either end, and bridged like a violin string. The performers on this primitive instrument held it in both hands clasped around the center while they twanged the bamboo strings with their fingers and danced a sort of crude quadrille to a quickening tempo. It was a most interesting performance. And while it could scarcely be called harmonious, neither was it discordant. Also, there was a very definite rhythm to both the dance and the music, the bell-like tones of the gongs being deeply resonant and musical. They had staged a royal welcome, indeed, for us, and one would hardly think that the Bagobos were, previously, probably the most savage of all the mountain tribes in the Philippine Archipelago. The next thing that attracted our attention was that all the men had their teeth filed to almost needle-like points — that being the prevailing style. We learned also that the fine clothing and dyeing was the work of the women who apparently took great pride in keeping their men-folks looking like Solomon in all his glory, with a more striking color scheme than they themselves affected. Lieutenant Cochran stepped forward and greeted the chiefs with a hearty hand-shake which they apparently understood as being good form amongst the white people and responded with great cordiality. The aquiline features of some of the young men, with their high foreheads and brilliant black eyes, would almost indicate the presence of Caucasian blood were it not for the well-known fact that the ancient laws of this tribe rendered such a possibility exceedingly remote. These people are sheer pagan, with many barbarous practices, especially human sacrifice which, it is said, still persists in their tribal ceremonies. It was not surprising, therefore, that their understanding of independence was that it was some material thing which, if planted with their corn, would greatly increase the size of the harvest — for this was the argument that had been advanced by the emissaries of Quézon — and the Bagobos were for it accordingly. After a two hours' pow-wow, they permitted us to take their photographs in company with Mr. Miller, which seemed to please them greatly. Returning to the ship, we bade good-bye to Lieutenant Cochran, who set off upstream in his launch to resume his lonely post at Tagun with a regret which we all shared. Is it possible, I wonder, that the Congress of the United States will permit the unselfish, devoted service of such men as these to be brought to naught, in the name of politics? God forbid!

Zamboanga! What memories it recalls! Perhaps the most interesting feature of this ancient Spanish town at the southern extremity of the western peninsula of Mindanao is the fact that General John J. Pershing, U.S.A. (retired), was stationed there as Military Governor of the Moro Province, in 1913, with the modest rank of Major. It is worthy of note that four years later he was in charge of the American Expeditionary Forces in France where he demonstrated the value of his Philippine experience. Major Pershing was in Zamboanga on our arrival and accorded us a very cordial welcome. He will be remembered in the Philippines for many years to come, not only as a great fighter, but a builder and constructor as well. He had just received his orders to return to the United States and was subsequently in command at the Presido in San Francisco.

'Zambo,' as it is familiarly dubbed in the Philippines, is the capital of the Moro Province and one of the most attractive towns in the archipelago. With a cooler climate than Manila and ideal sanitary conditions as a result of the American occupation, it has always been a much-coveted station by the army officers. As we neared the town, a flotilla of native outrigger boats came out to meet us, each of them containing its quota of gongs and tom-toms, with a great display of multi-colored flags. It was a most hearty

reception and we were glad of the opportunity to go ashore
under ideal conditions where we were entertained most cor-
dially by the officers and their wives. A motor ride followed, over as fine a ballasted boulevard as might be found
at home, taking in the new custom-house, piers, parks, and
bridges, including the Provincial Capitol, one of the finest
public buildings in the islands. Major Pershing showed us,
with no little pride, his recently constructed jail which was
open on all sides, thoroughly sanitary, and doubtless more
healthy and desirable quarters than the inmates had ever
known. The spacious parade ground, surrounded by palm
trees, on which the officers' quarters faced, was bordered by
a terraced canal of pure spring water conducted from the
hills, and the whole place filled to overflowing with flowering plants of infinite tropical variety. It was a perfect
haven of rest facing out upon the blue waters of the Sulu
Sea. A well-attended meeting was held on a sort of a common overlooking the sea, attended by both Moros and Filipinos. And it was odd enough to hear the former speak eloquently in their broken English of the security and peace
they enjoyed under the American flag which they hoped
would remain there forever — followed by a Filipino spell-
binder, properly coached, on the 'many blessings of independence.'

At the close of the meeting the Moros staged a mock
spear-fight which was not quite as much of a mockery as it
was supposed to be, in view of the fact that the contestants·
had to be separated. We had an idea that it was meant for
the especial benefit of the Filipinos present, as an earnest of
what they might expect under certain conditions. It must
be said that they looked none too comfortable. The usual
orchestra was on hand and the booming of the tom-toms accompanied by the deep-toned gongs was altogether too suggestive of the barbarism from which the warlike Moro is
slowly rising.

IN THE SUBURBS OF ZAMBOANGA

Sulu, the sinister — the island of subtlety and guile, whose ground has been drenched with blood from time immemorial. Well endowed for the propagation of the fanatical doctrines of the Koran in the fourteenth century. Born and bred to slaughter, innate hatred of the 'infidel,' utter indifference to death, which is simply regarded as the password to a typical Mohammedan paradise — the Sulu Moro including his Lake Lanao brethren, constituted in his day the most difficult problem of the Spanish Colonial Government and that of the United States as well. If those two comedians, Frank Daniels and George Ade, had had the slightest conception of the actual character of these sanguinary Malays, I am inclined to believe their humor would have oozed out long before they completed that delightful farrago of twenty years ago: 'The Sultan of Sulu.' At any rate, it was not a little interesting to me to behold the original of Daniels's drop-curtain as we came to anchor off the capital town of Jolo, eight hours' sail from Zamboanga.

Yes — there was the funny little concrete pier with its pair of rails extending clear out to the end. Just why they were there no one seemed to know. Almost any moment I expected to hear the clang of a trolley-car bell and to see the vehicle itself come careering down the street. Equally bizarre were the two concrete pillars on either side of the pier just where it joined the land, with empty lamps on their crests. Off to the right, outside of the city wall, was a well-protected bay filled with native outrigger fishing boats, while just back from the pier, on the left, was that ever-present eyesore of the Orient, the corrugated-iron-roofed Government building that has crowded out the more appropriate thatched product. Beyond the beautiful shade trees, for the distance of a couple of city blocks, could be seen the ancient Spanish wall built centuries agone for a safety which they never felt. A few miles back from the town we could see the forested heights of Bud Dajo, the extinct volcano into the crater of which the Sulu Moros and their fighting wives retreated in the last great fight of pacification the United States soldiers had to put up in 1906. I remember well the howl that went up all over the country here at home that our army boys were fighting women in the Philippines and how the newspapers took it up. The Moro figured that he had his fight with Spain to make all over again and he simply would not quit. He knew from experience that he could whip the Spaniard and he didn't figure a United States soldier any differently. That's exactly what he had to learn, and it took force to teach the lesson. When it comes to the Moro women, I'll content myself with quoting a verse from Kipling and you'll understand precisely what I mean. It will also explain how they came to be in the crater of Bud Dajo fighting with their men:

> When you're wounded and left on Afghanistan's plains,
> And the women come out to cut up what remains,
> Jest roll to your rifle and blow out your brains
>   An' go to your Gawd like a soldier.

It may be that in some distant Utopian day the Moro woman may become really civilized. What with the Spanish wars for over three centuries and the constant atmosphere of slaughter, she's no shrinking violet. She's as fierce a fighter as her husband and as much of a fatalist. To this very day the city gate is guarded as vigilantly as it was in the days of Spanish sovereignty, nor is a native Moro ever allowed inside without being first searched and disarmed. It would be strange, indeed, if the warlike tendencies of the Moro, built up through centuries of unbroken fighting in self-defense, could be done away with overnight. And — in the opinion of those who should know — this will be the first problem that a government by Filipinos will have to

face in event of independence being granted. Owing to
their absolute trust in the United States Government, the
Moros surrendered all their rifles and ammunition. It
wouldn't be long, however, before they would be as well
outfitted as ever. For years there has been constant smuggling of arms and ammunition into the Sulu Archipelago
from Singapore and Borneo. The armed Filipino Constabulary, which Harrison established in authority over the
Moro after the latter had given up his arms (to his later
bitter resentment), can maintain order just so long as the
United States Government is supreme. Let the United
States pull out, however, and we shall see the bloodiest
Moro uprising imaginable. They will wait just long enough
to fit themselves out with the necessary rifles and ammunition to make a Filipino massacre a dead-sure thing and
there will be a 'mopping-up' with a vengeance. It is a
matter of history that the Spanish conquest was the only
thing that confined the Moros to the southern islands.
Backed by Islam they already dominated the great island
of Mindanao and the Sulu Archipelago and were beginning
to spread northward. The difference between the Filipino
and the Moro merely as a fighting man is indicated by the
ease with which the Spanish established themselves in the
northern part of the archipelago and the unceasing warfare
which the Moros waged against them in the south. It was
only as recently as 1876, after constant fighting for over
three centuries, that Spain signed a treaty with the Moros
which secured to them the administration of their own af-
fairs and established their status as a protectorate, not a
dependency. That's all they wanted. That treaty Spain
observed scrupulously up to the time of the American occupation. The United States Government by its fair-dealing
won the confidence and made friends of the Moros. Harrison, determined to show, on paper, if not actually, a hom-

ogeneous Filipino Government, sent the ancient enemies of
the Moros down into their country practically as over-
lords, in the shape of the Filipino Constabulary: a gratui-
tous insult to a high-spirited, warlike race temporarily de-
prived of arms. One doesn't need to be a prophet to follow
this situation to its logical conclusion, once the Stars and
Stripes are pulled down in the Sulu Archipelago.

As our launch pulled up to the pier, we were welcomed
most heartily by a fine-looking six-footer in the person of
Civil Governor Vernon Whitney, who, I noticed, walked
with difficulty, dragging one foot along the ground as if he
had no power over it. Ordinarily there would be no point
whatever in mentioning a man's infirmity. The tragic
story back of that hamstrung leg, however — for that's
precisely what it was — has been lying in the back part of
my head for twelve years because Vernon Whitney asked
me not to tell it. He had an excellent reason for making the
request which, however, has long since passed into the
discard: nothing less than the Honorable William Jennings
Bryan, then Secretary of State under the Wilson Administration. I don't know where Vernon Whitney is to-day,
or whether he's alive or dead. It's time this story was told,
however, if for no other reason than to set forth the character of the men who figured in the pacification of the
Philippines a quarter of a century ago. Men who did their
duty as they saw it, accepted whatever consequences might
eventuate, and had but one unchanging prayer: that whatever they did might not reach the elongated ears of those
gentlemen in Washington 'dressed in a little brief authority' whose capacity for hampering a man in the performance
of his duty was unlimited.

According to Whitney, there had been a quarrel between
the members of a Moro fishing village a few miles up the
coast which bade fair to develop into something more

serious. Knowing the head-men quite well, he took a steam launch and a couple of soldiers and ran up with the expectation of straightening matters out. When he arrived there wasn't a native to be seen, which was good cause for suspicion and for caution as well. Beaching the launch, he left his two companions in charge and walked up into the village alone to investigate. Not a soul in sight. Appreciating the seriousness of the situation and his own danger, he turned to go back to the boat and found himself face to face with a couple of Moros with drawn bolos, who had been concealed behind some bushes. Noting that their eyebrows were shaven, he realized instantly that he was up against a pair of maniacs who were '*gone juramentado*' or running amuck. Among the Moros '*juramentado*' is an insane religious frenzy induced by chewing *bhang* or hashish — a narcotic drug made from the seed of wild hemp. It is accompanied by the dainty ceremony of knotting a green withe about the testicles and shaving the eyebrows. The final touch is administered by the priest whose anointing is supposed to render the gentleman invulnerable. Then he starts out on his holy mission to knife every 'infidel' in sight. Should anything happen to him, however, he is assured of a prompt admission into paradise where he will enjoy all the comforts of home, including a populous harem of very lovely houris. It was a rather dramatic situation for Whitney whose luck consisted in the fact that one of the lunatics was nearer by a few feet than the other. Pulling his revolver in the brief moment that was left him, he grappled with the nearest one over whose shoulder he shot his companion. Then pushing his immediate antagonist away he shot him also. In the few seconds that Whitney had held him close with his left arm, however, the Moro had a chance for a rear slashing blow with his bolo which severed Whitney's thigh muscle and left him a cripple for

life. His two companions ran up and assisted him into the
launch and they got away. It was Whitney's opinion that
the two men were about starting for Jolo with the expectation of picking up a soldier or two before they could be
stopped. I asked him if the incident ended there, and he
replied with a smile that a few soldiers marched up to the
village the next day, since which time they had had no
further trouble. It was the killing of these two madmen
that Whitney was anxious to keep from Mr. Bryan's ears.
He did not want to be identified with the wanton slaying of
our 'little brown brothers.'

Two brightly dressed Moros — one about thirty years,
with a rifle, the other about fifty — were squatting on their
hunker in Whitney's outer office, apparently waiting for
orders, although there seemed to be none forthcoming.
They excited my curiosity, especially the elder one who
wore a voluminous and parti-colored neckerchief in which
the lower part of his face was practically buried. Smelling
a story, I asked him about them. And there was a story in
very truth which involved them both in most interesting
adventures, the first one of which Whitney was particularly anxious should not reach any one active in the Department of State at Washington, for fear of their misunderstanding conditions.

'My great job here,' said he, 'is gathering in rifles from
the Moros up in the hills. It's comparatively easy to keep
them in line down here around Jolo where we can watch
them. During this last year fifteen hundred have been
turned in, and that's doing mighty well, considering that
they come all the way from Singapore and Borneo. This
young fellow in the outer office was one of the first to turn
his rifle in after the order went out. He came along with it
and stayed around saying that he wanted to be my 'boy.'
I told him I had no use for a 'boy' and no money to pay for

one if I needed him. That didn't seem to make any difference to him, and he made himself so useful in so many different ways that after about three months I gave his rifle back to him with a few rounds of ammunition just to assure him of my confidence. He scarcely ever lets it leave his hands.

'A few months ago news reached me that a " bad " Moro was shooting up a little town in the hills with a newly acquired rifle. It was a three-day trip to the place. I told the young man here to go up and get it. He was gone over a week and returned saying that the fellow wouldn't give it up. I sent him back a second time, and told him to get it without fail. And again he returned with the same report. I sent him a third time, with the added statement that if he didn't get that rifle I would take his away from him. Within ten days he returned with the rifle and the owner's head. I'll have to acknowledge he sprung something on me that I never dreamed of. But — that's the Moro's way, and I'd have a fine time explaining that to Washington. Needless to say, our friend outside retains his rifle. He's the most trustworthy " boy " I've ever known, but — I don't overlook the fact that he's a Moro.

'The old fellow there,' continued Whitney, 'has had an adventure that probably is without a parallel. He was a member of the Sultan's Council. It seemed that he repeated on the outside some "inside stuff." Shortly afterward a couple of our soldiers came across him with both cheeks slit from the corners of his mouth nearly to his ears. A couple of the Sultan's henchmen acting under orders had seized him and pushed a barong edgewise into his mouth, thereby giving him more room to talk, as the Sultan playfully put it. We sent him to the post hospital and sewed him up properly, since which time he has attached himself to me. The funny part of the whole story is: the Sultan restored him to his old place in his Council and he apparently stands in as well as ever. He's too proud, however, to show those wicked-looking scars on his face, so he always wears that big neckerchief tied in such a fashion that it just covers the lower half of his jaws.'

It was just as Whitney put it. That afternoon when the Sultan, dressed in a white duck suit with patent-leather shoes, a fez, and a cane, held an open meeting for the benefit of those who wished to express themselves to Mr. Miller on the subject of independence, sure enough, seated on the platform along with the rest of the elect, was our elderly friend with the sheet-like neckerchief submerging the lower part of his face. I noticed, however, that he had nothing to say. The consensus of the meeting was that the Jolo Moros didn't want any independence that necessitated any association with the Filipino. At its close, His Highness, Haji Mohammed Jamalulram, Sultan of Sulu, posed for his picture. He isn't a half-bad-looking fellow nor for that matter are the two loyal attendants of Governor Whitney.

Later in the day several of us, accompanied by a couple of soldiers, took a little walk into the native town outside of the walls and came across His Royal Highness clad in a much-soiled shirt, old knickerbockers, heavy shoes, and a pair of very much up-to-date garters worn on the outside of his trousers to hold up a pair of socks of United States manufacture. Not being able to speak the English language by reason of a mouthful of betel juice, he smiled affably and passed on. Having already secured his photograph in his 'glad rags,' I simply didn't have the nerve to train my camera on him clothed in his usual undress uniform, fearing he might feel a trifle sensitive. It isn't a nice thing to hurt the feelings of the Sultan of Sulu.

The army officers and their wives served a delightful luncheon at the Club overlooking the sea in the afternoon

THIS ONE TOOK THE BAD MAN'S HEAD

TWO DISTINGUISHED SULU MOROS

THIS ONE HAD HIS MOUTH SLIT

and we reciprocated by inviting them to an informal reception aboard *El Aguila*. I may have been mistaken, but — I thought I saw just a shade of a wistful expression on the faces of the ladies as they left the ship to return to the pier as we began hoisting the anchor. There is a great deal of glamour about these far-away places which stirs the uneasy foot. To visit them is a rare treat and most enlightening as well. I have never seen any woman, however, outside of an officer's wife, who could stand them as a steady diet. The glamour soon fades and the social limitations are great. Then, again, there's that ever-present tendency to let things slide. To perpetrate a bull: *Mañana* is the order of the day, and the sheltering palm soon loses its shade. Not an officer or his wife but regards each setting sun as 'a day's march nearer home' and lives in anticipation of orders from the War Department to report to some post in the United States. True — they get just as tired of the United States post as they do of the Oriental one and they finally settle down to living in their trunks. But — they *do* see the world, they *do* enlarge their mental horizon, their lives are *not* 'just one damned thing after another,' and they *are* vastly more entertaining to their friends than most of us.

Do you recall the thrill with which you used to pore over your old school-geography, and especially when you came across one of those illustrations of a couple of native huts perched on piling above the water, with the enthralling caption: 'Scene in the Philippines'? Well — I'll have to acknowledge that I had my eye peeled for one of those spots from the very day we left Manila. I had about reached the conclusion that there weren't 'no such animal,' when, on the morning after we left Jolo, we dropped anchor off the island of Siasi. There was my dream come true: a dozen crazy-looking shacks supported by equally crazy-looking spiles, with a dozen fishing boats in the shallow water below — and a most enchanting row of graceful palm trees on the beach. I swear I never expect to have another such thrill as surged through me on that glorious morning. Are not all such mornings glorious? This one was worth the price of the trip, and I went ashore in the launch with the most wonderful feeling of proprietorship that ever entered into an adventurer's soul. No boy ever raced through 'Robinson Crusoe' with any greater enthusiasm than I entered upon my possessions that eventful day. It was worth waiting a half-century for such a reward. Just imagine being able to drop out of the back door of your house onto the deck of your boat and go fishing! What a cinch for the lady of the house not to have any dusting or vacuum-cleaner stunts, no garbage-man, no plumber's bills, not even obliged to spend $900 per month for clothes! These Siasi natives are the Samal Moros who have lived in their sea-shacks from the most ancient times and gave the Spaniards some of the hardest fighting they had. And yet — when we reached the shore, we found a thriving native population in charge of one lonesome Constabulary officer. To my utter surprise, I learned that the occupants of the huts out over the water represented a very small percentage of the people who, under the benign government of the United States Army, and with nothing to fear, had given up their reef shacks for the greater creature comforts of the land and were living a happy, harmonious life.

Late that afternoon we hove in sight of the island of Bongao in the Tawi Tawi group. We could see the American flag flying from the only building in sight — that occupied by another lone Constabulary officer in charge of the Tawi Tawi tribes. It had come on to rain and we decided not to land. The apparent absence of any human life, however, was a bit puzzling, and Colonel Taylor went ashore to investigate. He found the man down with fever, entirely without help and all his quinine gone. It happened luckily that we had a supply on board and Taylor came back after it. Returning to the shore, he sat up with the sick man until daybreak when the ship sailed. The regular supply boat from Zamboanga was due in a few days when the poor fellow would be properly cared for. The quinine was all he needed, however, and he was correspondingly grateful. The Tawi Tawi tribes are a lot of bad actors, truculent in the extreme. The fact that the sick man had been deserted by his servant spoke volumes. He seemed to have no fear, however, and we proceeded on our way. Sandakan, British North Borneo, being but twelve hours' sail from Bongao, we decided to make that celebrated pest-hole a brief visit. From the standpoint of gathering in a lot of interesting information it was richly worth while. But — that's all.

CHAPTER XII

SANDAKAN — HELL'S OWN TOWN

Fifteen men on the Dead Man's Chest —
Yo-ho-ho and a bottle of rum!
Drink and the devil had done for the rest —
Yo-ho-ho and a bottle of rum!
We wrapped 'em all in a mains'l tight,
With twice ten turns of a hawser's bight,
And we heaved 'em over and out of sight —
With a yo-heave-ho
And a fare-you-well,
And a sullen plunge
In the sullen swell,
Ten fathoms deep on the road to Hell —
Yo-ho-ho and a bottle of rum!
                                    YOUNG EWING ALLISON

SANDAKAN is one of the few places on the face of the earth that should be razed to the ground — and, I almost said, including its population. It's a disgrace to the British nation under whose flag it carries on the vilest traffic known to man: the deliberate debauching of human beings as a factor in the opium traffic. In exact terminology, Sandakan is not a British colony. It is a British protectorate, however, being owned and governed by a private corporation — the British North Borneo Company — operating under a royal charter, with the power of life and death over thousands of defenseless natives and imported Chinese coolies whom it exploits with an abhorrent callousness and cruelty that is a blot on our civilization. And all in the name of creating dividends for stockholders in the British Isles. Why Great Britain does not rise in sheer loathing and wipe out this foul spot by revoking the charter which permits it to carry on, is a mystery to a white man. Here is a town of approximately fifteen thousand population with barely one hundred Europeans, among whom there may be a dozen women. With its picturesque and tropical setting so attractive to the eye as the steamer approaches its anchorage in the bay, it suggests a beautiful home with every creature comfort and luxury, situated over the vent of a foul latrine — with a distracted mother wondering why the children are continually down with malarial fever. Try and imagine a perfectly beautiful flower filling the whole house with its exquisite perfume only to discover that it has taken root in a putrid mass of unspeakable impurities beneath the foundation, the existence of which no one suspected. The difference between the simile and the actuality is that the Anglo-Saxon residents of this accurséd town are only too well aware of the reeking conditions by which they are surrounded, morally and physically, and are become either wholly indifferent to them or appreciate the utter futility of applying a remedy. Sandakan struck me as a town trying to escape from itself. It is founded in a series of open sewers in the native and Chinese section down near the water-front, accompanied by a string of ramshackle wooden platforms, which serve for homes, stretching along the water's edge for a half to three quarters of a mile — a section simply shot through and through with the foulest of opium dens, gambling-hells, and unspeakable native houses of prostitution — all run under the eyes and with the permission (if not coöperation) of the resident management of the British North Borneo Company. The place suggests a horror-stricken criminal with a ball and chain to his leg, doing his best to climb out and away from the terrible mess into which his own viciousness has buried him. As a matter of fact the frightful conditions would not indicate the presence of an Anglo-Saxon within a million of miles and the visitor is overcome with wonder to think that

there are not only white men in the neighborhood who
speak his language, but decent, respectable women as well.

Turning our backs on these sinks of iniquity, we climb
the hill to a small but scrupulously neat plaza or parade
ground on which the British North Borneo Company's
offices face, as well as the Planters' Club, both set off by
deep, comfortable verandas. Within a stone's throw are the
Protestant and Roman Catholic Missions and a Chinese
joss-house. Just what particular use the Chinese of that
crime-ridden town have for worship of any kind whatsoever, even of an otherwise respectable joss, is not apparent.
And even if it were — why the honorable British North
Borneo Company should allow a heathenish outfit like that
to locate itself cheek-by-jowl with two Christian missions is
a puzzle. It would almost seem that they had done it with
the idea of impressing upon those sodden wretches, at
whose physical and spiritual ruin they seem to be conniv-
ing, that their joss was on a par with any Christian mission
that might have the hardihood to attempt anything in the
way of regeneration in that noisome hole. Certainly the
Sandakan joss is the only deity (?) on the plaza that could
have any possible interest in the charnel-house down by
the waterside. It simply goes to show the depths to which
that unclean municipality has sunk.

Following a steep, winding road above the plaza we come
upon the picturesque bungalows of the resident Europeans,
surrounded by tropical vegetation: palms, flaming bougainvillea, blazing fire-trees, everything, in fact, that makes life
livable. True — one cannot wax enthusiastic over municipal problems with the thermometer at 110 and a fiendish
humidity that will separate the glued joints of a picture
frame and grow mould on one's shoes overnight. I can imagine the average resident and his wife consigning the native quarter to the nether regions, and can sympathize

with their frame of mind. There is a tremendous amount to
be said for the patient Britisher who accepts a job of that
character and whose equally patient wife goes along with
him into a climate that is going to make an old woman of
her before her time. Such people are a credit to any country. And to see these folk put on their dinner clothes every
night, despite the fact that ten minutes later they will be
hopelessly wilted in a profuse perspiration — is an inspiration. It's a part of the 'White Man's Burden' which they
accept with a philosophy that would feaze the average
American.

Native labor being comparatively worthless in British
North Borneo, the Company is obliged to depend upon Chinese coolies which it imports in large numbers, under pro-
mises of high wages, plenty of opium, and a fine healthy climate. These poor wretches are employed under the indenture system and their stay is limited to three hundred days,
at the end of which they can go back home if they have
money enough to pay their fare, or they can renew their indenture for another three hundred days which they generally
do. The coolie, on arrival, receives *an advance payment* of
twenty-five or thirty Singapore dollars which he is encour-
aged to spend in the native gambling-houses, dens of prostitution, and opium joints. A second advance is soon called
for which is willingly made — and sometimes a third. And
what the above-mentioned pest-holes do not get, the Company stores do, for supplies of all kinds, including medical
attendance. In the end the poor coolie is compelled to resort to the pawnshop which is also controlled by the Company — and you can picture the rest. In short, no matter
how his money goes — for food, clothes, medicine, gambling, prostitution, opium — it eventually finds its way into
the pockets of the Company to which the poor wretch
never is allowed to get out of debt. It is peonage in its

worst form. It traffics in the weakness of the indentured
man who comes there in health and is sent home, at the end
of two or three years, a physical wreck, riddled with disease and a confirmed drug fiend.

And now let's see just how the British Government fits
into this little scheme: The British North Borneo Company
buys its opium from the British Colonial Government of
the Straits Settlements. It pays for the drug at the rate of
$1.20 per tael, or one and one fifth ounces. After all kinds
of alleged adulterations, the Chartered Company sells the
product to the Chinese opium farmers at the modest figure
of $8.50 per tael. Take your pencil and figure the profit.
And the coolie pays a handsome profit on that figure to the
tenant of the Chartered Company who runs the 'hop
joint.' It surely is a fine business for the British Government to be in and takes us back to the situation in Hongkong and Canton. The Sandakan traffic in opium alone,
I was informed, nets the British Government over $500,000
annually.

One afternoon was quite long enough to spend in the
town. After having walked the length of Jalan Tiga, the
main street in the native section, about a quarter of a mile,
lined on both sides by gambling dens, my attention was
called to the streets running at right angles to it. These
were openly set apart for the opium and prostitution traffic
— each resort having its sign boldly hung out with a view
to attracting trade. A short walk therein was sufficient.
And when I was told that the Sultan of Sulu received a
subsidy of two hundred and fifty dollars per month from
the Chartered Company for certain territorial concessions
in North Borneo which had rested with the Sulu Government for hundreds of years, I understood the presence of his
boat which we passed coming into the harbor. Incidentally, I was informed that he always came in person to col-

lect it in order that he might leave it personally with the
Sandakan gambling-houses and thus be sure that his lib-
eral friends the British North Borneo Company got it back
without undue trouble. The writer, Colonel E. Alexander
Powell, who visited Sandakan several years afterward,
found the conditions unchanged. He has told the story in
far greater detail in his excellent book 'Where the Strange
Trails Go Down,' and closes with the following enlightening paragraph which will bear repetition. Here's hoping
that both his effort and my own as well may bear fruit some
not too-distant day. British Colonial Government is altogether too fine an institution to permit itself to be tin-
canned in this fashion simply for the sake of greed:

There is held each year, at one of the great London hotels,
the North Borneo Dinner. It is one of the most brilliant af-
fairs of the season. At the head of the long table, banked with
flowers and gleaming with glass and silver, sits the chairman of
the chartered company, flanked by cabinet ministers, arch-
bishops, ambassadors, admirals, field marshals. The speakers
work the audience into a fervor of patriotic pride by their
sonorous word-pictures of England's services to humanity in
bearing the white man's burden, and of the spread of enlight-
enment and progress under the Union Jack. But the heartiest
applause invariably greets the announcement that the North
Borneo Company has declared a dividend. Whence the money
to pay the dividend was derived is tactfully left unsaid. The
dinner always concludes with the singing of the anthem *Land
of Hope and Glory.* Yet they say that the English have no
sense of humor!

We pulled out of Sandakan that evening with a dark-
brown taste in our mouths — subjects for quarantine, as it
were. Not even in Canton had I seen anything that struck
me so sinisterly. We had visions of bubonic plague, yellow
fever, smallpox, and leprosy. It seemed as if we had brushed
against all of them in the dark. I question whether an individual in the whole party would have been willing to live

there for the income of the British North Borneo Company.
If it hadn't been for the prevalence of sharks we should
have all taken a plunge in the sea just for the cleansing
process. What a terrible thing is total depravity! And to
think of an Anglo-Saxon profiting financially from the out-
put of such an Augean Stable! It makes the Old Testament
narrative of Sodom and Gomorrah ring like a *Te Deum*.

El Aguila had reached her southernmost port and was
now headed for home. The middle of the next afternoon
found us off the little island of Cagayan Sulu, and at the
suggestion of the skipper we went ashore to see rather an
interesting freak of nature which no one has ever been able
to explain. About five hundred yards from the beach and
half as many high, there were two small lakes lying side by
side, in what appeared to be two craters separated only by
a narrow, rocky partition. One of these lakes was of fresh
water, the other of salt, and the level of one was about
twenty-five feet higher than the other. Neither had any
apparent inlet or outlet and they both maintained the same
general level all the time. Down on the beach was a large-
sized nipa-shack said to be the home of an American who
kept a stock of textiles of various sorts for sale to the natives
on neighboring islands. His stock looked to be worth about
$3.50. There was nobody about but a Moro boy, who said
the man was gone for the day, where he didn't know. It
looked to me like an instance of a man wanting to get away
from his kind and I felt quite sure he was in hiding on the
island.

What a strange, unaccountable creature is the animal,
man! And why shouldn't he hide himself if he wished?
Perhaps he knew we had come from Sandakan, in which
event he showed his wisdom. At any rate, it was a perfectly safe spot for a plunge and we made the most of it.

While we were at our bath a Moro outrigger canoe suddenly appeared from around one side of the island with a fine load of fruit of great variety. Where the fellow came from no one could imagine, least of all the skipper. There was no growth or cultivation of any kind on the island and no other islands in the immediate neighborhood. This native would have no excuse for hiding anyway. Our being in the vicinity was the merest chance. Maybe he was there with fruit for the American and took advantage of the opportunity to get a better price for it from our party. If so, he succeeded, and we laid in a fine stock of fresh fruit. Moral: don't hide when the greengrocer comes around.

One of the finest bits of constructive work done during the American occupation of the Philippines was the establishment of the Iwahig Penal Colony on Palawan Island. It was conceived and carried out under the Forbes administration in 1905, and consisted of the setting aside of eighty thousand acres of land, four thousand of which were cleared in a short time by fifty convicts sent there for that purpose. Followed the erection of an administration building, a hospital, a series of barracks, all surrounding and facing on an attractive plaza or parade ground. The first contingent consisted of twelve hundred long-term convicts among whom were a number of murderers with life sentences, with a record of two years' good behavior, who were given the privilege of either staying at Bilibid or going to Iwahig. Here they were organized into a sort of a George Junior Republic, under the supervision of Superintendent Lamb and his wife, choosing their own officers, judges, policemen, and running themselves on honor. For good behavior a convict earned the right to have a house of his own, to bring his family there, with a little farm to cultivate — half the proceeds going to the Government. When we were there,

there were eighty-seven families cultivating as many farms, a cocoanut-palm grove of fifty thousand trees, twenty-five thousand of which were bearing, and four thousand head of cattle. The place was being run by seven white men including Superintendent Lamb, and twelve convict sub-officials. There never had been an escape and quite a number of men whose terms had expired elected to stay there with their families and work on shares with the Government, their work being credited to the purchase of their farms. *El Aguila* anchored off Puerto Princesa while a launch manned entirely by convicts came down the river and took the party up for an inspection and a parade of the whole colony. It was a sight to remember for many a year.

And it should not be forgotten that practically not one of those men had any idea of industry of any kind when they were sent to Bilibid originally. They had virtually been made over and were doing their part as good citizens. One of the first things that Governor-General Harrison did after he took hold was to pardon approximately one hundred and fifty Bilibid and Iwahig prisoners, in the name of economy. Just get that — pardoning criminals, including murderers, in the name of economy!

A leisurely sail through the Visayan group brought us into Cebu for the night, and a short run over to the Isle of Mactan in the morning where Ferdinand Magellan is buried. At least he has a rather impressive-looking monument there and I hope, like those of the patriot Rizal, his bones are at rest. Magellan's trouble, after he got the head-man on Cebu converted and lined up in favor of his Catholic Majesty Charles V of Spain, was that he had to hustle over to little Mactan and corral the natives there as well. He didn't know that his supposed convert on Cebu was bluffing

and had sneaked around the back way to join hands with
the Mactan outfit. Together they slaughtered the old cir-
cumnavigator whose remains are supposed never to have
been removed from the little island. Then we slipped over
to Iloilo where the *presidente* gave us all a great welcome
and had a few *Independencia* orators on hand to provide a
little real entertainment. Also, he nearly poisoned the lot
of us with some native oysters. We should have known
better than to tackle such game as that. 'Twas about as
close a call for a family ptomaine party, as might be
imagined.

What a godlike thing it is for Science to lay her reassuring hand upon the fears of poor stricken humanity. I have
never ceased to be glad of our memorable visit to the Culion
Island Leper Colony. It brought back as nothing else could
have done the memories of childhood and the wonderful
Bible story of the ten lepers who were cleansed, there being
but one real gentleman in the lot and he a Samaritan: the
exception that proved the rule. If there are any successors
to Father Damien left in this old world, they are Governor-
General Leonard Wood and Dr. Victor G. Heiser, the latter
having instituted that wonderful colony. Dr. Heiser traveled the Philippines from one end to the other, gathering in
the unfortunates gently and kindly, as much for the possibilities of a personal cure as for the segregation of those who
were beyond it. He gained the confidence of those poor ignorant folk who had been hiding their afflicted ones away
in the hills, who had no conception of the benefits involved,
until he had assembled over five thousand on Culion.
Then he was practically forced out of the service because
of Harrison's plan for Filipinizing all public offices without
reference to the utter unfitness of the unsympathetic native
physician for the work in hand. We went ashore with just

the least bit of misgiving. We returned overflowing with enthusiastic praise. Nothing to disturb the most fastidious.
The location of the island is beautiful as well as its trees,
shrubs, etc. The plan of the houses is scientifically thought
out and the arrangements for those of the same family, similarly afflicted, to live together is most humanitarian. We
all stepped into a solution of bichloride of mercury before
we entered the enclosure, repeating the operation when we
departed. And now — Governor-General Wood is endeav-
oring to raise $1,000,000 fund here in the United States
which will enable him absolutely to drive the terrible disease out of the islands. This despite the opinion of the
native physicians in Manila that any money spent on the
cure of leprosy is wasted.

Romblon Island possesses three points of interest which
seemed to justify a brief visit for half an afternoon: first the
natives make a large variety of mats, table-covers, doilies,
wall-coverings, etc., of specially treated and finely woven
hemp fiber almost as soft and pliable as silk. The stuff was
so altogether enticing that we cleaned 'em out of everything
they had, good, bad, and indifferent. It was the first native
product we had seen that had any value beyond that of a
mere souvenir. Next in order was a fine bathing-beach of
which we all took quick advantage. And thirdly, was an
old Spanish church built in 1726 that we tried hard to en-
thuse over and couldn't. You see — we were getting near
home and it was much like the third week's daily inspection
of old cathedrals in Italy and France. Nevertheless, we were
courteously entertained by the *presidente* who made no
mention of '*Pendencia*,' for which we were all sincerely
grateful and wished him the same.

Our last port of call on this memorable voyage was at
Mariveles, just to the left of the entrance to Manila Bay

and almost in sight of Corregidor Island. Here we had a rather unusual session with a band of negritos or African dwarfs who had been coaxed down from the hills for the purpose. In ancient times the whole Philippine Archipelago was peopled with these folk. They were gradually driven out by the encroachments of the Malayan tribes until there are a bare twenty thousand of them left. A few scattering hundreds of them inhabit the mountainous portion of that peninsula which bounds Manila Bay on the west. They constitute the most primitive development of human life in the islands. Having no social or political organization, they move about from place to place, subsisting principally on fish and wild fruits of various sorts. Once in a while they will settle down for a few months, when they clear the jungle growth by fire, cultivate the ground with sharp-pointed stakes which they use for punching holes in which they plant *camotes*, a variety of sweet potato — also sugar cane and tobacco. They live principally in hollow trees and in wickiups of grass and brush. Their one weapon is the sumpitan or blow-gun with which poisoned arrows are used, both in hunting and in warfare. Similar to the Bagobos, they point their teeth, only they break the corners off with a heavy knife, instead of filing them. They also follow that most ancient and primitive method of ornamenting their bodies with scar designs, produced by cicatrizing the skin with a sharp piece of bamboo and rubbing dirt in the wound. This is unquestionably an inheritance from their African ancestry. Ordinarily they go perfectly nude. On the occasion of our visit, however, they were clad in cast-off white duck trousers and straw hats, doubtless furnished by *El Aguila's* crew, as a special concession to the amenities of polite society.

We docked at the Manila pier late in the afternoon of a

hot day in November, with more regret than we could well express. It seemed altogether more like a return to asphalt and macadam than we fancied. *El Aguila* had been gone five weeks during which time we had called at thirty different ports and visited in addition thereto twenty inland towns by motor-car. We had done approximately thirty-five hundred miles of sea-going, and I question whether any party ever journeyed through that great archipelago that saw more than we did in the time allowed or got a clearer conception of the hopes and fears of a more or less benighted people — not to mention the pagan and Mohammedan tribes. It isn't any unkindness to refer to them as a great congregation of overgrown children, with the merest smattering of knowledge on the part of a small percentage; all of them absolutely impractical, with no conception of civic requirements or progress and wholly lacking in initiative.

Whatever information they have acquired is grafted upon an Oriental mentality shot through with superstition and with a total lack of morale that unfits them hopelessly for self-government. With all of this, they are vain beyond words and easily led: the ideal prey of the self-seeking *politico* who winds them around his little finger by appealing to their sense of the dramatic and their unlimited egotism. Indeed, we Americans have contributed not a little to that unfortunate condition because of our unstinted praise of the very limited progress they have made under the watchful eye of every colonial administration from Taft to Forbes. In our desire to inspire them to added effort, we have slopped over in our commendations much as we might do with a defective pupil, in order that he should not become discouraged with his woeful lack of brain-power. We sowed the wind with our undeserved praise and are reaping the whirlwind of their having taken us literally. And such political tricksters as Quézon have been quick to avail themselves of a situation made to their very hands. Entirely apart from whatever material interests the United States has in the Philippines, which cannot be consigned to the scrap-heap with any degree of self-respect, the Filipinos are no more qualified to govern themselves than is any nation with its feet still clogged in superstition and ignorance, even though there may be an occasional emergence of some solitary head above the clouds. The only one up-to-date is that of Rizal, an intelligent patriot, who would most unquestionably have led his people out of medieval darkness into the light if the Spaniards had not stood him up in front of a firing squad. There are no present-day Rizals. The Rizals are not interested in spending the taxpayers' money to the tune of nine hundred dollars per month for clothing; in the little gifts like railroad presidencies from 'grateful' Governors-General who know when to 'look the other way'; in $500,000 annual *Independencia* funds to be spent without making any accounting to the same tax-ridden taxpayer. Dear God! I wonder if Quézon ever heard that eloquent ejaculation we have here in the States — 'Don't make me laugh'? His antics here in Washington and in the Philippine Senate would be funny if they weren't so terribly tragic for 'poor Juan' who is holding the bag in the Philippines.

Mr. Miller had one other place to visit before returning to the States: Baguio, the summer capital, up in the mountain-tops a day's ride from Manila. Baguio is in the Igorot country and just about the only place a white man can tolerate when Manila is in the throes of summer weather. We went with him — his little crowd was with him all the time — and no one seemed to enjoy it more than he, nor was there ever a more appreciative following than he had — peace to his ashes! Getting to Baguio is a real job. We

were called at 4.45 A.M. After a hurried breakfast, a car
was waiting to whirl us to Malolos (Aguinaldo's old stamp-
ing-ground), where we caught the train for Dagupan —
the end of the line. There we were met by motor-cars
which used up the balance of the day in reaching Baguio
after dark.

That ride will remain with us long after a lot of other
things of less importance are forgotten. It involved fording
rivers on bamboo rafts which didn't look as if they would
support a baby carriage, let alone a motor-car and its
human freight. But it did and with plenty to spare. In
other places we were carried across rivers in sedan chairs
with the carriers sinking just a little deeper at every step
until we began to think we'd better get out and walk too.
Crossing other rivers on bridge string pieces not more than
five inches wide — the planking having been washed away
in a heavy storm the day before. All this with an uncertain, nervous Filipino chauffeur. I think the fact of our
remaining in the car was all that enabled him to get
through. If we had got out, I'm afraid the apparent lack
of confidence would have cost us the car. And then that
wonderful Benguet motor road, the traffic on which was
controlled precisely the same as a railway train dispatcher
governs the movement of trains. For twenty miles the road
climbs up the mountain-side, over gorges, zigzagging back
and forth, doubling on itself repeatedly until it reaches the
summit, five thousand feet above sea-level. You'd think
you were in the States, so far as scenery is concerned, together with the character of the flora, etc. That night we
spent at Governor Forbes's fine bungalow, 'Topside,' under
the friendly ministrations of his Secretary Conrad Hatheway, who had remained behind to wind up his chief's af-
fairs — likewise under blankets. We should like to have
remained there a week, but time was fleeting and we con-

tented ourselves with three days. Mr. Miller went off into the wilderness with Colonel Taylor on horseback for a little talk with the Ifugaos, a more than half-wild tribe who still indulged that time-honored sport, head-hunting. The principal village of the Igorots, Bontoc, was near at hand, where we looked 'em over and witnessed some very original dancing. It just happened we spent a Saturday at Baguio and visited the dog-market. The Igorots are very fond of dog meat which they reserve for their Sunday dinners and other ceremonial functions. The less meat the animal carries around with him, the higher the price. This gives rise to a rather inhuman custom on the part of the purveyors of that market commodity: that of starving a dog almost to death before putting him on sale. The dogs are sold on the hoof, so to speak, and led back home by the buyer. It was not a particularly edifying experience, but then — we weren't looking for any among the Igorots. It must be said these wild folk are a fine lot of physical specimens — muscular and lithe, with splendidly proportioned figures. Clad only in a gee-string or diminutive breech-clout, they carried all their worldly possessions in a small cup-like basket which they skewered to their back-hair. This left them foot-loose and also free to use their spears at a moment's notice. An excellent school for Igorot children is conducted at Baguio. Camp John Hay is a permanent army institution (or was at that time). Many bungalow sites were purchased by Manila folk which, together with the transfer of the whole civil government force during the summer months, made a delightful colony. Harrison changed all that, however; he permitted only the more important officers to move up there, with a corresponding diminution in the health and efficiency of the service on the part of those compelled to remain in Manila. This was supposed to be an economical move.

Fifty miles south of Manila, in the Province of Batangas, there is a remarkable lake, Taal by name, eighteen miles long by twelve wide. The visitor would never dream that it occupies the crater of a tremendous volcano — one of the largest in the world. Still less would he imagine that the very ordinary-looking island in the center of the lake, barely a thousand feet high, was the active crater which had been pushed up from below, through the waters of the lake, in some early period of time. Twice in the history of the Province, Taal has had an eruption that wiped out the town: in 1754 and again in 1912. The loss of life during the latter was owing more to a tidal wave created by the eruption, which drowned over three thousand people living on the lake shore, than to the explosion itself. Very few travelers are told of this extraordinary spot and I was keen for a visit.

Accompanied by our popular conductor, Colonel Taylor, I spent the night at the house of a friend of his not far from the Constabulary Headquarters. Following the usual custom, we carried our canvas cots up on the roof and lay down in our pajamas, which were enough and to spare in the way of clothing. There was a glorious full moon, so wonderful, in fact, that we lay there and talked until almost daylight. Following an early breakfast we embarked in a boat manned by a couple of muscular Filipino Constabulary boys and rowed out to the island. There was every evidence of Taal having blown his blooming head off in that last eruption. That crater was half a mile in width at certain places and about a thousand feet deep. There was plenty of steam rising from a sizable lake down below and it was about as much of a volcanic exhibition as I cared for, having walked all of a mile and a half from the water's edge to the top of the cone, on a warm morning. There aren't such a profusion of volcanic craters within craters

and situated in the centers of large lakes in this little old
world of ours to render a visit to one of them a commonplace affair, and we both felt well repaid for the effort. 'Tis
a worth-while trip.

There is a Latin proverb, '*Festina lente*,' which, being
subject to a latter-day interpretation, might be translated
thus: 'Hasten slowly. He who travels too fast passes more
than he overtakes.' My visit to Lake Taal delayed our departure from the Philippines by three days and caused us to
take a Japanese freight steamer for Hongkong which did
not get away until late afternoon, with the result that we
saw a sunset over Mount Mariveles — the like of which I
have never seen before nor since. It was so unearthly in its
beauty as to lift us all completely out of ourselves. There
are not many experiences in this common, workaday life of
ours that bring us much nearer Infinity than a glorious
sunset. This one seemed to be a divine blending of Saint
John's vision on Patmos Isle and that of the man about
whom Saint Paul wrote as having been 'caught up into
paradise and heard unspeakable words which it is not law-
ful for a man to utter.' One does not watch with Buddhistic
composure the whole western horizon, almost to the very
zenith, burst into a volcanic explosion of color so vivid that
it can almost be heard. To behold Mount Mariveles'
lofty peak silhouetted for a few moments against the fiery
face of that molten planet descending like a glowing drop-
curtain, consumed in its own flames, was like being in-
ducted into one of Nature's mysteries. There were no
horizontal cloud strata, nor any variety of colors. It was
one vast, upward-shooting of flames, like unto a colossal
fan, the upper fringes of which tinted the billowy clouds
overhead and ringed their edges with gold. Had I seen the
words, 'Be still — and know that I am God,' emblazoned

across the sky I could not have been more deeply conscious
of the presence of the Unseen. I remember coming to myself in tears and unashamed. I remember feeling that most
of us find our souls with a club, that we are become so en-
meshed by material things that God has simply been compelled by our very indifference to leave us to ourselves. It
was a soul-journey we took across Manila Bay that wondrous evening. I expect never to duplicate it. The fact
that the vision returns at this late day speaks for itself.
And yet — I would rather lift the veil of a day to come than
look again upon the face of any day that is gone. There's a
Mount Mariveles sunset somewhere in your neighborhood
if you only know it. It's up to you to find it. If you fail to
locate it within, don't expect to find it in the Orient. That's
my sermon, brother.

CHAPTER XIII
IN THE STRAITS AT SINGAPORE

I want to go back to Singapore
      And up along the Straits,
To the bungalow that waits me by the tide;
Where the Tamil and Malay tell their lore
      At evening — and the fates
Have set no soothless canker at life's core.

I want to go back and mend my heart
      Beneath the tropic moon,
While the tamarind tree is whispering thoughts of sleep —
I want to believe that Earth again
      With Heaven is in tune —
I want to go back to Penang!   I want to go back!
                              CALE YOUNG RICE

WITH a three days' sail before you from Hongkong to Singapore, you'll appreciate the company of Joseph Conrad. Some of his stories will prove a fine introduction to the Straits Settlements and their romantic and sinister waterways. I might also suggest 'The Further Side of Silence,' a highly dramatic series of Malay stories written by Sir Hugh Clifford. By the time you reach the Straits, having 'done' Japan, China, and the Philippines, you'll need no arguments in favor of an Anglo-Saxon foothold in the Far East. You'll be glad that England is sitting pretty in Hongkong and in Singapore and you'll say to yourself something like this: 'What a pity that our Washington statesmen cannot see what it has meant to humanity for the white man to establish himself in these far corners of the earth. If they were wise, they would never listen to the cheap insincerities of those Filipino *caciqués* masquerading as patriots for the sole purpose of acquiring

for themselves the results of the white man's far-sighted-
ness, unflagging industry, and pride of performance. These
are the characteristics and qualifications which are so utterly lacking that they have neither the ability to keep the
machine running after it has been perfected and placed in
their hands nor the common, ordinary horse-sense to be
guided by the men who built it.'

In Singapore we have a brilliant example of the capacity
of one man: Sir Thomas Stamford Raffles, who, as the
representative of the British East India Company, established Great Britain's foothold there in 1819 by making a
deal with the Sultan of Johore, thus putting England on
the map for all time in the Straits and blocking Holland's
game for monopolizing the Indian Ocean and the Malayan
Archipelago. And after it was all over and he went back to
England, the Crown officials (probably composed of the
same kind of men we have in Washington to-day), in ca-
hoots with the British East India Company (in which most
of them were interested), made life so unbearable for him
that his health gave way and he died at the untimely age
of forty-five. Then they forced his widow to refund
$100,000 which Raffles had legitimately spent of the Com-
pany's money in putting over his plans. It never was con-
tended that he appropriated any of it to his own use.
Every dollar was accounted for. His was the unpardonable
sin of *doing the thing* for the good of his country and the
Company he represented only to have his estate mulcted
after he was dead. And then — Old England, running true
to form, gives him a tablet in Westminster and erects a
statue to his memory in the plaza at Singapore, sixty years
later, going on record on that occasion that 'In Raffles,
England had one of her greatest sons.' Just a bit late to be
of any comfort to the man who had really spent his life in
her service. You'll doubtless stop at the Raffles Hotel in

Singapore, or the del' Europe — they're both good. When you travel around, just remember that one hundred years ago Singapore was a mangrove swamp and harbored thousands of the most blood-thirsty pirates that the Seven Seas have ever known. To-day the city has a population of over four hundred thousand, with less than five thousand Europeans — the balance consisting of Chinese, Malays, and Hindus, all getting along very nicely together, thank you. And as long as Old England stays there on the job, midway between India and China, at the most important overnight station on the route to the Far East, and the United States maintains its foothold in the Philippines, the white man will get a square deal, and Japan won't get over-and-above gay. Believe me — that one thing is worth keeping in mind. No one knows how much money Great Britain has spent in fortifying that twenty-seven-mile-long sand-bank. But — it's quite enough to assure her supremacy from either side. And since the late World War, she's improving things a bit, much to Japan's disgust. Strange how much depends upon whose particular ox is gored.

The Raffles Museum in Singapore merits all the time you can give to it. Some of the finest-mounted trophies of the wild animal life in the Straits Settlements may be seen there, together with an unusually fine ethnological exhibit. Also, the Botanical Gardens. The most interesting place of all, however, is the Cavanagh Bridge over the Singapore River, with its motley multitude of Chinese junks, sampans, and every variety of river craft imaginable. Here is where the native life may be seen at its best and a leisurely stroll along the docks will repay the time. Good roads prevail and motor-cars plentiful as in any city in the United States. The Connaught and The Gap drives are beautiful and cool, passing along the sea-front and through some fine plantations with splendidly developed suburban estates and wealthy homes. Have your guide take you to one or two of the night-life restaurants in the Chinese quarter — they're worth seeing. Don't attempt to go anywhere alone after dark — it's an unnecessary risk and a very real one. There's one bit of a souvenir you might like to pick up in Singapore — the silver tical or bean-shaped coin current in Siam. It's money value is about sixty cents. Local jewelers have them in gold and silver. They make novel cuff-links or waistcoat buttons. Don't be deluded into crossing the strait for a visit to the palace of the Sultan of Johore. It's a tawdry affair, unworthy the time or the expense. Then again — you may have the Sultan all decked out in your mind as an Oriental potentate with an exotic harem, etc., when as a matter of fact he is thoroughly European in his amusements and spends the greater part of the year in London and Paris. You'll want to take a little ride in a *ticca gharry* or native horse-drawn taxi with an interior arrangement very much like a home-bred milk-wagon. Also, you'll find the native bullock-carts worth a passing glance with their great high wheels and undersized white bullocks with funny humps — the kind your mother used to take you to see at the circus where they were labeled 'The Zebu — India.' They're rather a remarkable and exceedingly valuable animal in that they are immune to rinderpest which carries off cattle by the thousands every year throughout the Orient.

I picked up the finest souvenir of the whole trip in Singapore. It consisted of a copy of Hilaire Belloc's 'The Four Men' which I found in the house of a friend. 'Twas my introduction to that wondrous craftsman with the King's English and was almost worth the price of the trip. What — you haven't read Belloc? Go and wash in the pool of Siloam.

Singapore being but an 'overnight' stop, as I've already

GREAT SHWE DAGON PAGODA — RANGOON, BURMAH

hinted, you'll probably catch the first steamer north for Rangoon, Burmah. Two or three hours at Penang next day will give you time to take a ride through the town, look in on a Mohammedan mosque, kodak the native children who get along without clothes and sport a silver disk about the size of a silver dollar, suspended around the waist by a little chain as a concession to the English population. You'll be quite ready to move on. It's a four days' run from Singapore to the mouth of the Rangoon River and then twenty miles up to Burmah's capital. If you are planning to go on to Mandalay, there is a waterway at Rangoon which connects the Rangoon River at high tide with the Irrawaddy which is navigable for nine hundred miles.

Much depends upon the direction in which you are traveling as to what you do in certain cities and countries. It is inevitable that a traveler who goes a pace at the outset will let down on the other end. If you approach Burmah from India, you will probably want to go up to Mandalay — an eighteen hours' trip by rail and between two and three days by steamer. If you're traveling in the opposite direction, it's exceedingly improbable that you'll go beyond Rangoon. The commercial importance of this city may be gathered from the fact that it exports close on to $100,-000,000 worth of rice annually. There are four things of importance to be seen. First of all is the Shwe Dagon Pagoda, the finest, the oldest, and the most venerated of all holy places in Indo-China. It derives its great sanctity from the fact that it is the only pagoda known that is credited with containing actual relics of Gautama Buddha: eight hairs, as well as equally credible relics of the three Buddhas who preceded him in this world.

There is nothing in the world to compare with this matchless pile. It is supposed to have been built six hundred years before Christ and stands on a terrace nine hundred feet long by six hundred and eighty-five feet wide and one hundred and sixty-six feet high. In itself it is three hundred and seventy feet high by thirteen hundred and fifty feet in circumference and is gold-plated from top to bottom. And when I say gold — I mean pure gold. It's actual value is absolutely incomputable. This gold-plating has been going on for centuries — once every generation. And there isn't a devout pilgrim in all Indo-China so poor but that he will bring his contribution to this work. You can imagine what it must look like glittering in the sun. During the native insurrection against England in 1885, the only way the British managed to maintain order was by keeping a cannon trained on the Shwe Dagon and threatening to blow it to pieces if they made any more trouble. At the pinnacle there is what is known as a *ti*, an umbrella-shaped series of iron rings from which are suspended hundreds of gold and silver bells most exquisitely jeweled, which was put up by popular subscription and is said to have cost close to half a million of dollars. These bells ring at every little breeze. The music is supposed to accomplish the same purpose of an ordinary temple bell which the worshiper pulls in order that the god or gods may be apprised of his presence and he acquire merit accordingly. Particularly is this the case all through India where the people worship the *nats* or spirits of the air whose propitiation is supposed to bring good luck. The main entrance to the pagoda is up a long and exceedingly filthy stairway of one hundred and sixty-six feet, broken into four sections or landings, and frequented by beggars of all sorts and descriptions, many afflicted with loathsome diseases. Booths for the sale of gold-leaf for use by the faithful and other little mementoes clutter the sides of the stairs. The gold-leaf is affixed to the outside of some particular shrine on the pedestal, as an offering. There are hundreds of these shrines, many of which have a Buddhist priest in charge for the purpose of expounding Buddhistic doctrine to the faithful who sit around him on the platform in rapt attention. Many are most beautifully carved and contain within a marble figure of the Buddha. They have been mostly erected by persons of wealth in an effort to acquire merit. Heavily timbered teakwood roofing covers the stairway, carved and painted with scenes from the life of the Buddha.

A certain situation has arisen in recent years, indicative of the strained feeling between the Burmese and the British Government. The Buddhistic authorities who control the Shwe Dagon have made a rule that no one shall ascend the stairs without removing both shoes and stockings. This being universal in its application eliminates any individual criticism, although it is known to be directed at the English, with a view to demonstrating to the natives the sovereignty of religious authority over the British Government and to embarrass the English residents and all European visitors. There really is no danger from any disease, although much talk is given to that subject. The principal discomfort lies in the fact that the sun-scorched platform is so hot that one's feet can hardly bear it. Some travelers have been clever enough to plaster the soles of their feet with surgeon's tape. Among those who have recently visited Rangoon without ascending to the Shwe Dagon platform are the Prince of Wales and the Prince of Siam. That the rule is purely political in character is shown by the fact that the Shwe Dagon is the only Buddhist temple in all Asia where it is in effect. Willy-nilly, I certainly should not permit it to keep me from a visit to that wonderful shrine. The game is surely worth the candle in this case.

'Elephints a-pilin' teak' is another point of real interest. They will be found busy enough in a local lumber yard in the suburbs of the city. It's a real stunt to see one of those great beasts find the point of balance in a teakwood log about the size and length of a telegraph pole, get his tusks under it, his trunk over it, carry it a couple of hundred feet and drop it on a pile of logs. That picture in your camera will repay you for the time you give to it.

Rangoon is one place where the bazaars should be visited, whether you wish to make any purchases or not. You will see the Burmese women sitting on the ground in all directions, surrounded by the various lines of native products they have for sale, and each smoking her 'whacking white cheroot' with a *savoir-faire* that is quite fetching. She's a better-looking person than her husband who piles his long hair in coils on top of his head just as you would expect her to do. Some of these market folk are reputed to be very wealthy. With a suspicious regard for fluctuating values of money and market products the average Burman invests practically all his money in rubies as fast as he accumulates it — that and jade being the two precious stones that Burmah produces. You'll find the Municipal Bazaars on the Strand Road, not far from your hotel and at Kemmendine, also the Suratee Bazaar on China Street. All three are worth while. In the Strand Road Bazaar silks and lacquerwork are on sale. The native shops in the city will better be avoided. Incidentally, if you are anxious for a camera shot at any of those latter-day 'Supiyawlats' in the bazaar, be sure to tip in advance. Being merely native Burmese apparently has not militated against these charming ladies accumulating a choice line of American profanity, in the use of which they are not at all backward. If your tip isn't sufficiently generous, you'll know it. And don't overlook the fact that your own countrymen created this situation. We are well known for this kind of foolishness all over the world. There's nothing particularly complimen-

'ELEPHINTS A-PILIN' TEAK '— RANGOON

INDULGING IN THE 'WHACKIN' WHITE CHEROOT,'
IN THE RANGOON BAZAAR

tary in being thought to have more money than brains —
but that's the American's reputation with many of the
natives and with the waiters in all lands. Think it over.

One more little matter you might keep in mind in Rangoon: ask at the hotel if there is a *Pwé* being given any
evening of your stay. This is the national amusement, so
common, in fact, that if you neglect to speak of it, no one
will think to tell you. It consists of acting, singing, dancing, and clowning. Take it all in all, it's an elaborate system of posturing, generally carried on by professional actors (?) who are paid by some wealthy person, the stage
being set in the open air and admission free. The 'curtain
rises' about 8 P.M. and lasts until morning. You'll bring a
cushion from the hotel and sit down on the ground opposite
the stage; that is, if you can find room. After you have
been there an hour or so and watched a lot of preliminary
stunts that will suggest the good old days of Harry Miner's,
you'll turn to your native guide and ask him when the show
begins and he'll tell you it has been going on for a couple of
hours. Then you'll get up and curse yourself all the way
back to the hotel and your guide will look much aggrieved.
But don't let that disturb you. You have already had lots
of company and will have plenty more.

Rangoon is a city of beautiful drives which should not be
missed under any circumstances. It will bring home to you
in no uncertain way just what the hand of the white man
has meant in making that country habitable. Take a car
out to the Cantonments — along Godwin Road, past the
Parade Ground and Race Course. Any good driver will
give you the proper directions, not only for that, but for
Dalhousie Park and out to Victoria Lake which supplies
the city with water. Not far from Victoria Lake is a fine
old temple and near by an immense reclining figure of the
Buddha which I have never seen mentioned in any guide-

book nor have I met a traveler who has visited it. The figure is a mammoth one, hewn out of the rock and mounted on a pedestal. It is not housed, but lies out in the open country, very easy of access and should be not missed. It is a holy place and very popular with Buddhistic pilgrims.

And now — if you happen to be a lover of Kipling's works, don't fall into the pit that yawns for every American traveler who reaches Rangoon. Don't try and learn the precise geographical location of the 'Old Moulmein Pagoda' nor endeavor to reconcile its eastward look with those points of the compass upon which Kipling impaled himself 'on the road to Mandalay.' Poetic license is a thoroughly respectable habit, old scout, and — if the redoubtable Rudyard elected to make 'the dawn come up like thunder outer China 'crost the bay,' why not let him get away with it? Of course, there's nothing to prevent you from journeying over to Moulmein and looking the ground over yourself. It's not very far off and you might enjoy having one 'on' Kipling, except that it's already been 'on' him so many years that he's got quite used to it. Also — if I have not tired you — may I suggest that we are on our way to Benares. There be those who have been so wondrously entranced with 'Kim' (and who could blame them?) that they spent the major part of their stay in that holy city trying to locate the 'Temple of the Tirthankers.' That's a right laudable pursuit, but you'll have a better chance of finding the Monkey Temple, which is infinitely more entertaining, because it exists somewhere else than in Mr. Kipling's imagination. Incidentally 'Mandalay' and 'Kim' are great testimonials to the hold that versatile artist has on his readers. We are so in the habit of thinking that the writer who draws on his imagination goes far afield, that we credit Kipling with writing fact instead of fiction simply

because he picks his 'high spots' from near by. More than
one traveler who has visited Moulmein has taken the time
when he got home to write the editor of his particular daily
paper that there wasn't any such thing as 'China 'crost the
bay' from Moulmein and that the dawn couldn't come up
from the direction of China, anyway, because it lay to the
north. Verily, truth is mighty, the realization of which has
given Mr. Kipling many a good laugh.

'Tis a full three days' run from Rangoon to Calcutta.
The trip through the Bay of Bengal is cool and delightful.
We lay in midstream off Rangoon from 10 A.M. for the
flood-tide at 2.30 before we got away. That's a way they
have on those British India steamers — they take no
chances of a late passenger delaying their start. One interesting feature of the trip is the opportunity for seeing the
constellation of the Southern Cross. If you're sufficiently
keen on the matter to stay up until 2 A.M., it's there. Take
a good look at the Hooghly River on your way up to Calcutta. There's only one hundred and twenty miles of it,
and it looks much like our own Mississippi, especially in the
matter of color. We reached the pier at four o'clock and
found our native servant waiting for us.

Entering India, the traveler must prepare for a deal of
railway travel the comfort of which will depend largely on
the amount of care he exercises at the start. In the first
place, a native servant is absolutely indispensable, and if
you secure a good one, he's a joy. Don't accept any man,
however, on your own judgment. Put it up to Thomas
Cook & Son. Inasmuch as you will doubtless have your
mail forwarded in the care of 'Cook's' wherever you go,
you will find that concern a great help at all times. They
are as universal throughout the Orient as a post-office, and
generally a mighty sight more reliable. They like to be

used in the best sense of the term, and there is scarcely a move you can make but will involve their service from the buying of a souvenir postal card to the cashing of a check. In the securing of railway transportation and hotel accommodations you cannot get along without them. Throughout Europe and the British Isles the American Express run them a good second. But in the Orient — 'Cook's.' No matter what city your train pulls into, you'll find a Cook man in uniform on the platform and you'll be surprised to see how often you'll call on him.

Your native servant will speak good English and doubtless will be a Mohammedan. This avoids any possible difficulties on account of caste. Also, he doubtless will inform you that, having but one God to worship as compared with the five or six thousand which the Hindu is obliged to keep in mind, he can render you better service. And it sounds reasonable. A good man will cost you about fifty dollars per month, including his food and railway fare, wherever you may go. He will be of more comfort to you and the whole party — women and children — than you can imagine, and will save you ten times his cost in pestiferous details and minor annoyances that would come near spoiling your trip. You'll find him just as necessary at your hotel as on the road. Furthermore, you must have your own bedding, especially for railway travel, and in some places for hotel and dak bungalow use as well. A dak bungalow is a Government rest-house where they have one attendant and beds minus bedding. Here it's a case of first come, first served and you cannot keep your room over twenty-four hours if there is anybody else needing one — and he has to give it up in his turn. In southern India the dak bungalow and the railway station hotel is the limit of your accommodations and you won't be sorry you have your own bedding with you. In all dry-goods shops throughout India you can purchase what is known as a *razai*, or cotton-wadded quilt, of any thickness. You will want two of these, to which you will add a pillow and a couple of calico sheets. You'll give the whole outfit to the guide when you are through, anyway, so you don't have to go to any great expense. But don't forget your waterproof cover for your bedding. Coolies are a bit careless and sometimes it rains in India. The best trains carry diners, but you can get good meals at the station dining-rooms. Hotels catering for tourist traffic take good care of their guests. It's only on the railway and in out-of-the-way places that you'll need your bedding. Lots of times your *razai* comes in very handy for day use. The upholstery of an Indian railway train has its limitations. In many ticket offices meal tickets are sold with the transportation, and you're supposed to notify the guard to wire ahead for restaurant reservations. Oh, there are lots of things that will be sprung on you in the nature of surprises, but none of them will be at all onerous. In fact, if you'll just enter into the spirit of the adventure, you'll have the time of your life, and you won't miss the industrious African who belabors you over the back with a whisk-broom just as your train is pulling into Grand Central Station when you haven't time to tell him what an utterly useless piece of furniture he is.

CHAPTER XIV

INDIA — ANCIENT OF DAYS

What matter all the creeds that come and go —
  The many gods of men?
My blood outcasts them from its joyous flow,
  And it is now as then:
The Pearl of Morning and the Sapphire Sea,
  The Diamond of Noon,
The Ruby of the Sunset — these shall be
  My creed, my Deity.
And I will take some old, forgotten tune
  And rhythm frolic-free,
And sing in little words thy wondrous boon,
  O Sunlight and O Sea.

JOHN RUNCIE

IN commencing this chapter on India, I would like to venture a prophecy. After you have spent a day wandering around Calcutta, taken a look-in at the slums, smelt the native quarter, gazed with open-eyed horror at the frightful physical wrecks and malformations that are dragged around the city as 'holy men' — you'll say it's a mighty good thing for India that she has a white man's government. And you won't envy England her job. Here we have a duplicate of the Philippine situation: an aggregation of practically helpless people who cannot possibly govern themselves and yet are unwilling that anybody else should govern them. The great difference between the two lies in the fact that it's thirty times worse in India, with her excess of 300,000,000 population as compared with the 11,000,000 in the Philippines. Whatever your preconceived opinions be, therefore, you'll reach the conclusion regardless of Britain's faults, that India is far better off with her than without her.

You will probably see all you want of Calcutta in two days or even less. Calcutta is not India by any manner of means. It's a big, widely spread-out city with a population of over 1,200,000 which has been aptly described by Kipling in his story 'The City of Dreadful Night.' By reason of that inborn love of sensation characteristic of the human race, Calcutta probably figures in more people's minds on account of the 'Black Hole' than anything else. And, as might be expected, it's the least important spot in the city. In fact, that's all it is — a spot, marked by a tablet, at the northern end the present post-office. The incident was not a nice one because it reflected on both the British and the Hindus and was more the result of stupidity than anything else. As a result of a quarrel between the British Governor Drake and Surajah Dowlah, a dissipated and arrogant Bengal prince, the latter marched on Calcutta with an army in June, 1756. Governor Drake abandoned the city without notice, being joined by the garrison commander with his troops, who deserted two hundred and fifty Europeans, including women and children. Of this number one hundred and forty-six were forced into the soldiers' lock-up in the fort for safe-keeping overnight. This room was twenty-two by fourteen feet in size with but two small barred windows. It was a hot June night, and when morning came only twenty-three remained alive. That's the 'Black Hole.' Though thoroughly characteristic of Hindu duplicity and cruelty, the centuries have woven a morbid sort of interest about the place and invested it with an importance it does not deserve. All that remains of it is a tablet.

After you have driven up the Chowringhee Road — Calcutta's principal boulevard — once or twice, taken a look at Government House from the car, given the modern Jain Temple a casual glance, visited the Zoölogical Gar-

dens, which are tremendously interesting, driven out to the
Botanical Gardens for a look at the big banyan tree, one
thousand feet in circumference, called at the post-office
and listened to a babu or native clerk display his pig-
headed ignorance for your especial benefit, there will be
one thing left for you to do which is worth the time: a visit
to the Imperial Museum — the point being that India's
past is a mighty sight more interesting than her present.

On the outskirts of the city it is quite possible you may
come across a holy man making a pilgrimage from some
distant point and acquiring merit by measuring his
length along the road in performance of a vow. He probably will have worn his nose off from burying his face in
the sand at every 'step,' said step being the length of his
body. Then you may also find another gentleman rolling
over and over in the road with the same object in view.
They all have attendants who do their begging for them,
by which they — the attendants — also acquire merit.

The most entertaining one of these traveling gentry that
I saw was a fellow who had managed to coax one leg up the
side of his body in such a fashion that he bent his knee
across the back of his neck, the foot hanging over the opposite shoulder. Not being able to walk on account of this
deep affliction, he was dragged about the town on a low
wagon with small wheels so as to facilitate his getting on
and off. I have often wondered since why he didn't have
the other leg similarly treated. Another joyous brother
had held his fist doubled up so long that his finger nails had
grown through the back of his hand. Still another had
looked at the sun so steadily that he had grown blind and
the muscles of his neck had become fixed with his face up-
turned. And just as if that wasn't holy enough, he had
held one arm in a vertical position so long that it had also
become permanently fixed. These scenes are not necessa-

rily confined to Calcutta, although it's a great town for alms-giving; hence the presence of these holy men who are treated with marked respect by all natives.

And now for a trip up to Darjiling and a look-off at Kinchen-janga and the Himalayan Range. Also, if you're keen enough to rise at 4 A.M. and drive out to Tiger Hill — a little run of six miles — you may have a glimpse of the tip end of Everest at sunrise. Don't minimize the importance of this trip. Don't say you care little or nothing for mountain scenery or you'll compel me to say that you have never seen any that will compare in the slightest degree with what awaits your wondering eyes in that spot. So — let us leave the major part of our baggage at either the Grand or the Continental Hotel (preferably the former) here in Calcutta, and take the sleeper for Siliguri. This is the junction point with the narrow-gauge railroad that takes you for an eight hours' climb over seven thousand feet up the foothills of the Himalayas, covering a distance of fifty miles, to a little town which you will learn to love in the brief one or two days you may remain there. I recall that I made a halting sort of an attempt at a description of a sunset over Mount Marivéles in the Philippines. There was some little excuse for that — it was within the limits of human effort. To essay a similar thing on Kinchen-janga's lofty height of twenty-eight thousand feet, with the valleys below in darkness, would simply be to court an anti-climax. That's something to see for yourself and to remember to your dying day. Darjiling is probably the only place in the world within your reach where such an unearthly glory may be seen, and it would be an unpardonable lapse for you to miss it. We reach Siliguri at five in the morning, tumble out for *chota hazri* (little breakfast of coffee and rolls) at the station, and then into the open cars of this most wonderful narrow-gauge line in the world. At Kurseong station, thirty miles farther on, we stop for a regular breakfast at the dak bungalow beside the track. The road turns and twists so constantly on its upward climb that there's not a moment of the time but some new and marvelous beauty unfolds itself. Sliding along the edge of precipices, running through both natural and blasted ravines, lofty trees and impenetrable jungle closing in on the road here and there, until at last you reach the summit and the magnificent peaks of the Himalayan Range break upon your enraptured view. You will scarcely credit the statement that they are forty-five miles away. Their immensity seems to fill the whole face of nature. And in between are diminutive ranges of twelve and thirteen thousand feet elevation that are dwarfed to little hills by the towering peaks above. In all this gorgeous world there is no mountain scenery that will even approximate the majesty of the view from the heights of Darjiling. Of course, you won't forget to bring plenty of warm clothing, also goggles for the railway ride — you'll need both. The most interesting spot in the town itself is the bazaar which is thronged on Sundays by picturesque natives from all sections: Tibetans, Nepalese, Bhutians, Lepchas, Paharis, and Limbus. It will be a field day for your camera. Gorgeously attired Tibetan women with long, black hair loaded down with a variety of native jewelry, peddle their wares on the streets and you'll never know when to stop buying. Remember — with all that's before you between Calcutta and Tuticorin at the very southern tip of the Indian peninsula, you won't duplicate the trip to Darjiling, the memory of which will remain after other places have faded. We shall spend but one night at the Woodlands Hotel, from which the views are exceptionally fine. You'll be glad to come in and hug the fire at nightfall and your servant will build a fire in your room before you arise in the morning. The train leaves at 2 P.M.,

making the descent by gravity, reaching Siliguri in time
for dinner and catching the night train back to Calcutta.
Incidentally, you'll enjoy the twenty-minute ferry ride
across the Ganges the next morning.

After one more day in Calcutta we are ready to start on
our eighteen-hundred-mile trip across India to Bombay,
to which we gave five weeks. A night's ride brings us to
Benares, on the river Ganges, India's great religious capital — from time without end the Holy City of the Hindus.
It is the great northern headquarters of the worship of Siva,
the Destroyer, one of the Hindu Trinity, and the most ancient exemplar of phallic veneration known to mankind.
Benares has not less than a million pilgrims annually, most
of whom bring along some kind of receptacle for the purpose
of carrying back home some water from the Ganges. It is
simply impossible for the European mind to conceive any
idea of the holiness of Benares and the Ganges to the Buddhistic pilgrim. It actually constitutes his gateway to heaven,
his release from the Wheel of life. All who die within its
sanctified precincts find their way direct to Nirvana and are
no more subject to reincarnation. For that reason you will
see amongst the pilgrims many very old and decrepit ones
who are scarcely able to move, who come there with the
fond hope that they may die within the limits of the sacred
city. And occasionally may be seen some stricken person
of wealth traveling in luxury (though on a stretcher) who
will be removed from the train by his attendants, with the
hope that he either may be cured of his malady or enjoy the
blessed privilege of dying there. In addition to bathing at
the five holy places along the river, known as *ghats* or land-
ing-piers, and worshiping at certain prescribed shrines, each
pilgrim is obliged to make the circuit of the Panch Kosi, a
forty-five-mile pilgrimage which includes all the holy places
within the city and takes six days to complete. As the long

train rolls slowly over the great Dufferin Bridge, you get a bird's-eye view of the river below which describes a wide crescent at that point. As far as the eye can reach, vari-colored temples, shrines, burning-ghats, and palaces line the shore. And in the water may be seen thousands of be-lievers drinking of the holy stream, lifting it up by the handfuls and pouring it over their heads, others standing waist-deep, utterly unconscious of all about them, wrapped in prayer. Within arm's length may be floating the remains of a more or less incomplete incineration of a dead body — but that means nothing beyond the fact that, being in the river, it is purified.

Not a train pulls into Benares any time of the day or night, from one end of the year to the other, but carries its quota of pilgrims. To see them surge out in families, from aged grandparents to children in arms, with their brass vessels and various trappings, including a vast array of turbans representing every color of the rainbow, is an un-forgettable sight. Not one of them, however, will either eat or rest until he has attained purification. Down they go to the ghats, over great flagstones leading to the river which have been worn smooth by the bare feet of countless millions through the centuries, past huge umbrellas under which hereditary priests hold forth, past phallic emblems, large and small, countless image houses and kiosks, to the bamboo platform from which they step into the water. And the look of ecstasy that comes over their faces leaves no room for doubt as to the sincerity of their belief.

The purification over the pilgrim turns to the priest who paints his caste mark on his forehead, the while he bows his head while the *mantra*, or charm peculiar to his sect, is pro-nounced. Then follows the purchase of flowers and fruit for the shrines and rice to throw into the begging-bowls of the holy men whom he will pass at every other step. With

BURNING GHATS ON THE BANKS OF THE GANGES
AT BENARES
Note in the left foreground the purification of the dead
by immersion before burning

his brass *lotah* filled with Ganges water, he is ready for the duties of the day. These generally begin with a mouthful of stagnant water from Siva's Well, which he drinks from the hand of the priest (a typhoid-breeder which has since been discontinued by Government order); he strings a few flowers around the neck of Ganesh, the elephant-headed, four-armed god of good luck; kneels to the ground and reverently kisses the footstep of Vishnu where he alighted from the heavens; joins an ecstatic throng in the Golden Temple; buys a diminutive portion of gingelly oil with which he anoints a huge stone reproduction of Nandi, Siva's kneeling bull; wanders into the shrine of Bhaironath under the tamarind tree, guarded by his grotesque dog in a niche, where the priest taps him with the peacock fan, thereby putting him on good terms with the god — for a small consideration. And so the day goes, spent in venerating an aggregation of obscenities which at one time were supposed to be susceptible to certain esoteric interpretations, about which neither he nor the priest knows any more than the man in the moon.

All this time, our devout pilgrim has been in charge of a *panda* — one of the most villainous scoundrels imaginable, scores of whom meet every train and impose themselves upon the unsuspecting devotee as duly certified and divinely approved priests who will put him on the most direct road to paradise. They herd the poor wretches in droves, knowing that they could not wring enough money out of anything less to make it pay. And when their pilgrimage is over, the panda has every *anna*, yea — every last *pice*— and the pilgrims generally walk back home.

To the traveler, the most interesting feature of a visit to Benares is the burning-ghats along the river. The best time to see them is in the morning. A river-boat which will accommodate from five to ten passengers may be hired for a small figure, in which you cruise up and down for a couple of hours and witness these strange ceremonies. Briefly — the swathed corpse, slung between two bamboo poles, is brought to the river by a couple of carriers and first of all immersed as a matter of purification. Then the relatives bargain with the dealers for enough wood to consume the body — and sometimes the haggling may be heard across the river. If they have enough money, they may buy a quantity of *ghee* or clarified butter which, liberally distributed over the funeral pyre, hastens the cremation. None but the lowest-caste folk attend to this work. The building of a pyre which will dispose of the remains expeditiously and uniformly, in the center of which the body is placed, is the first move. Next, a pouring on of *ghee*. Then the nearest of kin, generally a son or daughter, starts the flame with a lighted torch which is applied at the four corners.

It is all over in an hour or so, during which the relatives sit around on their hunkers and watch the operation to see to it that the attendants do not scant their work. The fire is supposed to release the spirit of the dead person which presumably inhabits the skull. Sometimes the head of the corpse is the last thing to yield to the flames, in which event the attendants assist the spirit's escape to heaven by bashing it in with a club. This seems to be accepted by the relatives as part of the ceremonies and occasions no comment. Then the ashes are swept off into the river and preparations made for the next comer. Sometimes there is a touch of pathos about these proceedings, as, for instance, one that I saw was attended by a young girl, all alone. She was led down the steps into the water for purification, a white cloth put around her shoulders and over her head as a mark of mourning, while the corpse was being prepared. Then she applied the torch and waited patiently until it was all over.

There are within the limits of the city some two thousand temples in addition to countless shrines. Scarcely a rajah in all India who is not represented by a temple of more or less magnificence. Along the river-bank there are some remarkably beautiful specimens of architecture which are well worth close examination. One in particular, known as the Scindia Ghat, which was commenced by the widowed Maharanee of Gwalior. It was either built too close to the river or the foundations were poor, with the result that the temple collapsed. All that may be seen now is a very beautifully carved turret above the water-level. Of course, such a strange happening had to be accounted for in some miraculous fashion, whence we have the following story which, of course, is accepted at its face value by all believers:

The masons at work on the foundation were alleged to have been troubled by a small underground stream which they overcame and the building proceeded. Later the difficulties reasserted themselves, and, while tracing the stream to its source, they came upon a cavern occupied by an aged hermit who began to question them about matters that had occurred two thousand years previously. When he found that Benares had passed under the government of a different race than his, he sprang into the Ganges and disappeared, following which the temple collapsed. The anti-English touch here is quite apparent.

The Mosque of Aurungzeb is the only Mohammedan temple on the river-bank. It is typically Mughal in its architecture, over three hundred years old and solid as a rock. A fine view, both up and down the river, may be had from the tops of the two minarets which rise one hundred and fifty feet above the ground, in which are winding stairways, well worth climbing. While up there, you will be surprised to note the numerous monkeys running about over the roofs of the houses. They are under the protection of

Hanuman, the Monkey God, one of the favorite Hindu deities.

One could spend a week in Benares and then not see half of its points of interest. It takes but a brief time to get fed-up on that sort of stuff, and you'll find yourself figuring the time-table. Don't leave, however, until you have visited the Golden Temple, the holiest place of all, where the bells ring all day and the pilgrims frequently have to crowd some vagrant bull out of the way in order to squeeze their passage through the narrow streets. On occasion the bull himself finds his way into the temple, following the trail of flowers which every devotee takes with him. The priest is the only one who dare lay hands on him because he's a very holy bull. He is led out into the street with great consideration accompanied by the most sincere apologies for thus disturbing his peregrinations amongst the shrines where his well-known powers are so deeply revered. The Durga Temple is another spot that you will wish to visit. It is the one temple in the city dedicated to Kali, the bloody goddess, in whose worship a goat is sacrificed daily. If you like to see such things, this is your chance. The temple itself, of red sandstone, is beautifully carved and located in an out-of-the-way spot where there is room for a little perspective. That's more than the narrow, dirty, and crowded lanes which pass for streets in the city proper will give you. Durga Temple is a great resort for the monkeys which frequent it in large numbers; hence it is known more familiarly as the 'Monkey' Temple than Durga's. Adjoining is the celebrated garden of the famous ascetic Bhaskaranand — by all means visit it. The easy way to do the temple district is to leave your boat at one of the lower ghats and have it meet you an hour later up the river. Then you can walk leisurely along the bank and see much that you would otherwise miss. There are those very interesting small *Sati*

monuments to the memory of certain well-born Hindu
widows who, in accordance with that barbarous custom of
earlier years, voluntarily sacrificed themselves upon the
pyres of their dead husbands. It may be said that there are
thousands of native women in India to-day who would do
the same thing were it not for the restraining hand of the
British Government. Then there is that ever-present eyesore, the *lingam-yoni* of Siva and Parvati, the significance
of which not one traveler in a hundred appreciates. It is
much in evidence at the Kedar Ghat, where barren women
come at dusk and indulge in certain rites that are beyond
description. 'Tis an utter travesty on words to classify
the rank and file of native Indians as Buddhists. Even
the Brahman priests have long since forgotten their presumably spiritual origin in Brahma, the chief figure in the
Indian Trinity, and, like their blind and sodden following,
have degenerated into phallic worshipers with all the in-
herent loathsomeness that accompanies the ritual in all
temples dedicated to Siva, the Reproducer. Strictly in line
with the Siva cult are the vile carvings on the Nepalese
Temple from which women are barred. Just why the authorities take it for granted that the animal man has a *flair*
for such things is a trifle beyond me. I've found him quite
a decent citizen.

You will wish to drive to Sarnath, the ancient site of
Benares, where Gautama Buddha started his teaching in
the sixth century B.C. 'Tis only four miles from Clark's
Hotel, where you will probably be staying, and you'll see
enough of antiquity, including Asoka's Pillar, to justify the
ride. That little experience will give you an idea of the age
of Buddhism. Ancient records show that there were three
Buddhas who preceded Gautama, who was born in 588 B.C.

Don't be led into buying anything more than souvenirs
in Benares. They are supposed to make a specialty of

brass-work, but it's poor. Wait until you reach Jeypore where the finest examples of brass enamel-work may be purchased at reasonable prices.

The morning train out of Benares lands you in Lucknow in the afternoon. If you have been reading up on the Great Mutiny of 1857, you will know what a hallowed spot this is and will be to the end of time to every man who speaks the English tongue. Even under the inspiration of Tennyson's and Lowell's heroic poems, with all the appreciation of the godlike bravery and indomitable will shown by the English during that hellish three months' siege, it is a vastly different thing to visit Lucknow than to read about it. For years I had been familiar with that oft-reproduced photograph of the riddled Residency with the British flag flying from the summit of the ruins. But — it seemed a very wonderful thing just to stand there and look at it and try to visualize what those devoted British men and women endured in that acid test. You'll want to explore every nook and cranny of that consecrated pile with your guide-book in your hand and a prayer of thanksgiving in your heart that there are enough English-speaking people on this old earth of ours properly to take care of its future if we have sufficient horse-sense to hang together. And I reckon we have. You'll put up at Wutzler's Hotel for one night or two at the outside. There's an interesting drive about the town and its suburbs. Don't overlook the great Imambarah and its mosque.

Leaving Lucknow in the morning, there will be time for a stop-over at Cawnpore. Visit the beautiful Gothic memorial of the Cawnpore massacre, erected over the well into which Nana Sahib threw one hundred and twenty-five men, women, and children, some of whom were alive, during that same bloody mutiny. Then read what Havelock's soldiers did to the mutineers on their arrival two hours later — and be glad you're a white man. You'll have time to drive over to the Sati Chaura Ghat on the Ganges where four hundred and fifty survivors — men, women, and children — embarked in boats, on the promise of Nana Sahib of a safe passage down the river to Allahabad — only to be shot down by soldiers waiting on both sides of the river as the boats floated on their way. It does a man good to read this kind of matter. He generally thinks more of his kind and less of himself by the time he's through. There is a good restaurant at the Cawnpore station where you may get a bite of lunch and rest awhile in the long, reclining chairs in the waiting-room — almost as comfortable as a bed.

On arrival at Agra to-night, we will put up either at Laurie's, the Metropole, or the Cecil. Here we are going to settle down for a few days and absorb the inexpressible beauty of one of the world's great wonders: the Taj Mahal. Thinking you may care to do a little reading, I will suggest the best novel of the Indian Mutiny ever written: 'On the Face of the Waters,' by Flora Annie Steel; Kipling's 'Kim' and 'Naulahka'; E. M. Forster's 'Passage to India,' and almost anything of Maud Diver's that you may get your hands on. It's surprising how a bit of fiction dealing with the country through which one is passing enhances the value of the trip and trebles personal interest.

CHAPTER XV

TAJ MAHAL — THE INCOMPARABLE

> And not in vain, from age to age,
>   In forms of grandeur and of grace,
> Is writ on more than History's page
>   The progress of the human race —
> The rise of mind and feeling, shown
> In golden poems made of stone.
>
> WILLIAM WINTER

TAJ MAHAL — the one tomb in all the world that suggests life, not death. Love incarnate, transmuted into marble. The religion of beauty, than which there is nothing more illusive or that exerts a more mystic and irresistible control. The one building against which you could almost lay your cheek and expect a corresponding thrill. Exquisitely feminine and chaste beyond words, arrayed in precious stones and samite and waiting for the bridegroom. I can imagine Shah Jehan, the crafty and sanguinary Emperor who was in love with beauty as well as with a woman, impatiently watching the slow development of this matchless jewel on the banks of the Jumna, at Agra, with a fierce resentment of the twenty-two years it took to complete it. And, too, I can imagine the swift death that would overtake the foolish craftsman who made haste at the expense of perfection. I can see him standing before the Grand Assize and hearing the words: 'His sins are forgiven, for he loved much.' This unquestioned mighty Mughal ruler of India for thirty-one years who founded the city of Delhi, India's present capital; conceived and occupied the famous 'Peacock Throne' in the Imperial Palace, reputed to have cost $35,000,000, also the magnificent mosque Jamma Masjid; whose reign

TAJ MAHAL — THE MOST BEAUTIFUL BUILDING IN THE WORLD —
AGRA

ushered in the golden age of Indian architecture — this is the man who poured out his soul in the creation of a dream of marble, the most beautiful thing of its kind in the world, recording for all time the undying love of a man for the woman of his choice.

Her name was Arjmand Banu, familiarly known as Mumtaz-i-Mahal, the 'Light of the Palace.' She died in childbirth in 1632. That same year the building of the Taj commenced. It is most beautifully situated in an immense Oriental garden across the river from the ancient palace in the great Red Fort where she dwelt in her youthful womanliness. Her sightly apartment, the Jasmine Tower, overlooking the river, is one of the chief charms of a visit to that historical spot.

The approach to the monument is through a superb gateway of red sandstone, inlaid with ornaments and inscriptions from the Koran, in white marble. A magnificent view of the Taj itself may be had from the top of the gate, which is reached by a ramp through the pillar on the left. You will need an attendant with a torch for this brief experience, not only to light the way up through Stygian darkness, but to keep off the bats as well. The glorious outlook from the top, however, will amply justify any temporary inconvenience in reaching it. The spaciousness of the garden below, nine hundred feet long by four hundred and fifty feet wide, filled with trees and flowering plants, with the river Jumna as a background, creates a setting of ravishing beauty for this incomparable jewel. It rests on a marble platform, twenty feet high and three hundred feet square.

The building itself is one hundred and eighty-six feet square, and the gold-tipped dome towers two hundred feet over all. In the interior is an octagonal chamber, each side measuring twenty-four feet, richly ornamented with

repoussé and that inlaid work so characteristic of the period.
Immediately under the dome lie the tombs of the Emperor
and his wife, surrounded by double grilles in marble of such
exquisite and varied pattern as to suggest the texture of a
cobweb. This for the purpose of tempering the light ad-
mitted from the entrances on all four sides — otherwise, the
glare of the sun would be intolerable. The tombs are covered with lace-like carvings of flowers, inlaid with semi-
precious stones: lapis-lazuli, malachite, agate, and carnelian. As if all this glory were insufficient to express the
feeling of this royal lover, he had made a canopy of pearls
which was spread over her casket on Friday nights (the
Mohammedan Sunday) and on the anniversary of their
wedding. This wondrous pall, worth a king's ransom, was
carried away along with the silver doors, which were originally a part of the memorial, during the Hindu raids which
followed the weak reign of Shah Jehan's son, Aurungzeb.
As is usual in Mughal sepulchers, the tombs within the
screens do not contain the actual remains which rest in a
vault immediately beneath, level with the surface of the
ground.

As you stand entranced by the overwhelming loveliness
of this chaste casket, you won't question that it cost over
ten millions of dollars and took twenty-two years to complete. The first time I saw it gleaming in the dazzling sunshine of an Indian morning, it resembled a jewel-encrusted
pearl that might have floated out of the sky and come to a
rest at that spot. So baffling was the sensation that I found
myself approaching it softly and speaking in a low tone
lest some unexpected thing might cause it to rise and float
away. So wonderful are its proportions and its symmetry
that it seemed instinct with life. I could not visualize it as
a tomb, nor can I now. There is no mortuary suggestion
unless it be the idea of resurrection, in that there should be
no extinction for such supernal loveliness.

Those inspiring lines from Whitman came singing through my brain:

> In this broad earth of ours,
> Amid the measureless grossness and the slag,
> Enclosed and safe within its central heart,
> Nestles the seed perfection.

Yea — here it was in far India. 'Twas no violation of old Walt's spirit to pin his exalted outburst to this miracle in marble. Neither did it occasion any surprise when I heard the legend that Shah Jehan had blinded Ustad Isa, the architect, after the completion of the monument, lest he be tempted to try to surpass himself.

Without doubt you will do as I did: you'll go back there again and again. You'll want to see it in every possible light. You'll take the little *batteau* near by and cross over for the purpose of getting a water-reflection view from the riverside. In the days that follow, you'll find yourself making provision for 'just one more look,' possibly by moonlight, when it is ethereal beyond words. I saw it for the last time just as the sun was setting — the long shadows creeping over the landscape like a veil of silver gray. Absolute silence reigned. Not even the subdued note of the bird as she finds her place for the night in some friendly tree. Then — with the outlines of the cypresses which border the tesselated pavement merging into the fast approaching dusk — for the first time it was suggestive of a tomb. But its message was Peace. Unearthly in its serenity, overwhelming in its impressiveness, the purple of evening mantling the horizon, stilling one's spirit into silence — it seemed there was never on sea or land anything so poignantly beautiful and so tragic. Of all the literature which this wondrous shrine has inspired, I know of nothing to equal the exquisite tenderness of that short story by L. Adams Beck, 'The Building of the Taj Mahal,' published in his well-known book, 'The Ninth Vibration,' from which I am glad to quote:

Now it is told that, on a certain night in summer, when the moon is full, a man who lingers by the straight water, where the cypresses stand over their own image, may see a strange marvel — may see the Palace of the Taj dissolve like a pearl, and so rise in a mist into the moonlight. And in its place, on her dais of white marble, he shall see the Lady Arjmand, Mumtaz-i-Mahal, the Chosen of the Palace, stand there in the white perfection of beauty, smiling as one who hath attained unto the Peace. For she is its soul. And kneeling before the dais, he shall see Ustad Isa, who made this body of her beauty. And his face is hidden in his hands.

When you visit the tremendous Red Fort, built by Akbar the Great, with its forty-foot walls, its circumference of a mile and a half, and its sightly outlook over the river, you will appreciate the tragedy of Shah Jehan's last years. Just as he had wrested the throne from his father Jahangir, even so his son Aurungzeb did with him. In 1658, four years after the completion of the Taj, he was deposed and imprisoned in a room formerly used by the ladies of the palace as a mosque. It has a glorious outlook over the river. For eight years thereafter all that remained for him was a daily vision of the beautiful casket he had watched for twenty-two years as it neared completion. It would appear to have been all-sufficient, because tradition has it that the Taj was the last thing his eyes rested upon before they were closed in death.

The points of interest at the Fort are too numerous for a detailed description. They are the Pearl Mosque, constructed throughout of the purest marble, white, blue-and-gray-veined, the floor of which is divided into arabesque-like sections, each just large enough for one person at prayer; the magnificent Hall of Audience; the Mina Masjid or tiny private mosque for the Emperor's use — the smallest in existence; the Hall of Private Audience, a miracle of exquisite carving; the Saman Burj, or retiring-room of the Emperor, overlooking the river, with its flooring of black-and-white marble made to represent a Parchisi Board, the game being played with beautiful girls as draughts, who moved in accordance with the fall of the dice; the Mirror Palace and the Jahangir Mahal with its famous Hindu carvings in red sandstone.

Outside of the Fort, the most important object is the tomb of I'timad ud Daulah, who was the grandfather of the Lady of the Taj. He was a sort of wandering Persian who came to Agra during the reign of Shah Jehan's father, with whom he established himself as the Royal Treasurer. He proved to be an able citizen by marrying off one of his daughters to his royal master. Like unto the ancient Egyptians, it was the custom of these royal Mughals and their dignitaries to build their own sepulchers in advance. The greater their means, the more elaborate the tomb, which was used as a place of entertainment prior to the death of the owner. This tomb of I'timad ud Daulah stands near the end of the pontoon bridge across the Jumna, surrounded on all four sides by exquisitely grilled walls of varying designs which admit the sunlight. The effect is extremely fine. It is said that each of these thousand and one, highly ornamented orifices in these grilled panels consumed thirty days to complete. One can well believe it. The floor is done in mosaic, showing graceful vines and flowers in a great variety of colors. In point of workmanship it stands next to the Taj Mahal.

In the vicinity of Agra there are two important points which should not be overlooked: the deserted city of Fatehpur-Sikri, twenty-three miles to the southwest, and the tomb of Akbar the Great at Sikandra, five miles distant, which you will pass on the road. It's a fine ride over a well-ballasted motor highway. How the renowned Akbar came to build this city and establish his capital there and then to desert it is an interesting story. It was formerly the site of an ancient village called Sikri, where a wandering Mussulman saint, Salim Chishti by name, took up his abode in a cave. He proved to be a man of great sanctity and — as will be noted — miraculous powers as well. Returning from a campaign, Akbar halted at Sikri to request the prayers of the saint on behalf of a son and an heir — he being at that time childless. The saint advised that he send his Hindu wife, Mariam Zamani, to reside at Sikri, which he did. A year later a son was born at Sikri, who afterwards became Shah Jahangir. In appreciation of the divine favor shown, Akbar built Fatehpur-Sikri and made it his capital for a number of years. Political conditions, however, caused him to resume his headquarters at Agra toward the end of his reign. With the departure of the Emperor, the splendid city was abandoned and became a resort of wild beasts and dangerous characters. In recent years, however, the British Government has restored it and keeps it in repair.

Fatehpur-Sikri is six miles in circumference and enclosed on three sides by high walls, each of which has three gates. The fourth side was formerly protected by an immense artificial lake which was drained many years ago. The finest feature of this ancient city is the great Gate of Victory in the southern wall, the largest and most imposing in all India if not in the world. It rises one hundred and thirty-five feet above the pavement and opens upon a vast flight of steps, making a total height from the outside of one hundred and sixty feet. The doors of this noble gateway are today studded with horseshoes, nailed there by the owners of sick horses who come to pray to the saint for their recovery. *Sic transit gloria!*

An odd-looking column known as the Hiran Minar stands just outside of the walls on the margin of what was formerly the lake. It is Akbar's old hunting-tower and bristles with stone reproductions of elephant tusks. From a protected cupola he used to shoot game as it was driven into range.

In the courtyard of the mosque, which is said to be a copy of the one at Mecca, will be found the tomb of the saint Salim Chishti — a fine specimen of Mughal carving in white marble with a gorgeous mother-of-pearl canopy over the cenotaph. Near by is the tomb of an infant said to be that of the saint's son whose life was sacrificed at the age of six months in order that Akbar's son (Jahangir) might live when born.

There is one spot in this deserted palace which throws a significant light on that divinity which is believed to hedge a king, but which does not always work. Every palace has two principal Halls, the first of Public and the second of Private Audience. In the former, the Emperors sat cross-legged on their thrones, surrounded by their nobles, and passed judgment on the various cases that were presented. In the Hall of Private Audience, however, there was always a chance for the unexpected happening, namely: assassination. The manner in which the wily Akbar circumvented any such possibility is interesting in the extreme and in itself would justify a visit to this deserted palace. At the first glance from the outside, this Private Hall would appear to have two stories. On entering, however, but a single apartment is found, in the middle of which rises a massive octagonal column of red sandstone, surmounted by an immense circular capital covered with elaborate carvings. The space at the top consists of a platform enclosed by the characteristic stone screens of that period. From this well-protected cubicle, four covered bridges extend to the windowed gallery which encircles the whole room. Within this isolated spot — completely out of harm's way — Akbar took his seat and listened to the lone petitioner, who was on the floor below. Incidentally, if said lone petitioner 'started anything,' even from that disadvantageous point, Akbar had his choice of four different runways to the protected gallery, through the outer windows of which he could give an alarm. In other words, he was taking no chances.

Unusual interest attaches to the tomb of Akbar at Sikandra because of the liberality of his religious belief. There are no more implacable bigots in the world than the followers of Mohammed. The wise Akbar, however, with an empire divided between Mohammedans and Hindus, did more to amalgamate the violently opposed religionists of both sides than any other Emperor. That there was more than mere administrative policy in his action is indicated in the location of his tomb, which faces the east instead of the west, or toward Mecca, in accordance with Mohammedan custom. The entrance to the garden enclosure is guarded by a magnificent gateway, from each corner of which rises a marble minaret two stories high. At the top of the gateway is an arched chamber where, in past centuries, drums were beat at sunrise and sunset in honor of the dead. This massive gateway is of red sandstone, profusely inlaid with Hindu writings upon white marble: further evidence of his leanings toward Buddhism.

The mausoleum itself consists of four stories, three of which are in red sandstone — the fourth, enclosing the cenotaph, being of white marble, surrounded by an exquisite cloister of grilled panels in squares of two feet — every square being of different design. In the center, mounted upon a marble platform, lies the magnificent cenotaph of the Emperor himself, at the head of which are boldly in-

scribed the words 'Allahu Akbar,' and, at the foot, 'Jalla
Jalalahu,' which being interpreted mean: 'God is Greatest,' and 'Magnificent is His Glory.' On the sides are engraved the ninety-nine glorious names of the Deity. A few
feet from the head of the tomb stands a richly ornamented,
white marble pillar, four feet high, with a recess in the top
which once contained the famous Kohinoor Diamond. In
the raids that followed the reign of Aurungzeb, Akbar's
tomb was looted along with the silver doors and pearl man-
tle of the Taj Mahal at Agra, including the jewel-studded
'Peacock Throne' at Delhi. A magnificent view of the
country roundabout is to be had from the roof of the
mausoleum, which is very easy of access. If you are pressed
for time, you can 'do' this tomb in fifteen minutes, and it
will be amply worth your while.

You doubtless will come across several snake-charmers
in Agra. They are a most interesting lot, each with his flat
basket containing a full-grown cobra which spreads his
hood and raises his head a foot or so from the basket as his
owner plays the queer gourd-like instrument, the droning
music of which they seem very fond. It's mighty good
camera material, and for a rupee each you can have as
many of them squatting around as your camera will accommodate. Also, there is the old man who carries with
him a cobra and a mongoose, between which he stages a
fight. He pegs the little mongoose out on a stout cord
about three feet long, gives Mr. Cobra the freedom of the
city — and let's them go to it. Mr. Mongoose, being just a
fraction of a second quicker than the snake, always beats
him out. And if it weren't for the fact that he had his
teeth drawn, he would kill him. With the exception of a
fatality once in a great while — just often enough to prove
the rule — these cobras are harmless. That is to say, they

have had their fangs removed. These fangs have a habit of growing again, however, and it occasionally happens that they reach maturity before the charmer appreciates it. Then the unexpected happens and there's one less snake-charmer in India. Without question, also, you will run across the juggler who will make a mango tree grow from a seed planted in the earth right in front of your very eyes — yes, sir. And before he's through, he'll have that blooming tree up as high as your knee. If he'd only quit the use of the big bandanna under which this fast-growing shrub is nursed along, it would be a trifle more entertaining. No — I didn't see the fellow who sends a kid climbing up out of sight on a rope which he throws in the air. You have probably heard the rest: how he gets tired of waiting for him to return, goes up after him with a long knife — and the next thing we know the ground is covered with the dismembered remains of the poor kid. It is said to be a case of mass-hypnotism. I've read about it many times, but I've never met any one who has seen the trick performed. These Indian jugglers are clever, indeed, and it might be a good plan for you to look one up. I've often wished I had done it. These are the little incidents we like to talk about when we get home. And you can't blame us.

DELHI

To undertake a detailed description of the ancient city of Delhi would simply be to set down a record of fire, murder, and sudden death, dating from certain historically established incidents as far back as the twelfth century and so far beyond as to be shrouded in impenetrable mystery. You may draw your own conclusions from the following chronicle: Sacked by Timur the Mughal in 1398; by Nadir Shah the Persian in 1739; by Ahmad Shah Durani the Afghan in 1756; captured by the Hindu chieftain Scindia in

1789; beseiged by Rao Holkar in 1804; and again at the outbreak of the Great Mutiny in 1857.

To the south lies an appalling area of ruin, covering
forty-five square miles, which includes the remains of no
less than seven different, fortified cities, with all of which
the ancient Delhi was identified at various periods preceding the twelfth century. This frightful district bears a close
resemblance to some of the battle-fields of France at the
close of the World War. As far as the eye can reach is a
dreadful holocaust of crumbling walls, scattered forts,
great gullies deep in dust and mud which once were streets.
It looks as though it might be the remains of a destroyed
world. There are two roads that run through this 'Valley
of Hinnom,' leading past breached walls, staggering pillars,
and half-filled, gaping vaults, which once were forts and
palaces. It is a salutary experience to drive through this
fearsome territory, if for no other reason than to realize the
exceeding thinness of humanity's veneer. In the course of
a few years the battle-fields of France will be covered with
farms, lush fields, and trees. Not so this spot. Beyond a
few stunted bushes here and there to show the direction of
the road, there isn't a plant nor a blade of grass to be seen,
and — so far as anybody knows — never has been.

Ten miles south stands the famous Tower of Victory,
Kutab Minar, in the midst of the ruins of an earlier Delhi.
It is one of the architectural wonders of India and said to
be the most perfect tower in the world. The Kutab was
built in the year 1200, and it stands to-day as bright and
fresh in its appearance as though it were finished within the
previous few weeks, instead of seven centuries ago. This
tower is two hundred and thirty-eight feet high and consists of five stories of alternating red sandstone and white
marble. A richly ornamented projecting balcony extends
around each story. The diameter at the base is forty-seven

feet and at the top, nine feet. A winding stairway of three hundred and eighty steps leads to the summit. A splendid view, however, may be had from the balcony of any one of the five stories. Near by are the remains of an elaborate mosque, built during the same period, within which stands one of the most curious antiquities of India — the Pillar of Rajah Dhava. It is a solid shaft of wrought iron, twenty-four feet high by sixteen inches in diameter. Wonderful to state, though having been exposed to the elements for seventeen hundred years, there is not a particle of rust on its surface. A thoroughly legible inscription in Sanskrit relates that 'The Pillar is the arm of Rajah Dhava, who obtained with his own arm an undivided sovereignty of the earth for a long period.'

Not far from the mosque is the imposing mausoleum of Adham Khan, which stands on a slight eminence. The manner of his death is more interesting than his tomb. And the fact that the narrative still persists, after all these centuries, is conclusive proof that 'the evil that men do lives after them.' Adham Khan, a typical Mughal general, was half-brother to the great Akbar. Jealous of Azam Khan, the great soldier and favorite of Akbar, he slew him in the Royal Palace at Agra. Assuming that his close relationship with the Emperor would ensure his pardon, he hastened to the royal apartment to tell the news and to sue for mercy. Akbar knocked him senseless with a mighty blow, and then caused his body to be twice flung from the high terrace of the palace to the court below, after which the remains of both slayer and slain were sent to Delhi for burial.

Outside the northwest corner of the mosque is the tomb of Altamsh — the oldest in India — dating from A.D. 1326. It is of the usual red sandstone, ornately etched and unlike any other tomb in India in that it is open at the top. Tradition has it that Altamsh was such a great lover of the outdoors that he wanted 'no roof but the sky.'

Returning to Delhi, the road leads by a hidden jewel, which would scarcely be discovered unless your attention was specifically drawn to it. It is the tomb of Nizam-ud-Din — the greatest of all the Chishti saints, who passed to his reward over two hundred and fifty years ago. You come upon the dusty track leading off from the roadside about three miles out from Delhi. To all appearances it loses itself in the desert waste through which you have been driving. Followed for a short distance, however, over crumbling stones and débris, it ends abruptly before a weather-beaten wall which looks as if it might have been left standing from the destruction of past centuries. Entering a narrow gateway one is ushered into a veritable grotto, in the center of which is a crystalline pool, fed by an unfailing spring — an absolute transition from the destructive area without. Beside the pool runs a well-worn pathway piercing an inner wall which opens into a quiet court of snow-white marble, in the center of which is the shrine of the holy saint, enclosed within a veranda of white pillars. Beautiful trees of great age overshadow the spot. Absolute quiet reigns. 'No rude alarms of raging foes.' No hint of the outer world. And the blue sky over all. Entering the tomb, you find a profusion of beautiful flowers filling the air with their exquisite perfume. And this has been going on for two hundred and fifty years — maintained by the descendants of this holy man, who live in the ruins near by. It is the most amazing tribute that I encountered on my long trip. Truly — 'the memory of the just is blessed.'

Within the enclosure are several other tombs, as well as a quiet mosque which has its occasional worshiper. In one lie the remains of the Princess Jahanara, the daughter of the Lady of the Taj, who followed her father into captivity and remained with him until he died. Hers is an eloquent epitaph:

> Save the green herb, place naught above my head —
> Such pall alone befits the lowly dead.

In another is the tomb of Khusrau, the Persian poet who died in 1324. His songs are still sung by the people of his country and his monument is still tended with the same loving care as that of the holy saint.

The architecture of the modern city of Delhi, which was founded by Shah Jehan, is largely a repetition of the great Red Fort and the Palace at Agra, lacking the same degree of perfection. Its most attractive feature — the finest thing in the palace, in fact — is the magnificent Hall of Private Audience which will bear close inspection. It was in this Hall that the 'Peacock Throne' stood, which was raped by Nadir Shah in 1739, broken up, and carried off to Persia. The throne derived its name from having the figures of two peacocks standing behind it, with expanded tails inlaid with sapphires, diamonds, rubies, pearls, emeralds, and other precious stones in colors appropriate to the design. In the center was a life-size parrot cut from a single emerald. The throne was in the shape of a bed, six feet by four in size, supported by four solid gold feet twenty-five inches high. From the structure rose twelve columns which supported a magnificent canopy, the bars of which were decorated with crosses set in precious stones. In all there were over two hundred and fifty large rubies and emeralds, with pearls. 'Tis said to have cost thirty millions of dollars. No wonder Nadir Shah carried it off!

This hall has been restored by the British Government, and, with the exception of the semi-precious stones in which the walls and pillars were originally inlaid, stands

'FRIDAY MOSQUE,' OR SABBATH SERVICES IN THE JAMMA

MASJID — DELHI

just as it did in Shah Jehan's time. His was the most sumptuous court of his day and without an equal in history. In those good old times there was a stream of water flowing beneath the floor to cool the atmosphere when the Emperor was holding court. You may still see the open conduits passing under an arch into the ladies' apartments, which are screened off by a wonderful bit of open grille-work in marble, in the center of which is a small window. A pair of scales is carved in marble above the window. Just what their significance is does not appear. They can have nothing to do with the dispensing of justice because all that commodity emanated from the Peacock Throne.

The principal hotels in Delhi are Maiden's and the Cecil. The business street is the Chandni Chauk. It is about three quarters of a mile long and leads from the Fort to the Lahore Gate. A beautiful row of pipal and neem trees divide the street down the center, creating a charming effect. Chandni Chauk is the headquarters in all India for gold and silversmith work and the finest of native jewelry. You probably will be surprised to know that in those bare, unpretentious shops, minus any display, may be found some of the most precious gems and exquisite specimens of the jeweler's art. Take plenty of cash with you if you contemplate any worth-while purchases in this famous mart.

Should you happen to be in Delhi on Friday — the Mohammedan Sunday — I would suggest a visit to the Jamma Masjid, or Great Mosque, as an exceedingly worth-while experience. If you will get there about eleven o'clock and cultivate the friendship of the *moulvie*, or priest, he will take you into a little relic-house, where you will see a red hair from the Prophet's beard, a print of his foot in stone, a slipper he wore, and a quotation from the Koran in his own handwriting, etc. If you are duly impressed to the point of crossing his palm with a bit of silver, the priest will place you at a strategic point of observation on the tower over the eastern gateway, facing the pulpit. Then you'l' realize, as never before, the difference between Moslem and Christian worship.

There are no slackers in Mohammedanism. Doctors, lawyers, shopkeepers, and laborers, all leave their work for prayer. Below me on the floor of the mosque, which is three hundred and twenty-five feet square, was a veritable sea of turbans. In all that vast space there was not a vacant spot. As the worshipers entered, each and every one made hasty ablution in the marble tank in the courtyard before taking his place with the congregation. Followed the sermon by the Imam, after which he called the *takbir:* 'Allaho-Akbar, Allaho-Akbar.' As the voice of the preacher rose, the vast audience rose with it as one man, swayed forward, and then every forehead was pressed against the pavement below. Not a head was seen — only a prodigious display of backs and soles of the feet. To attempt any more of a description of this tremendous spectacle would be an anti-climax. There is just one place in the world where it can be seen, and that is in Delhi's Great Mosque. Delhi being India's capital and British territory, the lines between Islam and the Christian 'infidel' are not drawn so tightly as in other Moslem centers. Otherwise no European 'pagan' would ever have the opportunity for witnessing a Mohammedan service.

CHAPTER XVI

IN RAJPUTANA

A band of years has flogged me out — an exile's fate is mine,
To sit with mumbling crones and still a heart that cries with
    youth —
But — oh, to walk in Babylon, in Babylon, in Babylon,
The happy streets in Babylon, where once the dream was truth.

                                          VIOLA TAYLOR

PRECISELY what actuated Jey Singh II, the celebrated Rajput Maharajah and astronomer, to desert the ancient city of Amber and build the gingerbread city of Jeypore back in 1728, will never be known. Amber was founded in the first century of the Christian era and had been a Rajput stronghold since 1037. The town, including the palace, lies on a mountain-side about five miles from Jeypore, at the foot of which is a charming little lake, and dominated by a massive old fort on a hilltop about a thousand feet above the valley. It is a deserted city in the most eloquent sense of the term. This impression is heightened by the fact that the present Maharajah of Jeypore keeps the palace in excellent repair. For a number of years (on request) he has placed an elephant at the disposal of travelers who wish to visit it. The proprietor at either the New Hotel or the Kaiser-i-Hind Hotel will gladly attend to this.

You drive out to the foot of the mountain, preferably early in the morning, where you will be met by the elephant and his keeper and taken up to the palace over a massively paved roadway that has been in use for centuries. The whole mountain-side below the wide verandas is covered with tier on tier of typical native stucco houses lining the usual narrow streets. For the moment there's no evi-

dence of destruction and you wonder at the deathlike stillness of the place. As you take in the scene, you fully expect any moment to see people come out of their houses and
start walking here and there, to hear dogs bark and the
ringing of the temple bells. Putting your binoculars to your
eyes, however, you note that the roofs have fallen in, that
growing trees have split the walls apart, that the windows
are covered with wood-tangle, that the streets which were
so plainly defined to the eye are filled with cactus and the
débris of collapsed houses, and that the only sign of life is
the kites and the crows. It is, indeed, a deserted city that
has been sleeping for two hundred years and will never
waken. Your first impulse is that you would like to go
down and walk through the streets. The 'close-up' that
you get from your glasses, however, changes your mind.
You're quite willing to complete your sight-seeing right
there in the palace. As you return to the plain you notice
that the beautiful little lake is a ruin — you didn't quite
catch it on the way up. It's so wretched it hurts.

Possibly you may arrive at the time of the daily sacrifice
of a goat to the Goddess Kali. A genial lady, this Hindu
deity. Her breast is garnished with human heads. Around
her waist hangs a girdle of human hands. She is always
painted bloody red — and altogether she is anything but
an inviting goddess. It is said that she has never been
truly happy since they changed her daily sacrifice from a
human being to a goat. It's an ill wind that blows nobody
any good, however: the goats for the sacrifices to Kali,
throughout India, are all supplied by the natives, to whom
the carcass is returned, the temple priest retaining a small
piece of meat for himself and the head as an added decora-
tion to Kali's shrine. So, you see, the native gets his butch-
ering done free and Kali's appetite is satisfied. You won't
need any blatant announcement of this latter fact on draw-

ing near to any shrine to Kali throughout the country.

Also — the priest has an ingenious way of disposing of the goat. The animal is tied; an attendant takes him by the hind legs and lifts his rear end off of the ground so that he may not be tempted to run around during the ceremony. Then the holy man takes a long, heavy, two-handed knife resembling a Philippine bolo, and delicately removes the head with one stroke — all of which is supposed to pave the natives' way to heaven. It's an exceedingly interesting ceremony — to those who like it, and suggestive of the ritual of the stock-yards.

The Amber Palace, which was begun in 1600, ranks second to that of Gwalior, the most magnificent in the country. Its distinguishing feature is its Hall of Public Audience with its forty elaborately carved, sandstone pillars — exemplifying the finest craftsmanship in the Empire. Shah Jehangir, learning that he had been surpassed in magnificence by his vassal, Mirza Rajah, at Amber, became bitterly jealous. Accordingly, he sent commissioners with instructions to destroy the offending forty pillars. Mirza Rajah, however, in order to avoid the inevitable, had the columns plastered with stucco. When Jehangir's walking delegates arrived, therefore, they found nothing to justify their master's jealousy and reported to him at Agra accordingly. It is a strange thing that in the intervening years none of those in authority has been sufficiently interested to remove the stucco from these columns and thereby bring to light this superb work. You will note in some spots that the stucco has been scraped off and the sculpture beneath is as perfect as on the day it was carved.

Returning to Jeypore, we find a pale pink city. Laid out in rectangular blocks and divided by cross-streets into six equal portions, the main streets being one hundred and eleven feet wide and paved — it is the only place of its kind in all India. Try and imagine this 'city of magnificent distances' filled with two-story houses built of pink stucco and green blinds, the upper stories lavishly covered with geometrical designs and crude drawings of elephants, peacocks, and rajahs going to war, all canopied by the flawless blue of an Indian sky. That is the prevailing color scheme of Jeypore and harmonizes effectively with the sandy desert by which it is surrounded. It is notable, indeed, that the idea of a city of these proportions should have found expression through a Hindu potentate in 1728. If our national capital had been in existence at that time, one might think that Jey Singh II had evolved Jeypore as the result of a visit. It is an odd experience to walk down the main street and be elbowed off the curb onto the pavement by a sacred bull who has just wandered up on the sidewalk in order to sample the vegetable-man's display. If you could understand Hindustani — the native language — you would hear him say, 'Welcome, brother!' His eyes, however, would give the lie to his speech, notwithstanding which he wouldn't dare remove the greens. And all this by reason of the great sanctity of Mr. Bull.

You will find yourself picking your way amongst the grain merchants with their goods spread all over the sidewalk, and women in the midst grinding — two each — at an ancient hand-mill, thus literally picturing the Scriptural quotation: 'Two women will be grinding at the mill.' You will see women in the middle of the street drying long sections of newly dyed fabric for *saris* — the native dress in which a native woman can swathe herself most gracefully in less time than it takes to tell it. Meantime, a police officer on a camel ambles leisurely through the crowd, while veritable clouds of pigeons settle in the public square where they are fed by the children. In fact I have seen the sky almost blotted out for a moment by the thousands of pigeons that cover Jeypore's streets. They make the plaza of Saint Mark's, Venice, look infantile by comparison. Raising your eyes you will see a huge electric sign of the word 'Welcome' on the crest of a mountain overlooking the city. Just about the time that you are congratulating yourself upon Jeypore's recognition of your importance, your guide will probably tell you that sign was erected in honor of the Prince of Wales's visit several years ago.

I have said that Jey Singh II was an astronomer. He was more — he reformed the calendar. You will doubtless want to visit his observatory. It is an open courtyard, taking up half the space of a city block, filled with curious and fantastic instruments which he designed. Antiquated as they are, they are adequate to the calculating of eclipses. Also, his zodiacal dial enabled him to find the moment of exact noon any day in the year: the first instance on record of a Rajput chieftain being pressed for time. It is well worth a visit.

A permit, which is easily secured, admits you to the grounds of the Maharajah's palace, at the foot of which is a large artificial lake. Laden with a half-dozen chunks of raw meat, your conductor, taking his place on the parapet overlooking the lake, will call loudly, in the native dialect: 'Brother!' Immediately, a half-dozen hungry, twenty-foot crocodiles will slide off the mud flat on the far side of the lake and come to the call. The expertness with which they catch the meat thrown them indicates their familiarity with the term 'brother' and inspires a correspondingly wholesome respect on your part for the relationship. It is almost too real to be comfortable.

One of the most pretentious buildings on the public square is a four-story, garishly ornamented and turreted building erected by the Maharajah, known as the 'Hall of the Winds.' It is well named, because above the first floor the whole structure is nothing but a profusely pierced false front. Just what purpose it serves, no one seems to know further than that it constitutes an added point of interest. Jeypore is the center of some of the finest tiger-hunting in all India. The Maharajah has three magnificent specimens, thoroughly caged, which are worth seeing. Jeypore also boasts one of the finest, most complete and thoroughly catalogued museums in the Empire.

The Chattries or cenotaphs of the Maharajahs are just outside of the city walls. They are in the midst of well-watered, well-planted gardens, the trees of which are full of gray-headed monkeys of solemn visage. It will take only a few moments to drive out there, and, if you limit yourself to the inspection of Jey Singh's monument alone, it will be worth your while. This is a tomb of pure white marble, supported by twenty exquisitely carved pillars, ornamented with scenes from Hindu mythology.

The Jeypore bazaar is a place of lively interest. Here you see a variety of native manufactures going on, especially the brass enamel-work, which is the finest in all India; the cutting and the setting of garnets; rug-weaving and the printing of cloths and muslins. Taken all in all, this is one of the most entertaining cities on the trip across country — a fascinating combination of the old and the new that will justify all the time you can give to it.

UDAIPUR AND CHITOR

When you enter India, let me suggest that you purchase an abridged copy of Tod's 'Annals of Rajasthan.' It is a small book and will contribute greatly to your understanding and appreciation of the ancient State of Rajputana. If it accomplishes nothing more than to induce you to spend a couple of days at Udaipur and Chitor in Mewar Province, it will be worth while. You will find a rest-house ample for all necessities in both places.

A prouder and more haughty race than the Rajputs would be difficult to imagine. When you realize that up to twenty-five years ago the Maharana of the province had succeeded in preventing the building of a railroad to his capital city Udaipur, you can form some idea of their exclusive character. Practically all there is of the city of Udaipur is the Maharana's Palace and its immediate surroundings on the shores of beautiful Pichola Lake — an artificial body of water hemmed in by mountain ranges. Here the Maharana reigns as a benevolent despot, even to the point of having his own particular mint. The Palace is a mammoth pile of white marble and every building in the town is whitewashed. In view of the further fact that practically all the towns in Mewar, and Udaipur in particular, surmount hill-tops, you may gather an impression of their extreme sightliness. Pichola Lake is two and a quarter miles long by one and a quarter wide. It is deep and intensely blue. In the center are two islands, each containing a beautiful marble palace, one of which was built in 1628 and the other in 1734. Covering all the space on the islands, they create the impression of having floated down from the sky and alighted on the water. It is one of the most romantic landscapes imaginable. The passing years have brought about a more tolerant attitude toward visitors so that now one may be conducted through the Palace and rowed out to these dainty *chefs d'œuvres*. They have not been used for years, but they are kept up with the most scrupulous care. Every detail of the marble work of these exquisite fabrics, together with the massive masonry of the Maharana's Palace on the opposite shore, is mirrored in the glassy surface of the bright blue waters of the lake.

Udaipur has no business of its own. It is a tradition in human pride. You don't seem at all surprised to meet a Rajput cavalier with his long, curved sword. The Maharana of Mewar is the only Hindu potentate in all India whose family has never given a daughter in marriage to the Mughals. He is the spiritual as well as the feudal head of his people. And he's a benevolent monarch as well. The Palace includes the various governmental departments, a coöperative store, and a spacious arena for elephant fights. Lying but seventy-nine miles from Ajmere on the main line of the railroad, it is easy of access and one city of a thousand the traveler should not miss.

A short twenty-five miles from Udaipur, on the line of the railway, lies the ancient stronghold of Chitor, the former capital of Mewar, which dates from the first century. The tragic history of this fortress is the epitome of Rajput unyielding pride and warlike chivalry. This terrific ruin surmounts a precipitous rock formation three miles long by one and a half wide. It rises five hundred feet from the plain and is approached by a great causeway which zigzags up the face of the cliff, passing beneath seven tremendous gateways. It was held by the Rajputs for over six hundred years and was supposed to be invulnerable. The last two hundred and twenty-five years of this period, however, was given up to a constant warfare of defense from attacks by the Mughal hordes. Tod's narrative of the three sackings of Chitor over this period reads like a romance from the 'Arabian Nights.' Three times the royal family, princes and princesses, the finest of the race, were annihilated both in action and by that characteristic self-immolation by fire rather than fall into the hands of the invader. In each case, however, a royal male infant was spirited away and concealed in the mountain caves for years until he reached manhood, when the fight was renewed.

During these long periods, the survivors, hidden away in the mountains, deliberately laid waste their own lands

THE MAHARANA'S PALACE ON LAKE PICHOLA, UDAIPUR

so that there might be no subsistence for a foe, meanwhile holding to their oaths that they would sleep on straw and live on what they could forage until the city on the rock was restored. In short, none would accept a survival that involved dishonor. The city was finally wiped out by Akbar in 1568, with an army that covered the plain for ten miles. Facing the inevitable, as before, the women, led by the Queen and her princesses, passed into a subterranean sepulcher of flame and were consumed by the thousands, while the men rushed into the thick of the battle and died on the field. And when Akbar marched into Chitor, he entered a city of the dead. From 1568 down to the present time, it has lain uninhabited and undisturbed — one of the most majestic ruins on the face of the earth. There still stands in the center of the ancient city the great Temple of Vriji with its tremendous tower, undisturbed and virtually unimpaired after nearly five hundred years. Also the celebrated Tower of Victory celebrating former conquests, both of which the British Government keep in repair. It is an opportunity that the traveler should not miss, to go swinging up that ancient causeway on the back of an elephant for a brief visit to one of the most ancient and historical spots in all India. No road in all Christendom has been so saturated with blood. Visitors leaving the train at Chitor will find a dak bungalow a mile from the station where application must be made on the spot for permission to visit the deserted city, for which elephant transportation will be furnished.

I have already spoken of the Rajput pride. There is more than that to be said. In point of etiquette they are the most punctilious of all the Indian people. The tradition of common ancestry with the Maharajah permits the poorest and humblest Rajput to consider himself as well-born as the wealthiest landholder of his clan and vastly superior to any official in the profession classes. They are experts in sword-making and in swordsmanship and form one of the main recruiting fields for the British-Indian army to-day. Their loyalty has never been questioned. In the Great Mutiny of 1857, they stood pat. They consider any occupation outside of the army or Government service as beneath their dignity. No one ever heard of a Rajput, however, no matter how wretchedly poor he might be, accepting a tip of any kind. I well remember a little personal experience with the brakeman on the train that took us down from Ajmere to Udaipur. He did me an unexpected courtesy and I offered him a tip. He declined it with a smile and said he would take a cigarette if I had one to spare. It wouldn't do any harm if we could import a few like this to the United States.

MOUNT ABU

A sojourn at Mount Abu, four hundred and twenty-five miles east of Bombay, will be a welcome change for the traveler who has been reasonably busy since leaving Calcutta. An elevation of five thousand feet, with all the pure mountain air that goes with it, will 'listen fine' after several weeks down on the plains. You leave the train at Abu Road station and make a sixteen-mile climb over a perfectly good road in a *tonga* drawn by two horses. This is a two-wheeled, covered vehicle, with two seats for three persons each, facing front and back. The driver and our hand-baggage occupied the front seat, with my women-folks and myself in the rear. The customary thing is to keep these horses on a constant gallop, changing them for fresh animals four times during the course of the trip. From the standpoint of physical comfort, it isn't half bad, and it constitutes a most interesting change because this will probably be the only spot in all India where you will see such remarkable temples or use this kind of transportation. There is a good dining-room at the railroad station and a good hotel at the summit — the Rajputana. Don't forget to make reservations in advance.

Mount Abu is the home of Jainism. The Jain is a most interesting vegetarian. He will not take the life even of an insect. His religion carries him to the extreme of avoiding the possible swallowing of the animalculæ in the air. If, therefore, you meet some bareheaded men in white flowing garments, with close-cropped hair, wearing a white screen over their mouths tied by a piece of string around back of their ears like an eye-shade, just as if there was an epidemic of influenza, you may know they are Jains. You'll be surprised to learn that the sect originated six hundred years B.C. — just a trifle in advance of the Christian era. One of their ancient kings kept his army in camp all through the rainy season because it was impossible to march without killing the various worms, bugs, and insects that are found on the ground at that season. Oil-mills and potters' wheels are shut off entirely from June until October, lest the moths who flourish at that time of the year be caught in the flames. In various places throughout India, Jains will be found feeding the ants by the roadside. At Ahmedabad and other cities where the sect flourishes, certain houses are set aside for the special benefit of insects, in which these charitable penitents spend certain hours, devoting their own bodies to the feast. They never wash because they might kill a microbe in the water. Wherever the Jain goes, he carries with him a soft mop in order that he may brush all insect life from his path. There is a certain inconsistency in the Jain religion, however, in that history proves him to have been a good fighter and not averse to taking the life of his brother-man. He has been a bit of a problem to the British Government by reason of his exceeding humane attitude to rats, notwithstanding the fact that they carry bubonic germs. In certain cities they have established municipal rat-houses in charge of a Jain caretaker. This was as near as the Government officers got in the way of a compromise with these kind-hearted folk. Bubonic plague or not, they wouldn't allow the rats to be killed in their houses. They would willingly have perished rather than to have injured a single germ. They did allow cages to be set, however, with the understanding that the rats should be housed and fed outside the city.

The two celebrated Dilwarra Jain temples of Mount Abu are marvels of elaborate carvings. They were started in the year 1197 by two brothers and were completed fourteen years later at a cost of six millions of dollars. For delicacy of carving and beauty of detail, they stand unrivaled in all India. These temples are dedicated to Nemnath, the twenty-second Tirthankara, a saintly leader of thought, contemporary with Gautama Buddha. There are twelve niches or cells in each of these temples, all of which are devoted to glass-eyed statues of the same Tirthankara, Nemnath. He has been carved out of white marble and sits there in the usual cross-legged style, looking straight out through what is nothing more or less than a barred door, the reason for which I could not learn. Certainly, there was nothing to steal nor anything that invited tampering of any kind.

These figures, however, are the least of the attraction. The wondrously carved marble on pillars, walls, and ceilings has become soft and cream-colored with age and contains representations of every saintly figure remotely connected with the fanciful system of Jain metaphysics. In view of the fact that there is no such thing as a Jain heaven or hell, one wonders why he should be so particular as to insect life, especially that particular breed to which he submits himself occasionally in an insect 'rest-house.' However, there's no accounting for taste. A few miles farther up the mountain there are two other Jain temples dedicated to Achilgar. The carving in these temples, however, is not equal to that of the Dilwarra nor are they as accessible. A pass is necessary for admission to both temples which may be secured without any difficulty from the hotel manager.

Mount Abu is a lovely place to settle down for two or three days and invite your soul, without reference to any further temple-gazing until you reach Bombay, and not even then. It is also a good place to sort o' take account of stock. You practically say good-bye to northern India here. You won't see any more of the same kind of native, the same kind of temples, nor the same kind of towns. Bombay, like Calcutta, is not India. It's just a big overgrown city, on the western coast at the terminus of the transcontinental railway and, so to speak, is neither Orient nor Occident nor good red herring. Your attention will have been attracted to many things during the past few weeks which will now take their places in your mind as memories. You will recall how many pretty Hindu women you saw adorned with the nose rings, some expensively jeweled and others plain brass, and how it changed the whole appearance of their faces. You will remember the splendid figures and the inimitable grace of the *sudra* women — the lowest caste in the Empire — as they stopped to gather up with one hand the manure just dropped from a bullock in the road, mixing it with a bit of dust before dropping it into the baskets on their heads without removing them. You'll recall the thousands of native shacks you have seen with manure cakes plastered against the walls, drying in the sun, to be sold for fuel. It will be months before you will get the acrid odor of burning manure out of your nose — and, let

me tell you, you'll miss it — because it's India. And a few
months after you have put India behind you, you'll be
wondering just how you are going to get back there for
another visit. You'll think of so many, many things you
didn't have a chance to do, and you want to do them.
That's India. You'll recall the hundreds of irrigating wells
you saw as your train sped through the country. A pair of
bullocks on a tow-rope that seemed endless, before a whop-
ping bullock-hide 'bucket' made its appearance underneath the windlass and the water was poured forth over a
parched field which sopped it up like a sponge. That's
India.

Your mind will be constantly calling up the crowds of
natives, with their sad, expressionless faces, forever coming
and forever going — God only knows where. You'll remember that you never approached a railway station but
that there were a score of them sitting around on their
hunkers on the platform waiting for a train that was not
due for ten hours. Oh, how you'll recall the colors, and
how they transformed the poorest, most poverty-stricken-
looking mother you ever saw as she strode gracefully along
the road with an overgrown child astraddle of one hip!
That's India. And you'll want to go back. You'll remember the myriads of mina birds and how they resembled our
own beloved robin redbreast — and it made you long for
home at the time — but, you want to go back now. And
the shrill piping of the kites all over God's creation and how
you cursed them — yes, and the gray-headed crows and
monkeys too — they made you tired. But now — yes, it's
different, and you wish you had stayed a little longer.
That's India. And oh, those gorgeous blue jays, the like of
which you never saw in your born days. A streak of electric
blue flashing through the air and dropping on the ground
within twenty-five feet of you. No such blue jays as those

in the United States — they fairly made your eyes ache with their blinding brilliancy. Even the damned-fool babu ticket agent, post-office clerk, hotel clerk, and what not, who is still amazed 'that one small head could carry all he knew' will, now that it is all put behind you, 'implore the passing tribute of a sigh.' For, brother, that's India. And to your dying day, you'll never get the ichor out of your veins. So — make the most of your opportunities when in that wondrous country because, just so sure as you curse its heat, its dust, its temples, its frightful ignorance and superstition — you'll want to go back. *You'll want to go back.*

CHAPTER XVII

BOMBAY TO CEYLON'S ISLE

> Oh, for the trail, wherever it may lead,
> From small credulity to larger creed,
> Till we behold this world without detraction
> As God did seven times with satisfaction.
>
> BLISS CARMAN

To the traveler who has seen as much of the real India as the foregoing pages present, Bombay will have comparatively little to offer. It is a big overgrown city of great wealth with a population approximating a million, having a greater diversity of racial types than any city in the world. One thoroughly enjoyable experience is a leisurely walk through the native city, so-called. Here may be seen specimens of every race and nation of the immemorial East: Afghans from the northern frontier; Persians from the Gulf; black, shaggy Beluchis; Arabs from Mucsat; Zanzibar negroes, Malays, Chinese, Jews, Lascars, in addition to the Parsees who, by reason of their great wealth and ability, control the city financially. Special mention might be made of the Arab horse mart in the Bhendi Bazaar, which is worth an early morning visit. Here you may see some of the finest bred horses in the Orient, including the picturesque Arabs who bring them to Bombay for sale. After a drive to Malabar Hill which includes the residential section, there remain but two points worthy of serious consideration: the Parsee Towers of Silence and the Island of Elephanta.

The Parsees, as a people, are more interesting than anything else in Bombay. They are descended from the ancient Persians who emigrated to India in the eighth century.

You'll recognize them on the street, with their long cloaks, olive complexion, aquiline features, black, snappy, penetrating eyes, small black mustaches, and odd-looking, shiny turbans resembling a Derby hat minus a brim, with a retreating crown. They are good-looking, well set-up, and probably the keenest business men in the world, which latter has earned them the colloquial appellation of 'The Jews of the Orient.' Several of them have amassed great fortunes and are widely known for their great charities.

A Parsee must be born on the ground floor of the house, his religious teachings being that only through humility and a clean life can he attain any elevated position either in this world or the next. On the seventh day after birth an astrologer is called in to cast his horoscope. At the age of seven he goes through his first religious ceremony — purification by washing in cow urine, followed by his being invested with the *kusti* or girdle of his faith — a cord of seventy-two threads representing the seventy-two chapters of the Zend-Avesta, in the sanctity of which he is bound and received into the Zoroastrian religion. From that time on he is morally responsible for his own acts. Parsee funeral ceremonies are among the most characteristic feature of Bombay life. Something closely resembling extreme unction is administered to the dying man, after which an appropriate sermon is delivered by the priest. The body is then taken to the ground floor where it was born — washed, perfumed, and laid on an iron bier. A dog is brought in to take a last look at his deceased master in order to drive away the evil spirits. When put on the bier, the remains are completely covered and turned over to professional pall-bearers, clad in white. A procession is formed by the male friends, headed by the priests in full dress, which proceeds to the Towers of Silence, in a beautiful garden covering several acres on the summit of Malabar Hill, the trees of which

swarm with vultures. There are five of these towers, constructed of stone, cylindrical in shape, about two hundred
and seventy-five feet in circumference and twenty-five feet
high. The interior is like unto a gridiron in three circular
sections, separated by walls with footpaths on the top, the
gratings all slanting toward the center in which is a deep
well five feet in diameter. And right here is where the
Parsee's religion comes in. Being practically worshiper of
fire, earth, and water, he does not believe that any of those
elements should be polluted by the disposition of a dead
body and so — he commits his dead to the vultures. Having arrived at the Towers of Silence, the cortège is joined
by two bearded men who carry the remains up a flight of
steps and through a small gateway in the wall upon which,
in the meantime, a flock of vultures have taken their accustomed perch in anticipation of the feast. The bodies
are arranged as follows: men on the outer row of gratings,
women next, and children nearest the center. It takes
about half an hour for the vultures to devour one body.
The bones are left exposed until thoroughly dry, after
which the bearded men, who are the only ones allowed to
enter the enclosure, go in with tongs and cast them into the
well in the center where they crumble into dust. Thus they
literally fulfill one of the tenets of their belief: that both the
rich and the poor must meet in death, which, so far as the
observation of a Philistine like myself goes, is about the
only place they ever do meet on a par. Just at the foot of
the hill on which the Towers of Silence stand, there is a
Parsee almshouse which will accommodate two hundred
inmates. One must at least admire the efficiency of these
remarkable people. There is no lost motion between the
inmates of the 'Parsee Dharmasala' — the reverberating
name by which this institution goes — and the hearty welcome that awaits them on the hill-top after it's all over.

Fed-up with temples as you may be, you must, nevertheless, visit the Caves of Elephanta on Elephanta Island, about six miles from Bombay. It is a pleasant trip in a motor-boat — which Cook's will furnish — and you'll be glad you went. This remarkable spot was discovered about the middle of the eighth century. The term 'cave' is a trifle misleading. It consists of a series of shrines to the Hindu deity Siva that have been hewn out of the solid rock in different rooms, so to speak, of fifteen to seventeen feet in height and one hundred to one hundred and fifty feet square. These shrines are filled with heroic sculptures and carvings of great antiquity, including Siva's usual phallic trade-mark in a separate and enclosed niche. In fact, no one knows how old they are. The workmanship is unusually fine, particularly the supporting pillars of the caves, around which the excavations were made. There are but two cave temples of note in all India: Elephanta and Ellora. The chances of your seeing the latter are a bit slender as you have left them behind. Elephanta being close at hand should not be overlooked. You will doubtless have your guide-book which will give you all the necessary details impossible in a book of this character. It is a mistake to go anywhere without that invaluable help, whether it happens to be by a well-known author or a purely local product. It sometimes happens that the latter are more reliable for the reason that certain guide-books covering the Far East are written by persons who have never been there, who glean their material from a variety of sources generally close at hand. There are two excellent guides published covering India: Murray's Handbook which includes Burmah and Ceylon, and the little brochures published by Major H. A. Newell of the Indian Army, which cost but a few pennies. You can get them both at almost any of Cook's offices or at your hotel, which will probably be either the Great Western, or the Taj Mahal, the latter having a fine outlook on the bay.

There are two different departures from Bombay west, open to the traveler: he may sail direct for the Suez Canal, or via Ceylon. If he elects the latter, he has the choice of going by steamer to Colombo or down through southern India to the very end of the peninsula by rail. We chose the latter, notwithstanding the fact that there is not a real hotel south of Madras. There are, however, thoroughly satisfactory rest-houses and dak bungalows in every city. We got along splendidly and were mighty glad we went. That portion of India from Madras south, known as the Carnatic or lowlands district, is the 'India's coral strand' of the old missionary hymn. It is the southern headquarters of the worship of Siva as Benares is of the north. The same old degenerate orgies resulting from phallic adoration are carried on here to an even greater extent than in the north.

The Dravidian architecture of the temples, and their general plan and scope, are entirely different from those of northern India, just as the Tamil or southern Hindu is an entirely different breed from his northern brother. Also, it may be said that there are exceeding few Mohammedans in the south, whereas in the north it is almost an even break between them and the Buddhists. The temples are commonly built in the middle of a quadrangle equivalent in area to several city blocks, and enclosed by walls from fifteen to twenty-five feet high, which conceal them completely from the public view, as they are never raised above it. Each outer wall has one entrance consisting of an immense pyramidal stone pylon or gateway from one hundred to one hundred and fifty feet in height, known as a *gopuram*, on which are displayed a vast

variety of carved and colored figures depicting alleged
scenes from the lives of gods and goddesses, etc. The low-
lying character of the country and its tendency toward
fever-breeding has had a great deal to do with the scarcity
of Europeans. In fact, there are practically none to be
found except those who are engaged in missionary work.
All these reasons are adequate for the traveler's choice of
this trip. It can be done in a week from Bombay and includes three exceedingly worth-while stop-overs in addition to Madras, where we will break our journey at either
the Connemara Hotel or the Buckingham Hotel, after a
ride approximating six hundred miles.

TRICHINOPOLY

Our first stop after Madras is Trichinopoly, a run of
two hundred and fifty miles. This is a town of considerably
over a million population, in which the famous Lord Clive
made his headquarters during his administration of the
British East India Company in the eighteenth century. It
is famed particularly for its temple to Ganesh, the corpu-
lent, elephant-headed god, on the summit of a huge granite
rock which rises two hundred and sixty feet from the level
of the plain. A flight of steps, vertically striped in red and
white — Siva's colors — are cut into the solid rock leading
to the top through a covered passage. On the way up you
will pass huge stone elephants, primitively carved pillars,
and various reproductions of a long list of deities. In front
of the temple is a huge granite 'Nandi,' or Siva's bull, covered with silver plates. He has a very valuable hide, at
least.

This temple was built in 1660, and is one of the most popular in southern India because of the popularity of Ganesh,
who is the good-luck deity of the Hindus. Important parts
of the sanctuary occupy the south and west sides of the

rock, where are found two caves, in one of which will be found an inscription dating from the beginning of the seventh century; the other containing a record of the ninth. On the plain below is a handsome Teppakulum, or sacred bathing-tank, used on festival days.

Three miles from Trichinopoly, on an island in the Cauvery River, is the famous Vishnu Temple of Sri Rangam — the largest in India and one of the very holiest, as witness the following extract from one of the ancient records: 'Those who visit Sri Rangam, those who remain there even for a few seconds, and those who only see the place, will not alone be saved from Hell, the abode of Yama, God of Death, but will be free from disease and agony at the time of death, and will be preserved from a death untimely.' Rather a large order! However — we don't go a-visiting temples in a carping frame of mind. This famous temple measures 3072 feet by 2521. It was commenced in 1700 A.D and has four huge, unfinished *gopurams* facing to the four points of the compass. It had not been finished, however, in 1753, at which time war broke out between rival native chieftains, in which both the French and the English took a hand, converting the big temple into a fortress for the time being. Whether for lack of funds or because the temple had been defiled by the presence of the soldiers, no one knows, but no further efforts were made after that date to complete it. Tremendous monoliths are used as uprights in the construction, some of them being over forty feet high. Equally huge stones constitute the roof, while the one inside of the arch at the entrance is thirty feet long by eight feet thick. The massive teak door in the second entrance, with its closely set panels of wrought iron, studded with huge nails that are as useful as they are ornamental, is worthy of a 'close-up.'

Beyond the third gateway stands one of the great cars

used in the annual festival in December and January. If
you attended Sunday-School when you were a youngster,
you probably will remember the kind of book they gave you
to read during the week, consisting principally of stories of
missionary life in India. Do you recall some of the harrow-
ing pictures of the car of Juggernaut, under the wheels of
which the crazed devotees of the god threw themselves in
their excess of holy zeal? Well — it's just such a car as this
that you'll find at Sri Rangam and it will bear close examination. The car itself is of teakwood, every square inch of
which has been elaborately and deeply carved in scenes
representing incidents in the lives of the various deities, in
which rearing horses and martial-looking figures predom-
inate.

This ponderous car is trundled about on massive wheels
fully eight feet high, made of hardwood and braced with
wrought-iron plates secured by tremendous knobheaded
spikes. During festival seasons it is dragged out on the
highway by long ropes, drawn by anywhere from five to
seven hundred Hindus who fight amongst themselves for
the privilege of a place on the rope, through which they acquire merit. Meanwhile, those who fail to get a ropehold,
acquire their modicum of merit by throwing flowers in
front of the moving car. It is strongly suggestive of boy-
hood's halcyon days, when our greatest privilege was to
secure a similar position on the long rope by which we
dragged the brand-new fire engine around town on Decora-
tion Day and the Fourth of July.

In an octagonal-shaped, gorgeously decorated pavilion on
top of the car sit the god and goddess, laden down with jew-
els and beautiful flowers. In short, Mr. and Mrs. Vishnu,
of Sri Rangam, when they go visiting, travel in style, with
a display of precious stones and jewelry fabulous in value.
There is a tradition that the famous Orloff Diamond, for so

many years the pride of the Russian Czar, once masquer-
aded as an eye in the great idol at Sri Rangam. It was supposed to have been stolen by a soldier during the French
occupation of the temple. It is an unusual mark of great
favor for the god to pay an especial visit of ten days or so
to some very wealthy actual or prospective patron of the
temple. The canny priests can be trusted to select the
proper citizen for such high preference. In view of the fact
that these annual feasts are kept up for sixty days, there is
ample opportunity for the extension of these special favors
to those who are able to express adequate financial appreciation.

TANJORE

To the intense satisfaction of the traveler, the great Siva
Temple at Tanjore is not considered particularly sacred for
the same reason that applies to the temple at Sri Rangam:
it was converted into an arsenal by the French in 1772.
This means that you can visit the finest specimen of Dravidian architecture in all India without being pestered to
death by priests, temple attendants, and beggars. Not a
booth is to be found within its walls. It is, without question, the best-regulated and most attractive shrine on the
Indian peninsula. Out of a population of sixty thousand in
Tanjore, one third at least are followers of Vishnu, who may
be distinguished from those of Siva by the caste-mark on
the forehead. The Saivites draw three horizontal bars
across the forehead with the sacred ashes of cow dung, with
a small circular spot of red between the eyebrows. The
votaries of Vishnu draw a curiously shaped V in white in
the center of their foreheads, divided by a vertical red
stripe.

As you enter the enclosure, note on the left and right the
two small shrines dedicated to Ganesh and Subrahmanya,

DRAVIDIAN TEMPLE TO SIVA — TANJORE

the two sons of Siva. Ganesh you have already met. He is to be found at the entrance of every Hindu temple throughout India — all religious ceremonies commencing with an invocation to him. Subrahmanya, Siva's second son, carries six faces, five in front and one behind. He invariably rides on a peacock and is worshiped particularly by those who are desirous of subjugating matter to mind. As you walk in, you will encounter on the right, under a gayly painted and whitewashed pavilion, a very ancient, crudely wrought, mammoth statue in granite of Siva's favorite bull 'Nandi.' He is twenty feet long by eight wide, and over twelve feet high. He has been affectionately slathered with gingelly oil by admiring female devotees of the temple for so many years that his color has been changed to a light brown.

As might be imagined, Nandi pulls a strong oar in this phallic worship game and is very highly esteemed. Among the various legends that have sprung up among the faithful is that Nandi was not created. He just naturally grew up from the earth by divine influence. This particular Nandi at Tanjore increased in size so rapidly that the Rajah, alarmed lest he should outgrow the temple itself, consulted the chief priest who explained the situation by stating that there was a living toad inside of the bull, the steady growth of which caused Nandi's increasing size. Of course, the Rajah ordered the toad to be killed and the royal mandate was executed. If you have a native attendant on your visit, he will point out to you a crack in the back of the statue as convincing evidence of the truth of the story. It is also said that blood continues to trickle from the old wound, thus proving that, though severely injured, the toad is still alive after a lapse of nearly a thousand years.

A short distance beyond Nandi's pavilion rises the mag-

nificent temple tower which, despite its massive proportions, is a marvel of symmetry. From a wondrously carved
sandstone pediment ninety-six feet square, it towers two
hundred and sixteen feet to a gold-tipped dome carved from
a single block of granite, weighing eighty tons. This gigantic capstone was brought from the village of Sarapal-
lam, four miles distant, and raised to the summit by means
of an inclined plane made of earth. The two operations, it
is said, required twelve years to complete. The exterior of
the tower is covered with a myriad of decorations concerning the adventures of Siva, in red, buff, and blue stucco.
In the northwest corner of the outer enclosure will be
found the beautifully carved main shrine of Subrahmanya,
one of the most exquisite bits of decorative architecture in
the Empire. It is only fifty feet high, superimposed upon
a base forty-five feet square, effectively adorned with pillars and pilasters, and different in every respect from any
shrine in either northern or southern India.

Deep within the interior of both Siva's and Subraman-
yah's shrines is the very holy of holies where the *lingam-
yoni* is enthroned. This emblem — a marble combination
of the male and female generative organs, similar to those
found on the banks of the Ganges at Benares — is the most
deeply revered symbol of the Hindu religion. The source of
physical life being the ancient's highest conception of God,
accounts for phallic worship in past centuries. Since the
Brahman priest discovered, years and years ago, however,
the stronghold this primitive doctrine still had upon the
imagination of his ignorant followers, he has exploited it in
the most shameless fashion, until it has degenerated into an
endless succession of disgusting and orgiastic rites which
are kept under cover in their temples. Local Hindu guides
with over-stimulated imaginations are in the habit of hand-
ing out highly colored narratives which are worse than the

rites themselves, if such a thing were possible. At any rate, the traveler who has been led to believe that the phallic worship of the ancients has been consigned to the limbo of forgotten centuries has but to journey through India to learn that it is as popular now, in the twentieth century, as it was in the days of Greece. Of course, the Eleusinian rites are lacking and the ceremonies much tempered, owing to long contact with the restraining power of the British Government. And again — education has done a great deal for those natives who have been interested in acquiring one. The great rank and file, however, are still weighed down with this terrible incubus of superstition and ignorance which is utilized by conscienceless priests on every hand under the guise of religion.

In temples, cemeteries, ancient palaces, native monuments and memorials of every sort — in fact wherever Siva worship is practiced, the traveler will encounter this crude emblem all over India. In a long open corridor lining the inside wall of the main enclosure of the Tanjore Temple will be found a procession of them. In one corner of this corridor, there is a separate chamber containing upwards of one hundred reproductions, bunched together, although to what purpose is beyond the wildest imagination. One would think that these Saivite priests had been sitting at the feet of some of our theatrical producers in New York. At all events, if the future holds any prospect of uplift for India's three hundred millions, their emancipation from the nauseating ceremonies of Siva worship will be one of the first, if not the first, move.

MADURA

Here is an ancient city which has been flourishing since the fifth century before Christ. With an active, industrious population of over 110,000, including possibly a dozen

Europeans, it is the most remarkable combination of past and present of any city in India. Madura's crowning glory is its tremendous Dravidian Temple to Siva and his consort Minakshi — one of the largest and most populous temples in the world. It is eight hundred and fifty feet long by seven hundred and thirty feet wide, covering an area of over fourteen acres, and surrounded by a high wall. These Dravidian temples consist of vast enclosures rather than great buildings, although the actual temples themselves are far from small. This one would accommodate every temple in the ancient city of Benares and have room to spare. Its four walls are pierced by as many gates surmounted by massive *gopurams* or pyramidal stone towers over one hundred and fifty feet in height, in addition to nine lesser ones which ornament the gateways to temples and various shrines within the enclosure. One would never gather the idea that he was entering a place of worship from the surroundings of this immense caravansery. Its gloomy, labyrinthine corridors are choked with shops of every imaginable character — cheap brummagem toys, fruits, sweetmeats, paper flowers, and cutlery — anything, in fact, that will yield a revenue seems welcome. The enclosure is filled from morning till night, day in and day out, not so much by visiting pilgrims as by the townsfolk themselves. In short the temple is more of a club than anything else, and everybody is 'on the make.'

The Golden Lily Pool or temple tank is thronged with bathers all day long, the cloisters on the side being preempted by sleek, practically naked priests who circulate among the crowds looking for the chance to perform some alleged holy office for a fee. Here the temple elephants come and go, in charge of their keepers, who are as keen for a tip in return for the privilege of taking a photograph of their burly charges as any New York waiter. Just what

DRAVIDIAN TEMPLE TO SIVA AND MINAKSHI — MADURA

the elephants were doing with a great big caste-mark of
Vishnu on their foreheads, in a temple to Siva, was a bit beyond me, especially since one of the shrines formerly dedicated to that deity has been closed for years, owing to some
internal row.

There is even more activity at night than during the
day. Indeed, that is the better time to see the temple life.
Thousands of little saucer lamps give a glow to those almost
endless and depressing halls which appear anything but
reassuring during the day. This seems to be the time for
the women, who arrive by the hundreds with the coming
of darkness. After a visit to the main shrine, they repair to
an altar consisting of a great slab which looks more like a
flat tombstone than anything else, over which the priests
preside, and around which the devotees march nine times
after pouring oil into a brazier opposite. Beyond a constant
mumbling by the priests, one could not make head or tail
out of the ritual. Even my guide could not enlighten me.
The flickering lights, deep shadows, and pungent odor of
burning gingelly oil were more suggestive of Black Magic
and Walpurgis Night than anything I have ever seen, and
one had to pinch himself to be sure he had not drifted out
of the twentieth century back into an earlier incarnation.

The inner corridors of the temple are more or less
shrouded in gloom as you approach Siva's shrine in the
center. The eye strives ineffectively to pierce the shadow
that lies beyond the outer portal. That this is a theatrically
conceived idea of the priests, there can be no question.
You catch a glimmer of a high-light which your attendant
will tell you is the altar cloth upon which the *lingam*
stands. You are properly impressed up to the moment that
he informs you, with considerable pride, that each succeeding day the emblem is reverently washed with Ganges
water, brought from Benares, the sale of which constitutes

no mean percentage of the income of the temple. God save us all!

The most interesting feature of this great temple to Siva is the devotion of the worshipers to his consort Minakshi, the fish-eyed goddess. Minakshi was a local Dravidian deity supposed to have been the daughter of one of the earlier kings, and very popular with the Madura folk. Tradition has it that she was born with three breasts, much to the horror of her parents. They were comforted, however, by a priestly prophecy that one of them would disappear as soon as she met her future husband. It would seem that the priest was a good guesser, because it wasn't long before she met our highly eligible friend Siva, who fell for her very heavily and wanted to adopt her immediately.

From where the Tanjore Saivite priests stood, Minakshi was small fish, indeed, and not in the same class with the Siva family, even if she were a goddess. Furthermore, they didn't fancy hooking up with that new-fangled Dravidian cult which was a bit new and untried. They didn't know whether they could make it pay its way or not. With all the Dravidians of southern India strong for Minakshi, however, not to mention the hundred thousand odd in Madura alone, they had to work fast. Accordingly, they held a solemn conclave; and with that characteristic adaptability of all Brahman priests, wherever money or power weighs in the balance, they decided to scrap their scruples and do the thing right. So — instead of making an ordinary, common, garden variety second-rater of Minakshi by adding her to Siva's harem, they arranged for a real, honest-to-god wedding with that gay Lothario, and gave her a fairly good percentage of the gate receipts from the Madura Temple, although they couldn't go quite so far as to dedicate it to her. Whereupon the lady's third breast disappeared as by magic. Then, these wise priests, not overlooking any bets, made a spread-eagle announcement of the wedding ceremonies, accompanied by official statements that the Minakshi-Siva nuptials united the old faith with the new in the strongest possible bonds. And thus they have held the solid Dravidian vote from those trying times down to the present day.

Over in the southeast corner of the town is a magnificent sacred tank, a thousand feet square, faced with granite, with three separate flights of stone steps on either side leading down to the water's edge. It was built in the seventeenth century and is connected with a neighboring river by a channel. That these ancient builders had an eye for beauty is indicated by the exquisite little tropical island that rises from the middle of this tank. It is a perfect bower of flowering shrubs, palms, and other native trees, with a diminutive temple in the center, the spire of which towers over all. On certain annual festival days, the enthusiastic devotees of Siva and Minakshi, each of whom has been playing a lone hand for a year, convey their respective statues from the temple to the lake, where a raft awaits them.

Just as soon as darkness falls, a half-dozen semi-naked priests board the raft with a paddle each and give Siva and Minakshi the ride of their lives around the tank to the accompaniment of red fire and much beating of drums and the wild approval of the assembled multitude. After the excitement is all over, they escort the devoted pair to the sanctuary on the little island, where they spend the night together in divine contemplation or words to that effect. The next day finds them back on the job in the temple. There are a number of other worth-while attractions in the Madura Temple, and in the town as well, which you will appreciate, including the Hall of a Thousand Pillars, a remarkable exhibition of fine carvings. And now we will take the train to the railway terminus at Tuticorin, where the Colombo steamer is waiting to ferry us across the straits.

CEYLON

After a week on the train and in the rest-houses and dak bungalows of southern India, the approach to Ceylon's Isle is all that the imagination has ever pictured. There are the immemorial palms, the long stretch of rose-tinted, shelving sea-beach, fleecy clouds floating in the brightest of blue skies backed by the lofty mountain peaks in the interior — everything in fact that suggests the *dolce far niente* of the tropics without any of its drawbacks. And just a little exercise of the imagination will materialize those 'spicy breezes' of the old hymn in a most startling fashion.

Our vessel comes to an anchor off Colombo, within a magnificent harbor with an area of over six hundred acres, protected by two of the most remarkable jetties or break-waters in the world, with an aggregate length of nearly eight thousand feet, including a lighthouse which can be seen from a distance of eighteen miles, constructed at tremendous expense by Great Britain years ago. This is the way that great Colonial Government does things in the Orient. The seas that are kicked up in those latitudes by the monsoon rendered these constructions absolutely vital to safe harbor. There are three good hotels in Colombo, two of which are situated in the center of the town: the Grand Oriental and the Bristol. There is another — the Galle Face — a mile and a half out of town, situated on the beach and overlooking an Orient sea. Let's go out there and invite our souls for a day or two.

A couple of drives will give you all there is of any particular interest in Colombo. They will be just a little different, however, from any drives you probably have ever

WHEN THE MONSOON BLOWS — COLOMBO

taken. The fascinating glimpses of a sapphire sea through the most gorgeous tropical growth, and wild flowers of the most exquisite beauty, as you traverse a motor highway as smooth as the palm of your hand, will give you a slant on Ceylon that you'll never forget. The primitive native huts under the cocoa palms as you draw out into the country a bit will make you wonder that such things can possibly exist along with the wear and tear of the twentieth century.

Yes — and you'll like the smiling faces of the Sinhalese, both men and women. Nor will their bright coloring, either of skin or clothing, be lost upon you. Also, you'll wonder by what particular dispensation a man wears the kind of a comb affected by your women-folks at home. And the picturesque native catamarans drawn up on the sea-beach, too. It isn't natural that you should return from a drive that brings you so close to Nature's heart to settle down to an outlook over paved streets. That's why I want you to luxuriate for a day or two under the palm-tree shadows of this most beautifully located Galle Face hostelry. Of course, if you're only going to stop over for a steamer, you probably will prefer the town. But you will miss half the beauty of a sojourn in Ceylon unless you go up-country, which you will enjoy all the more by taking your fill of a very wonderful seascape.

To those who have never visited the tropics, the seventy-five mile trip from Colombo to ancient Kandy, seventeen hundred feet above the sea-level, will be a genuine eye-opener. A marvel of engineering skill, that railroad, which makes its tortuous way up the side of one of the most amazingly beautiful tropical gorges imaginable, past vast rice paddies extending in terraces from the crest of the gorge to its depths — endless vistas of the most vivid green, through groves of breadfruit and frangipani trees and clumps of cocoa-palm. Myriad streams and cascades find their way

down the sides of the gorge to swell the winding river in the
bottomlands far below. A veritable embarrassment of
riches in tropical beauty. If you did no more than go up to
Kandy to remain one night, it would be worth your while.
But you won't do that. You'll want to settle down in
Kandy, in the Queen's Hotel, beside a beautiful lake. Its
shores are covered with royal palms and wide-spreading
tamarind trees, with the dainty bungalows of resident tea-
planters peeping out here and there.

Within a stone's throw is the celebrated Buddhist 'Temple of the Tooth.' This is the only temple you will have to
visit in Ceylon. You are going to be a trifle surprised when
you first view this celebrated relic, which rests on a lotus
flower of pure gold, beneath seven concentric, bell-shaped,
metal shrines, gorgeously bejeweled. The fact that it is a
piece of discolored ivory two inches long and a little less
than an inch in diameter, and looks as if it might have
once graced the jaw of a prehistoric, saber-toothed tiger,
cuts no figure in the mind of your priestly guide who will
most solemnly assure you that it was at one time part of the
dental make-up of Gautama Buddha. There never was any
question as to the genuineness of the original sacred tooth,
which was brought from Kalinga, India, to Ceylon in
311 A.D. by a Sinhalese princess who concealed it in her
hair. There followed more bloody wars over that relic than
were ever fought in the Crusades. It was regained by the
Malabars a thousand years later and carried back to India;
recovered by a Sinhalese king and hidden until 1560; discovered then by the Portuguese, it was taken to Goa where
it was burned by the Archbishop of the Holy Roman
Church. That, however, was a mere matter of detail —
the Sinhalese just had to have their 'sacred tooth,' so they
proceeded to make another, and this is the one you'll see.
It's old enough in all conscience. It has lain uncomplain-

ingly on that golden lotus flower since the latter part of the sixteenth century. Once a year they take it out and give it a ride on an elephant in a parade. You are supposed to look properly impressed when you view this emblem. To say the least, it's infinitely preferable to Siva's.

Another interesting feature of this celebrated temple is its sacred elephants, which are bathed regularly by their keepers in a near-by stream. If there is any animal that enjoys a bath more than an elephant, I don't know it, nor one that apparently experiences a more ecstatic sensation as his keeper massages him from stem to stern with half a cocoanut shell. This is another of these Oriental sights that is very much worth seeing. It takes place every day, and the rickshaw man will run you down from the hotel to the river in a very few minutes.

There is a beautiful drive around the lake, bordered by royal palms, which extends well out into the country and affords some fine mountain scenery. Kandy's greatest attraction, however, is the Royal Botanical Garden at Peradeniya, four miles distant. This wondrous garden covers one hundred and fifty acres and is encircled by a beautiful river. There is scarcely a tree, flower, or plant native to the Far East but will be found in this beautiful spot. If you have time for nothing else, give Peradeniya the preference.

The early morning services at the Temple of the Tooth start off somewhere in the neighborhood of five o'clock, accompanied by a native band of music consisting entirely of bass-drums. You won't need any call to breakfast at the Queen's Hotel.

There are many indications in the island of Ceylon of its prehistoric settlement. It is also noted for its buried cities, the principal one of which is Anuradhapura, eighty-four miles distant by rail, with a very comfortable rest-house at the end of the journey. This city — the most famous in the world for its ancient monuments — was the capital of Ceylon in the fifth century, B.C. It attained its greatest grandeur about the commencement of the Christian era. In its colossal proportions it ranked with Nineveh and Babylon, being surrounded by four walls each sixteen miles long enclosing a territory of two hundred and fifty-six square miles. As a result of repeated invasions by the Tamils, who came over from India in a war of conquest, Anuradhapura was finally deserted as a royal residence in the eighth century. In the centuries that followed it was completely overrun by the jungle and blotted from sight. It was rediscovered in 1872, the tropical growth cleared away, and the magnificent ruins laid bare. There is good authority for the statement that there are sufficient remains of former temples to build a town of fifty thousand population.

The restorations in this ancient spot consist for the most part of necessary water tanks and dagobas — a bell-shaped structure erected in commemoration of some revered relic, surmounted by a lofty spire. The most typical and oldest of these is the Thuparama Dagoba, which has been thoroughly restored and will be immediately recognizable by its new appearance. It was built in 307 B.C. by one of the ancient kings as a shrine for the right collar-bone of the Buddha. The number of these structures is legion, varying from a few feet to over eleven hundred feet in circumference.

There are two remarkable relics in Anuradhapura which are bound to impress the most sophisticated traveler: first, the ancient Pipal or Bo tree — the oldest historical tree in existence and most deeply revered by the followers of Gautama Buddha. This tree was brought from Buddh Gaya, India, not far from Benares, and planted on its present spot in 245 B.C. It was a cutting from the original Bo tree at Gaya under which Gautama Buddha inaugurated his teachings. While probably not more than a fragment of the original tree exists at Anuradhapura, its geniuneness is attested by definite records extending from 288 B.C. to 1739 A.D., showing that it has been watched over for all these centuries by an unbroken succession of guardians. The tree stands upon a terraced mound about fifteen feet high, completely covered by its wide-spreading branches. This mound is doubtless the result of the earth having been heaped up around the original trunk in previous centuries in order to protect it. This is further indicated by the presence of many small trees on the terrace which have doubtless sprung up from roots thrown out by the parent trunk.

The rescue of this ancient city from its overwhelming tropical growth was accompanied by the cutting-out of certain well-defined pathways for the convenience of the traveler. They have been kept clear. In following one of these footpaths I came upon a dark granite, weather-beaten, seated statue of the Buddha, one hand resting in the other in the characteristic attitude of contemplation. As a bit of sculpture it was of no particular interest beyond the fact that one would hardly expect to encounter a solitary statue of the Buddha or any one else in the depths of a jungle, far separated from all other evidences of the hand of man. It was the cast of countenance that riveted my attention: a composure so absolute that one immediately perceived the absence of anything of the kind in himself; almost, a mobile play of features and a startling lifelike expression in the downcast eyes. The deep hush of the forest, the immemorial trees, the consciousness of the unbroken silence which had brooded over the spot for untold centuries — all called for self-effacement. And yet — I could not help but feel that if he could communicate his secret it would probably lose its value. Poor, puny mind setting itself up as an analyst in the presence of immanent spirit. Scarcely enough sense left to render unto Cæsar the things which were Cæsar's. I had come upon a mystery and wanted to argue about it. Emerson furnished the answer and humbled me in the dust: 'A man may set his own rate. Let him be great and love shall follow him.' Truly I had got more than I dreamed of when I ventured into that deserted spot. My day at Anuradhapura was crowned. Who was it said:

> There will always be one or two who hold
> Earth's coin of less account than fairy gold;
> Their treasure, not the spoils of crowns and kings,
> But the dim beauty at the heart of things?

CHAPTER XVIII
EGYPT AND THE HOME TRAIL

Spendthrift of life, they ravish
The days of an endless store,
And ever the more they lavish
The heap of the hoard is more.
For joy and love and vision
Are alive and breed and stay
When dust shall hold in derision
The misers of a day.

RICHARD HOVEY

TWELVE long beautiful days from Colombo to Cairo,
through the Indian Ocean, the Straits of Bab el Mandeb,
the Red Sea, and the Suez Canal. Don't those names sound
fine? Much has been written of the infernal heat of these
latitudes and especially the Red Sea. So far as we were
concerned, however, they were figments of a disordered
imagination. More perfect weather than was vouchsafed
to us on that particular run could not be imagined. We
were traveling on a German vessel homeward bound from
Australia. Just as we dropped anchor off Aden for a two or
three hours' stop-over in order to put in a supply of coal,
the British fort started target practice with some of the
smaller guns. 'They always do that when a German pulls
in,' said one of the ship's officers; 'they don't want us to
forget that this is British territory and that their guns
command the Straits.' Well, I rather imagine that our old
friend John Bull finally got the idea over to Fritz and it is
barely possible that he remembers it even at this late date.

Having a little money left, we went ashore and did some
shopping with the Arab merchants. It might be well to
remember that nothing will take the place of gold for a bit

of fast work with these fellows. They know the American tendency for souvenirs and they hoist the price of everything about three hundred per cent for the unwary traveler who wishes to buy something worth while and hasn't time to argue over the attempted larceny. They have some fine feather fans worth about five dollars for which they will ask ten or fifteen dollars without batting an eye. You may have some Indian rupees which they will gladly take but they cut no figure when it comes to driving a bargain. Fish a British sovereign, worth $4.86 or less, out of your pocket and offer it to Mr. Arab for his $15 fan, and he'll take it from you so quickly that you'll wonder if you haven't stuck yourself after all. Did I say it was cool in the Red Sea? Well — I'll make an exception of Aden. All the old moss-covered jokes about heat, such, for instance, as the soldier from a station in the tropics who woke up in hell and wanted to go back to his last post after his blanket — are quite *passé* in Aden. Even the Arabs are wise to 'em. Don't waste time searching in the back parlors of your memory for similes. Just buy your fan and go back to the ship and change your clothes. When the thermometer registers 110° in the shade (which there isn't any in Aden) they say it's quite comfortable. When it's really hot, the thermometer doesn't register — the mercury just naturally burbles out over the top of the tube.

When your vessel pulls into Port Said, you'll see old Ferdinand de Lesseps's bronze statue looming up at the end of the canal. That little strip of water, one hundred miles long, three hundred and ten feet wide, and thirty-one feet deep cost the neat little sum of $153,000,000 or over $1,500,000 per mile. And it was nothing but a sand-dredging proposition. 'They say' that over half that modest appropriation went for graft in Paris and Constantinople.

Certainly poor old de Lesseps didn't get much of it, for he died a pauper and in an insane asylum. The cleverest of them all — and playing a strictly clean game at that — was Britain's Jewish Prime Minister Disraeli, who outwitted France and Turkey, which is why John Bull controls the old ditch to-day, including the Assuan Dam. Does he hold the whip-hand in Egypt? Well — I guess he does. Long may he wave! If he ever gets the taint of opium out of his clothes, he'll be ready for translation.

From Port Said to Cairo is a quick journey of one hundred and forty-five miles, through the typical flat, treeless, and desert Egyptian country. After establishing yourself at either Shepheard's, the Savoy or the Continental Hotel, the first thing you will need to do is to make your arrangements for your Nile trip. Unless you have practically unlimited time and wish to travel in your own *dahabeah*, with your own crew, there is just one satisfactory method of seeing Egypt and the Nile: take one of the steamers of the Cook flotilla at Assiut and settle yourself for twenty-one days. Assiut is reached by rail, two hundred and fifty miles south of Cairo, where the Nile is dammed in order to supply Egypt's great irrigation canal — Bahr Yusuf. From Assiut you will have a leisurely river trip of two hundred miles to the Assuan Dam which (going and returning) will enable you to visit all the famous temples on both sides of the river, including Karnak and Luxor.

If you wish to go about one hundred and fifty miles beyond the First Cataract and pay a visit to the splendid temple of Abu Simbel, you can do it by the Sudan boat, and for which you should allow four additional days. The probabilities are that you will have two or three days in Cairo before going up-river, which you can put in most profitably. Without question your first move will be either to trolley or motor seven miles out to Gizeh for a day at the

pyramids and a few words with the Sphinx. You'll want to
climb the four hundred and fifty feet of old Cheops as well
as to go down into the crypt — and you should do both.
With a couple of Arab 'boys' to help — one pulling and the
other pushing — you'll make the summit of Cheops in a
few minutes and the view will more than justify the effort.
Why do you need Arab boys to help? Because the stones
of which this tremendous pyramid is built are about three
feet square and you'll appreciate both the push and the pull
on the way up.

Cairo is credited with having about four hundred
mosques. A visit to two or three will be all-sufficient. The
first in point of antiquity is that of Ahmed, founded in
879 A.D., from the summit of which may be had one of the
finest views of the city, including the citadel. In point of
architectural beauty that of Sultan Hassam surpasses
them all, with its richly ornamented porch, spacious court,
and towering walls. Here we have a survival of one of the
oldest of Oriental traditions: that the king ordered the hand
of the architect cut off lest he should attempt to produce
something yet finer. Then there is the Azhar, or 'Splendid,' Mosque, which includes the Cairo College, where
hundreds of the youth of the city repair daily for the study
of the Koran. This is well worth a visit if for no other
reason than to see these cross-legged youngsters spread all
over the court, droning away over the precepts of Mohammed. Practically all the mosques have been more or less
restored with stones filched from the pyramids. In all the
world there is no more interesting museum than that of
Cairo, with its priceless archæological and historical relics
from the tombs of the ancient kings. Here are innumerable treasures so eld and inestimable in value as to be beyond all comparison. One whole day would not be too
much for the visitor to devote to this remarkable display.

You will, of course, have secured your dragoman or native guide for your stay in the city. Don't try to get along without him. He will have been worth ten times over what you pay him by the time you are ready to leave. These men will be found in waiting in the hotel corridors or at Cook's, and may be depended upon for good and reliable service. If you think you would enjoy a day's camel ride on the desert — and I am sure you will — get your dragoman to arrange for a camel and a boy to meet the early morning train at the little station Bedreshen, fourteen miles south of Cairo, and visit the ruins of ancient Memphis and the step-pyramid of Sakkara, the oldest in Egypt.

You will find it difficult to imagine, as you walk around on that pile of rubbish under the palm trees, that it was once the site of the capital of Upper and Lower Egypt, second in importance only to Alexandria; that it was founded four thousand years before the Christian era, and that King Mena changed the course of the Nile in order to build on that spot. The imagination limps in the face of such remoteness, and the references to this ancient city, in the Old Testament, by Hosea, Ezekiel, Isaiah, and Jeremiah, under the names of Moph and Noph, seem recent by comparison. There are three mementoes remaining of its former greatness which are worth seeing: two tremendous monoliths of Rameses II, Israel's oppressor, one prostrate and one erect; also an immense sphinx, all of which were supposed to have been a part of the ancient temple to Ptah. The absence of any further remains is explained by the fact that Memphis was for many years the quarry from which Cairo got most of its building material. Not very romantic — but such are the facts. In the old Sakkara cemetery near by will be found the famous Serapeum or underground tombs of the sacred bulls connected with the temple in those days — a series of spacious vaults containing immense sarcophagi of polished granite, each of which housed at one time a mummied bull. Imagine a sarcophagus fourteen feet long by eleven high, hewn out of a solid piece of granite. Then think of the Copts, those early Christians in Egypt, who raided these tombs, stealing even the mummied remains of the bulls — twenty-four in all. There's but one reason why they left behind the granite sarcophagi: the same one that keeps a latter-day thief from stealing a red-hot stove. Crossing the desert from Bedreshen, the present village on the site of Memphis, you will arrive in Gizeh in the late afternoon and dismiss your camels, returning to Cairo by trolley-car. As a matter of fact, you can make this trip and 'do' Gizeh on the same day if you are pressed for time. It's a novel experience and you will find nothing uncomfortable about camel-riding. After you have driven around that most colorful city, Cairo, visited its bazaars and seen a little of its night life, you'll be ready for your trip up the Nile which, I predict, will be one of the most enjoyable of your long journey. In accordance with the time the steamboat makes, based upon the number of sandbars on which you will get stuck, you will be escorted at least twice a day to some ancient temple not far from the banks of the river, by the steamboat's dragoman — a gorgeously togged-out Arab — who has learned his lesson well and who knows the 'high-spots' of every temple.

It's a regular 'Cook's Tour' proposition and most intelligently carried out. What the dragoman has forgotten, you won't know anything about. And you'd forget it in the next half-hour, anyway. For anybody but a 'nut' archæologist who might be slightly inclined toward the sky-pointing nose with a Cook's dragoman, this method of seeing Egypt's monuments is as satisfactory as anything I

HOUR OF PRAYER IN THE DESERT

RUINS OF MEMPHIS
'Lo, all our pomp of yesterday
Is one with Nineveh and Tyre.'

know. If inclined, you can read up during the hours in between on the boat for which I would suggest some of those old-time novels by George Ebers — 'Uarda,' for instance; also 'The Spell of Egypt,' by Robert Hichens, and 'Egypt,' an anthology of prose collated by Esther Singleton. Both these latter books consist of short stories, and will give you a better bird's-eye view of Egypt and her temples than any half-dozen books you'll get your hands on. And listen — when your old boat slides her snubby nose on a sandbar and you begin to wonder just when she's going to slide off, like a lot of other folks, you'll probably go snooping around a-looking for the captain. And it will suddenly occur to you that you haven't met him. Then, for the first time, you will learn that he's a foxy old Arab and keeps himself on the upper deck, in the pilot-house, where he belongs. Furthermore, that there's no passageway up to where he is — that the old rascal climbs up a stanchion from the deck below: a stunt that you are not likely to undertake — and he knows it. If, however, you should happen to catch him sliding down his stanchion, while yet the gallant craft is hugging the sandbar, and ask him the 'damphool' question that comes to your and all other travelers' minds at such a moment — he will assure you with deep gravity that 'it is as Allah wills.' And before you can make the second crack, the old fellow will have slid down the other stanchion, to the deck below, for a word with the engineer. Inshallah! — but he's a wise old skipper and knows the Nile as you know the midnight route to the refrigerator in the kitchen. There's nothing in the world quite like the boat-life on the Nile. The velvety black of an Egyptian night comes down like a swift-falling curtain, by which time the anchor should be in the bed of the river. For there is no traffic after sundown. Most suggestive of those lines from Knibbs —

The harbor of the broad lagoon,
The darkening shore, the early star,
The magic of the tropic moon —
New fortunes in a land afar.

And then to be wakened in the morning by the strangest
undertone of an Arab chantey — the deck-hands, in squads
of five, working rhythmically with their brooms, as they
wash down the deck to a tune that never was on sea or land
and to which you will find yourself keeping time. Oh —
there's something more in the Nile than water.

Let no one beguile you with that immemorial lie about
the monotonous sameness of the Nile. People who talk
that way are either cursed with dyspepsia or the well-
springs which God originally planted within them are dried
up. How can there be monotony where feathery palms lean
gracefully over a jumble of mud huts, with the creak and
drone in your ears of the camel-operated *sakiyeh* or native
irrigation well on one bank of the river, two fellahin hoisting water with their imitation well-sweep *shadoof*, on the
other; a red lateen sail in the foreground, a camel and a
donkey hitched to a primitive plough in the background;
old Sol doing his damdest, with a white temple just beyond under the most blinding blue sky that your fettered
imagination can conjure up. In Heaven's name, what is
monotony? 'What went ye out for to see?' Shall the Nile
pipe unto you and shall you not dance? Verily I say unto
you, it shall be more tolerable for Sodom and Gomorrah
in the day of the smiting than for the guy who goes up the
Nile with a market report in his hand. If you're in a hurry,
stay away from Egypt. If you cannot get the rattle of the
stock-ticker out of your brain, go to Atlantic City and
revel in the glories of a wheel chair. But — remember, old
scout: 'There's no pocket in a shroud.' The usual offering
will now be taken and — brethren, don't forget the Foreign

Missions. They, at least, have furnished us a speaking acquaintance with the heathen who happen to be a lot more entertaining than some speedy friends we could mention.

Let us go into the temple of Edfu, the best preserved and the most noble of them all. It is over two thousand years old and took nearly two hundred years to build. The very first thought that finds its way into the consciousness of him who hath ears to hear is that he would like to enter into the inner sanctuary of so marvelous a shrine. Nothing could more eloquently picture the upreaching of mankind toward the beauty of holiness than the measureless dignity and perfect serenity of this spiritual building made with hands. The thought of its having been built for pagan worship in the dawn of time will not occur to you. You could no more raise your voice or indulge in frivolous conversation in this place than you could in Saint Peter's in Rome. Just as the Ark of the Covenant was concealed behind the veil in the Tabernacle which Moses built for the ancient children of Israel, even so will the inner sanctuary of all these Nile temples be found deep in the very heart of the structure: a low, small-sized, rectangular chamber which, even in those prehistoric days, was devoid of either statue or emblem. It contained simply the sacred bark or tabernacle of patined wood mounted on a pedestal. In other words, the all-important object was the creation of an atmosphere of divine worship, unencumbered with material accessories, to whatever gods might be. What more will you find in any church or cathedral of the present day? Evidently they appreciated, possibly as much as we do in this enlightened age, that 'The letter killeth, but the spirit giveth life.'

Arranged about the sanctuary was a series of rooms used for storing ceremonial paraphernalia such as golden vessels, flowers, robes, and perfumes employed in various sacrificial services, etc. Then came an inner vestibule of columns, next an outer courtyard sacred to the priests — the whole being surrounded by a colonnade in which the worshipers assembled. Rather a high-church proceeding, as it were. It was only outside and beyond these limits that even the mighty Pharaohs of that day could make additions of vast porticoes, courtyards, halls, pylons, etc., redounding to their own personal splendor, the best examples of which are found in those vast temple remains at Luxor and Karnak. Every succeeding Pharaoh went the limit in celebrating some great victory by making an addition to the temple. But — he kept on the outside. He never even approached the colonnade where the people assembled for service, let alone the inner sanctuary. If you will keep these few suggestions in mind, you will get a clearer conception of the basic plan upon which all the Nile temples were built.

At Dendera will be found the one temple on the Nile in which there has been any attempt at sculpturing a face. Out of four different full-face carvings of the Goddess Hathor (she who presided in the under-world) at the top of each of the six immense columns which support the façade of the temple, there is just one which has not been destroyed. This was the work of the Copts, those early Christians who took it upon themselves to rebuke the paganism of the Egyptians by hacking to ruin many of the wondrous carvings on these temples. It fairly makes one's blood boil to see such criminal vandalism even though it is centuries old. The one face left practically unharmed out of the twenty-four looks as if Hathor might have been a rosy, fat-cheeked girl. The sculptor, whoever he was, has given her a pair of rather voluptuous lips, widely separated eyes, and an oval face with high cheek-bones. She's a mighty attractive goddess, if you leave it to my estimate, and I should imagine she'd be as popular in the upper world as apparently she was in the lower where they probably

TEMPLE AT PHILÆ — SUBMERGED IN THE ASSUAN DAM

needed her more. Another good feature of the Dendera temple is the fact that it is scrupulously clean, inside and out. There are two flights of stairs which lead to the roof from which a most sightly view may be had. Eighteen massive columns support the ceiling which, including the whole interior as well as the exterior of the temple, are most elaborately carved. Conventional figures of Cleopatra and her son appear on the rear exterior — the only representation on any temple in Egypt of that redoubtable queen. Owing to its compactness and orderliness, this temple offers a better opportunity for close observation than any in the Nile district. It will prove a thoroughly satisfactory visit, whether you are an archæologist in the bud or just an ordinary sight-seer like the writer.

And so you will find some one particular feature of each temple along this great waterway which will appeal. Few of us realize that practically every temple and desert city throughout Egypt is built upon the remains of earlier dynasties which latter, frequently, in their turn, top those of yet more ancient character. Note particularly, when you are at Luxor, the site of the Mohammedan mosque above the top of the temple columns, outside of the excavated area. This has been one of the difficulties Egyptologists have had to face: the Moslem objection to any excavations that might disturb their mosques, all of which are built over the tops of ancient sand-buried temples.

In those early times then it was the custom of each Egyptian king to destroy the temples of his predecessor in order that he might have room to spread himself and leave behind a still greater reputation. Thus you will see in many different places the cartouche of Rameses II, the genial Pharaoh who compelled the Israelites to make bricks without straw. You will note that this gentleman was not satisfied to trade-mark the temples which he actually built, but frequently imprinted his own cartouche over that of his predecessor — a reprehensible practice that is not altogether unknown in these more enlightened times.

As you stand on the deck of the steamboat moored to the river-bank at ancient Luxor, it will be difficult for your imagination to picture the extent of ancient Thebes: three miles square, taking in both sides of the river. 'Twill be more difficult yet for you to realize that all that territory lying between the river and the Libyan Hills was thickly covered with temples of every description, dedicated to the thousand and one local gods of each individual 'congregation.' Oh — they were as denominational in those days as the present-day towns of fifteen hundred population which support a county jail, an insane asylum, three lodges, and the Second Presbyterian Church, and, as the oldest resident boasted, 'enjoyed the advantages of all of 'em.'

When you ride muleback for that mile-and-a-half that separates Luxor and the great temple of Karnak, just remember that those two magnificent temples were formerly connected with an avenue bordered on both sides by innumerable monuments of sphinxes and rams, and that the very marked depression in the land off to one side and in between was a splendid lake. The temple at Karnak is of immemorial antiquity — probably the oldest in all Egypt — and — if I may be pardoned a digression — the flies come next. You won't need anybody to call your attention to them. However, you're not going to make your residence in Karnak, so cheer up and don't stay away on that account. And then remember that Thebes was completely destroyed during the reign of the Roman Emperor Augustus 30 B.C. Despite the fact that since that day its remains have proved an inexhaustible supply for native mill-stones and lime-burners, Thebes still represents the greatest collection of monumental ruins in the world. You'll appreci-

ate the great Colossi of Memnon across the river more if
you'll remember that they once graced the entrance to a
magnificent temple, not a stone of which remains. On the
walls of the Deir el Bahri temple to Hathor, excavated from
the sands of the desert over against the cliffs of the Libyan
Hills, your attention will be called to a most interesting
record of Queen Hatshepsut's seafaring expedition to the
Land of Punt in search of incense. There being nothing in
these wall records to indicate that the Egyptians ever built
a seagoing vessel, the location of the Land of Punt was a
mystery for many years to all Egyptologists. They finally
fixed it in what is to-day known as Somaliland on the north-
eastern coast of Africa, thus indicating that the flotilla
made its way through the Red Sea and out into the Indian
Ocean. Quite an undertaking for the kind of vessels that
are pictured on temple walls. Incidentally, the expedition
was a great success, hence the prideful account by Queen
Hatshepsut. And so the days will go: you will find something of individual interest in every temple you visit: Abydos, Kom Ombos and Philæ — the temple now partially
submerged beneath the waters of the Assuan Dam —
through which you will be rowed — because the Egyptian
Government wasn't sufficiently interested in that wonderful pile to save it by removal; the Ramesseum and Medinet
Habu, the latter of which has a fine sculptured representation of a battle on its exterior walls, with old Rameses II
in full action and going strong. It's muchly worth a visit.

If you can slip up to Abu Simbel, by all means do so.
That is the one temple that has been hewn out of the mountain-side. It is the most highly individualized of them all
and, as might be imagined, the work of our modest friend
Rameses II. There are three of them, all recessed out of the
solid rock and overlooking the Nile. We will content ourselves with a brief description of the principal one which is,

without doubt, the greatest rock-hewn monument in the world. The outer platform or court is reached by a flight of steps leading up from the river. On either side of the entrance are two tremendous seated colossi of Rameses II (one of which has fallen down), sixty-five feet in height above the pedestals on which they are placed, with a placidity and benignancy of countenance that belie that old war-horse's real character. Running true to form, he has his wife and children distributed here and there between his various legs. Just as a matter of interesting proportion: they, as standing figures, are mostly less than half the height of his knees. He's a very self-effacing old fellow, this Rameses II, with an ear three feet five inches long, a fifteen-foot elbow, and a forefinger of three feet. He hated himself. The temple is dedicated to the Egyptian sun god, Amen Ra, and faces the east at such an angle that the rising sun's rays illuminate the two great halls in the depths of the mountain to their full extent, over two hundred feet. They include the sanctuary as well and fall gently on the two central figures in the interior: Amen Ra and that same shrinking violet, Rameses II, flanked on either side by the gods of Memphis. A portion of the highly interesting painted sculpture and frescoes of the interior show Rameses the king making offerings to himself as a god. Could innate modesty go further! Never mind, brother, he's been dead a long time — ever since 1250 B.C. in fact. You'll be as dead as he five minutes after your heart stops beating. If you're going to Abu Simbel, you have very little time to lose. And the probabilities are that your business will be run better in your absence than when you're on the job.

While you are at Luxor, you doubtless will go over into the Valley of the Tombs of the Kings, and it's barely possible you may acquire the necessary imagination to hark back anywhere from two to six thousand years. It cannot

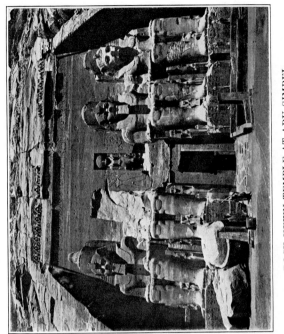

ROCK-HEWN TEMPLE AT ABU SIMBEL

be done merely by looking at the figures and repeating them aloud. That's the wizardry of Egypt. There's no use trying to visualize a civilization that produced such marvels as you will visit along the Nile. All that you can do is to look at them as intelligently as possible and be thankful that you're alive. In this latter peculiarity you have considerable of an advantage over Rameses II, Tutankhamen, and the rest of that imperial bunch of swashbucklers who have afforded you a lot of real entertainment and enlarged your horizon by just that much. And that is what travel is supposed to do, the best evidence of which being that you will want to go back and do it all over again.

Having had our hand-baggage thoroughly rifled by the porters at the National Hotel on our return to Cairo, we were ready to say good-bye to that ancient city, as the one place in a ten months' trip around the world where we had encountered thieves. We had been warned that Cairo was as full of thieves as a successful career is of blunders, and we had kept our bags locked every moment of our absence up the Nile. On arrival at the railway station in Cairo on our return, we opened them to stow away some travel toggery. Knowing that we should be in our hotel in ten or fifteen minutes, it never occurred to us to lock them for that brief period. Being broad daylight, we didn't hesitate to let them ride on top of the bus. We saw them put there and saw them taken off and placed in the entrance to the hotel. They seemed to be a bit of a long time on their way up to our rooms, with the best of good reasons: they had been plundered en route and in the dark. The only things stolen were articles enclosed in leather, which included some valuable stick-pins, shirt-studs, cuff-links, etc., not to mention a case of razors rolled in chamois. I mention these details for the benefit of my readers. It was a master hand

that pillaged those bags — one owned by a thief who knew
the feel of fine leather and what it generally contained.
When I reported our loss to the proprietor, he was very
polite and confirmed our previous warning that there were
many thieves in Cairo — but that was as far as it went. A
word to the wise is sufficient. The next afternoon found us
on our way to Alexandria by rail where we caught the
steamer for Naples. Were we ready for home, you ask?
Well — you have a home, in all probability — you answer
that question. We were just so ready that, instead of waiting for a couple of days to catch our scheduled steamer by
the southern route, we took the first train out for Paris and
caught the first steamer for the little old United States,
leaving from Cherbourg. Then her name was the *Imperator*. She has changed owners since. To-day her name is
the *Berengaria*. It must be stated, however, that under her
present flag she lacks one feature that was very much in
evidence under her former registration: a very swell oil
painting at the head of the grand staircase of the then most
puissant German Kaiser. You don't hear so much about
him now. There were those on the vessel who figured some
family connection between the painting and the vessel's
name. I was so glad to be getting home that I let them get
away with it.

Yes — we are going to do it all over again. The same
splendid pair of pals — wife and daughter — whose feet
are tuned to all trails, who know the Rules of the Game
and observe them —

Till the last adventure calls us from the old, the vain desires,
To a trail that's still untrodden, though aglow with little fires:
Where no wanderer grows weary and a man is free to roam,
Or hang his hat upon a star and call the planet 'Home.'

THE END

INDEX

INDEX

INDEX

Abu Simbel, temple of, 293, 303, 304.

Abydos, temple, 303.

Aden, 291, 292.

Adham Khan, mausoleum of, 248.

Agra, hotels at, 235; the Taj Mahal, 236–40; the Red Fort, 240; the tomb of I'timad ud Daulah, 241; points in the vicinity of (Fatehpur-Sikri and the tomb of Akbar the Great), 242–45.

Aguila, El, cruise of, 156–201.

Aguinaldo, 145.

Ahmedabad, 263.

Akbar the Great, his hunting-tower, 243; his manner of circumventing assassination, 243, 244; his tomb, 244, 245; defeats the Rajputs at Chitor, 261.

Alcoholic liquors, use of, in the Orient, 127–29.

Algué, Father, director of the Manila Meteorological Observatory, 154.

Altamsh, tomb of, 248.

Amber, deserted city of Rajputana, 253–55.

American Express Co., 220.

Ancestry-worship, of the Chinese, 122, 137.

Anglo-Saxon in the Far East, the tragedy of, 172, 173.

Antung, 83, 84.

Anuradhapura, ruins of, 287, 288; dagobas at, 288; ancient Bo tree in, 288, 289; a statue of Buddha in, 289, 290.

Arizona, Petrified Forests of, 4.

Arjmand Banu, the Taj Mahal a monument to, 237–40.

Around-the-world journey, cost of, 3, 4; direction of, 4.

Asano, Mr., multi-millionaire, 27.

Asoka's Pillar, 233.

Assuan Dam, 293, 303.

Assiut, 293.

Astronomical University, at Peking, 102; at Jeypore, 257.

Babies, Japanese, 66, 67.

Bagobos, native tribe in Mindanao, 171, 174–77.

Baguio, 203–05.

Bahr Yusuf, 293.

Bathing, in Japan, 66.

Bats, in Philippines, 171.

Bay of Bengal, 219.

Bazaars, at Rangoon, 216; at Jeypore, 258.

Beck, L. Adams, his *The Building of the Taj Mahal*, 239, 240.

Bedreshen, 295.

Bell, General J. Franklin, places *El Aguila* at Congressman Miller's disposal, 156, 157.

Bell, Temple of the Great. *See* Temple of the Great Bell.

Belloc, Hilaire, his *The Four Men*, 212.

Benares, and the 'Temple of the Tirthankers' in *Kim,* 218; the holiness of, 227; the pilgrims to, 227–29; phallic worship at, 227, 229, 233; burning-ghats at, 229, 230; temples at, 231–33; the Scindia Ghat, 231; the Mosque of Aurungzeb, 231; the Durga Temple, 232;

the *Sati* monuments, 232, 233; the ancient site of (Sarnath), 233; hotel at, 233.

Benet, Stephen, quoted, 85, 86.

Bengal, Bay of, 219.

Bilibid Prison, Manila, 154.

Binzuru, Japanese god, 62, 63.

Black Hole, Calcutta, 223.

Bo tree, oldest historical tree in existence, 288.

Bombay, the population of, 268; the Parsee Towers of Silence, 268–70; the Caves of Elephanta, 271; hotels in, 271, 272.

Bongao, 188, 189.

Books, Japanese, 67.

Borneo, British North. *See* British North Borneo.

Bowring, Sir John, hymn written by, 140.

Boxer Rebellion, 93, 96, 97, 99.

Brass enamel-work, of Jeypore, 234, 258.

British East India Company, and Singapore, 210.

British North Borneo, Sandakan, 189–96.

British North Borneo Company, 190–96.

Brocades, at Shanghai, 130.

Bryan, William Jennings, 182.

Bud Dajo, volcano on Sulu, 180.

Buddha, bronze statue of (the Daibutsu), 18–20, 72; a statue of, in Anuradhapura, 289, 290. *See* Guatama Buddha.

Buddhism, the age of, 233.

Burmah, 213–19.

Burmese, and British Government, strained feeling between, connected with the Shwe Dagon Pagoda, 215.

Burning-ghats, 229, 230.

Bushell, Dr., of the British Consular Service in Peking, 124.

Cagayan Sulu, 196, 197.

Cairo, hotels at, 293, 305, 306; trips from, 293; mosques of, 294; museum at, 294; native guides at, 295; bazaars and night life of, 296; thievery in, 305.

Calcutta, arrival at, 219; the sights of, 222–24; the Black Hole, 223; hotels of, 225.

California, big trees of, 4, 5.

Camarines, the, 162.

Camoens, grotto of, 140.

Camp John Hay, at Baguio, 205.

Camp Keithley, Mindanao, 164.

Camp Overton, Mindanao, 164.

Camp Vickers, Mindanao, 166.

Campbell, Tim, Congressman, 20.

Canton, character of, 132–35; the standard bill of fare in, 135; pagodas in, 136; the old Execution Ground, 136; the City of the Dead, 136–38.

Cavité, 145.

Cawnpore, 234, 235.

Cebu, 198.

Celebes Sea, 169.

Cemetery, burial place of the Forty-Seven Ronins, 27–30; in Manila, 154.

Ceylon, Island of, approach to, 284; drives in, 284, 285; trip to Kandia, 285–87; indication of its prehistoric settlement, 287; ruins of Anuradhapura, 287, 288; relics at, 288–90.

Chefoo, 126.

China, North, controlled by Japan, 84; from Dalny to Tientsin by boat, 85–87; Peking, 87–113, 121; the Imperial family of, 92, 93, 96, 97, 100, 101; since the death of the Empress Dowager, 93, 94; temples in, 97–99, 101, 102, 121–23; municipal examinations in, 102, 103; Christianity necessary for civic progress in, 104; defenseless condition of, due to social system, 110; protected by the 'open door,' 110, 139; explanation of partitioning of, 110; household servants in, 112; the Great Wall, 114–17; the Ming Tombs, 117–21; shiftlessness and lethargy of, 120; pagodas of, 123, 136; the Pearl River, 130–32; Canton, 132–39; gambling-houses in, 140; Hongkong, 140–43.

Chinese, their character, 89; typical method of disposing of difficult political problems of, 104, 105; their method of trading, 105–09; face-saving of, 105–13; social system and business principles of, 109; 'squeeze,' their custom of, 111–13.

Chion-in, temple, in Kyoto, 64.

Chitor, 260, 261.

Chosen. *See* Korea.

Clifford, Sir Hugh, his *The Further Side of Silence*, 209.

Clubs, in Oriental countries, 128, 129.

Cochero, the, of Manila, 150, 151.

Cochran, Lieutenant, Constabulary officer at Tagun, Mindanao, 170, 171, 176, 177.

Cock-fighting, at Manila, 155.

Coleridge, Samuel T., his poem *Kublai Khan*, 124; quoted, 125.

Colombo, approach to, 284; hotels in, 284, 285.

Colorado, Grand Canyon of, 4.

Colossi of Memnon, 303.

Conrad, Joseph, stories of, as introduction to the Straits Settlements, 209.

Convicts, penal settlement of, on Palawan Island, 197, 198.

Cook (Thomas) & Son, serviceable, 219, 220.

Cork helmet, need of, from Hongkong to Egypt, 130, 131.

Cormorant fishing, in Japan, 48–50.

Cotabato River, Mindanao, 168, 169.

Courtesans, Japanese, 30–34.

Cremation, customary in Japan, 66.

Cryptomeria trees, 43–46.

Culion Island Leper Colony, 199, 200.

Cuspidors in Japan, 66.

Daibutsu, bronze statue of Buddha, 18–20, 72.

Dak bungalow, a Government rest-house, 220.

Dalaion, Mindanao, 174–77.

Dalny, 84, 85.

Daniels, Frank, and George Ade, their *The Sultan of Sulu*, 179.

Darjiling, 225, 226.

Dansalan, Moro village, 165.

Davao, 170–73.

Davao, Gulf of, 169.

Deir el Bahri temple, 303.

Delhi, founded by Shah Jehan, 236, 250; Peacock Throne at, 236, 245, 250; the chronicle of, 246; the ruins of, 247; the Tower of Victory, 247; the Pillar of Rajah Dhava, 248; the mausoleum of Adham Khan, 248; the tomb of Altamsh, 248; the tomb of Nizam-ud-Din, 249; the tomb of the Princess Jahanara, 249; the tomb of Khusran, 250; architecture of, 250; Hall of Private Audience, 250; hotels of, 251; business street of, 251; the Jamma Masjid, 251, 252.

Dendera, temple at, 300, 301.

Dining, in Japan, 67.
Disraeli, Benjamin, 293.
Diver, Maud, 235.
Divorces, in Japan, 68.
Dog-market, at Baguio, 205.
Dollar Line of Pacific steamships, 6.
Drake, Governor of India, 223.
Dravidian architecture, 272, 276, 280.
Dwarfs, African, original inhabitants of the Philippine Archipelago, 201.

Eastman, Max, quoted, 12.
Ebers, George, novels of, 297.
Edfu, temple of, 299.
Elephanta, the Caves of, 271.
Elephants, teak logs carried by, 215, 216.
Ellora, cave temple of, 271.
Empress Dowager of China. *See* Old Buddha.

Face-saving, the Japanese and Chinese method of, 54, 105–13.
Fatehpur-Sikri, 241–44.
Filipino Constabulary, established by Harrison over the Moros, 181, 182; lone officer of, at Siasi, 188.
Fog, a, in the Pacific, 6.
Forbes, Governor, his bungalow 'Topside,' 204.
Forster, E. M., his *Passage to India*, 235.
Forty-Seven Ronins, story of the, 27–30.
Fox, the, in Japanese religion, 59–61.
Fujiyama, 15, 17.
Fundamentalists in legislatures, 129.
Flying-fox, the, 171.
Fruit-bat, the, 171.
Fung-Shui, geomancy, 137–39.
Fusan, 78.

Gambling-houses in China, 140.
Ganesh, temple of, 273; found at entrance of all Hindu temples in India, 277.
Ganges, the, 227.
Gecko, the, 172.
Geomancy, Chinese belief in, 137.
Gifu, 48.
Gilbert, Newton W., Vice-Governor-General of the Philippines, 152.
Gilhouser, Major, resident Governor at Mindanao, 165.
Gizeh, 293, 296.
Golden Gate. sunset at, 5.
Graft, custom of, in China, 111–13.
Grass-Lark, Japanese, 70, 71.
Great Britain, and the opium trade, 141–43, 190–96; at Hongkong. 141–43; at Singapore, 210, 211; and Burmese, strained feeling between, connected with the Shwe Dagon Pagoda, 215; in India, 222; *Sati* custom forbidden by, 233; in Egypt, 293.
Great Wall of China, the, 114–17.
Guatama Buddha, relics of, 213, 286; started his teaching at Sarnath in sixth century B.C., 233, 289.
Guide-books, of India and the East, 271.

Hai-fuki, Japanese cuspidor, 66.
Hall of Private Audience, Delhi, 250.
Hamaguchi, landlord of Miyako Hotel, Kyoto, 20.
Hanna, Mark, 157.
Harriman, E. H., anecdote of, 19, 20.
Harrison, Francis Burton, Governor-General of the Philip-

pines, 145, 149; address made
by, at banquet in Manila, 156,
157; reverses policy of Wood
and Pershing, 163; Filipino
Constabulary established over
the Moros by, 181, 182; pardons criminals in the name of
economy, 198; forces Dr. Heiser out of Culion Island Leper
Colony, 199; diminishes health
and efficiency of the Philippine service in name of economy, 205.
Hatheway, Conrad, Secretary
of Governor Forbes, 204.
Hathor, the Goddess, 300.
Hatshepsut, Queen, 303.
Hawaii, a day in, 7–13; arrival
at, 7; Pearl Harbor, 8, 9; Diamond Head, 9; Waikiki Beach,
10; Kapiolani Park, 11; departure from, 12, 13.
Hawaiians, the, 12, 13.
Heiser, Dr. Victor G., founder
of Culion Island Leper Colony,
199.
Hemp-raising, at Dalaion, Mindanao, 174.
Hichens, Robert, his *The Spell of
Egypt*, 297.
Higashi Hongwanji, temple, 64,
65.
Himalayas, the, 225, 226.
Hindus, and Mohammedans,
272.
Hiran Minar, column near Agra
(Akbar's hunting-tower), 243.
'Holy men' of India, 222, 224,
225.
Hongkong, 130, 140–43; hotels
at, 143.
Honolulu, a day in, 8–13. *See*
Hawaii.
Hooghly River, 219.
Hovey, Richard, quoted, 2.
Human Bullets, by a Japanese
officer, 84.

Hunt, Moses H., purser of the
Mongolia, 7, 8, 11–13.

Ifugaos, the, 205.
Igorots, the, 203–05.
Iguana, the, 172.
Iligan Bay, Mindanao, 163.
Iloilo, 199.
Imperator, the, 306.
Inari, the goddess, 59–61.
Inari Temple, in Kyoto, 59,
60.
Indenture system, at work in
British North Borneo, 193.
India, railway travel in, 219,
221; need of a native servant
in, 219, 220; personal bedding
necessary in, 220, 221; better
off with than without Great
Britain, 222; 'holy men' of,
222, 224, 225; Calcutta, 222–
25; Darjiling, 225–27; Benares, 227–34; phallic worship
in, 227, 229, 233, 271–73, 276–
79; Lucknow and Cawnpore,
234, 235; Agra, 235–45; snakecharmers and jugglers of,
245, 246; Delhi, 246–52; Mohammedan service in, 252;
Rajputana, 253–65; characteristic features of, 265–67;
women of, 265; Bombay,
268–72; guide-books to, 271;
Southern, characteristics of,
272, 273; Mohammedans and
Buddhists in, 272; Trinchinopoly, 273–76; Tanjore, 276–
79; superstition and ignorance
of the natives of, 279; Madura, 279–84; the Island of
Ceylon, 284–90.
Inland Sea, Japan, 72–74.
Insect-dealers' shops, in Kyoto,
70, 71.
Irrigating wells, of India, 266;
of Egypt, 298.
Irrigation canal, in Egypt, 293.

I'timad ud Daulah, tomb of, at Agra, 241.

Itozaki, 72.

Ivory carving, at Shanghai, 127.

Iwahig Penal Colony, Palawan Island, 197, 198.

Iyemitsu, mausoleum, 36.

Iyeyasu, mausoleum of, 36, 40; castle built by, 56.

Jade, of Canton, 136; of Burmah, 216.

Jahanara, Princess, tomb of, 249.

Jainism, 263, 264; temples of, 264, 265.

Japan, Yokohama, 15–17, 22–25; Tokaido Road, 16; Miyanoshita, 16, 17; Lake Hakone, 16, 17; Kamakura, 16–22; Miyajima, 21, 72–74; Tokyo, 22–34; Nikko, 35–46; cryptomeria trees in, 43–46; Lake Chuzenji, 46, 47; trout-fishing in, 47–50; Kyoto, 51–71; the Inland Sea, 72–74; her military rule of Korea, 75–78; controls northern China, 84, 85; the British at Singapore not a delight to, 211.

Japanese, fishermen, 21; dress, 22, 23; attitude toward women, 22, 24, 31, 38; courtesans, 30–34; temples, 36, 57–65, 72; royalty, 37, 38; circumscribed spiritual vision, 46; pilgrimages, 57; prayers, 58, 63; massagers, 65; customs, 66–69; wrestlers, 69, 70; their method of trading, 52–55; face-saving of, 54; social system and business principles of, 109, 110.

Jehol, 124, 125.

Jewelry, at Shanghai, 127; fine native Indian, at Delhi, 251.

Jey Singh II, 253, 256–58.

Jeypore, brass enamel-work of, 234, 258; hotels at, 253; color scheme of, 255, 256; sights in, 256, 257; observatory in, 257; the Maharajah's palace, 257; the Hall of the Winds, 257, 258; center of tiger-hunting, 258; museum of, 258; cenotaphs of the Maharajahs at, 258; bazaar, 258.

Jizo, Japanese god, 64.

Johore, Sultan of, 212.

Juggernaut, car of, 275.

Jugglers, Indian, 246.

Jujutsu, 70.

Juramentado, religious frenzy among the Moros, 183.

Kali, the Goddess, 254, 255.

Kamakura, 16–22.

Kandy, 285–90.

Karasaki, 56.

Karnak, 293, 300, 302.

Kegon Falls, 47.

Keithley, Camp, Mindanao, 164.

Khusrau, Persian poet, tomb of, 250.

Kienlung, Chinese Emperor, 122.

Kinchen-janga, 225, 226.

Kipling, Rudyard, quoted, 1, 14, 180; his *The English Flag*, 159, 160; licenses of, in *Mandalay* and *Kim*, 218, 219; his *The City of Dreadful Night*, 223; his *Kim* and *Naulahka*, 235.

Kiyomizu-dera, temple of, 61–64.

Knibbs, H. H., quoted, 2, 43, 298.

Knives, used in native Philippine warfare, 167.

Kobe, 72.

Kohinoor Diamond, the, 245.

Kom Ombos, temple, 303.

Korakuen, garden of, at Okayama, 72.
Korea, her unhappy lot under
Japan rule, 75–78; Seoul, 78–
83; tomb of kings of, 81, 82.
Koreans, their dress, 79, 80;
character, 80, 81.
Kublai Khan, 90, 91, 102;
builds the Peking Wall, 90, 91;
builds the Astronomical Observatory at Peking, 102;
Coleridge's poem about, 124.
Kusa Hibari, the Grass-Lark,
70, 71.
Kutab Minar, Delhi, 247.
Kwang Hsu, Chinese Emperor,
92, 93, 101.
Kwannon, shrine of, at Kamakura, 22; temple of, at Kyoto,
61, 64.
Kyoto, character of, 51; hotels,
51; shopping at, 52–55; Imperial Palace at, 55, 56; Shogun castle at, 56; Lake Biwa
and Karasaki near, 56; temples at, 57–65; massagers of,
65; insect-dealers' shops at,
70, 71.

Lake Biwa, 56.
Lake Chuzenji, 46, 47.
Lake Hakone, 16, 17.
Lake Lanao, Mindanao, 164,
166.
Lake Pichola, 259.
Lake Taal, 206.
Lakes, a freak of nature in, 196.
Lamb, Charles, 8.
Lamb, Mr., Superintendent of
the Iwahig Penal Colony,
Palawan Island, 197, 198.
Legazpi, in the Philippines, 162.
Leper-colony, on Culion Island,
199, 200.
de Lesseps, Ferdinand, 292.
Liaotung Peninsula, 85.
Lingam-yoni, the, 233, 278.

Lizards, in the Philippines, 172.
Lucknow, 234.
Luxor, 293, 300–02, 304.
Lyons, Nobert, quoted on the
cochero of Manila, 151.

Macao, Portuguese settlement
in China, 139, 140.
Mactan, Isle of, 198.
Madras, hotels in, 273.
Madura, 279–84.
Magellan, Ferdinand, burial
place of, 198, 199.
Malabang, Mindanao, 166.
Manchuria, 84, 85.
Mandalay, 213.
Manila, arrival at, 144, 145;
what American government
has meant to, 145–47; hotel
at, 146; sights in, 150, 151;
description of, 153; cemetery
in, 154; the Bilibid Prison, 154;
cock-fighting at, 155; Aqua-
rium, 155.
Manila Bay, sunset in, 6.
Marahin Island, Lake Lanao,
Mindanao, 166.
Marco Polo, 91.
Maria Cristina, waterfall in
Mindanao, 164.
Mariam Zamani, 242.
Mariposa Grove of Big Trees,
4, 5.
Mariveles, 200, 207, 208.
Marquis, Don, quoted, 2.
Marriage, in Japan, 68, 69.
Masefield, John, quoted, 2.
Massagers, Japanese, 65.
Medinet Habu, temple, 303.
Memphis, 295.
Miller, Congressman Clarence
B., his visit to the Philippines,
147; cruising on El Aguila,
156–201; visits Baguio and the
Igorots, 203–05.
Minakshi, 282, 283.
Mindanao, Iligan Bay, 163;

muleback trip across, 164–67;
Lake Lanao, 164, 166; Dansalan, 165; Cotabato River,
168, 169; Davao, 169, 170,
172, 173; Tagun, 170; the
Bagobos, 171, 174–77; Dalaion, 174–77; Zamboanga,
177, 178.
Ming Tombs, the, 117–21.
Mirza Rajah, 255.
Miyajima, 21, 72–74.
Miyanoshita, 16, 17.
Mohammedan service, a, at
Delhi, 252.
Mohammedans, and Hindus, in
India, 272.
Mongolia, the, Pacific Mail
steamship, 6, 7, 12, 14.
Mongoose, the, 245.
Moros, 163–65, 168–70, 178;
their method of fighting, 167,
168; a mock spear-fight of,
178; of Sulu, 179–86; *juramentado* among, 183; the story
of two, 184–86; of Siasi,
188.
Mosques at Cairo, 294.
Moulmein, 218, 219.
Mount Abu, journey to, 262;
hotel on, 263; the home of
Jainism, 263, 264; Jain temples
of, 264, 265.
Mount Mariveles, a sunset at,
207, 208.
Mount Mayon, in the Philippines, 162.
Mount Nantai-Zan, 47.
Mukden, 84.
Muntaz-i-Mahal. *See* Arjmand
Banu.
Murray's Handbook of India,
271.
Mutsuhito, Emperor, 38.

Nadir Shah, plunderer of the
Peacock Throne, 250.
Nagara River, fishing in, 48–50.

Nagasaki, 71.
Nagoya, 48.
Nandi, Siva's favorite bull, 229,
273, 277.
Nanking, Treaty of, 141.
Nankow, 117.
Nankow Pass, 115.
Nara, 72.
Newell, Major H. A., his
guides to India, 271.
Nikko, religious center, 35, 36;
the mountain and shrines at,
36, 40–42; the town, 39; hotels
in, 39; the tolling of the bell at,
42; the cryptomeria trees at,
43–46.
Nile trip, the, 293, 296–305.
Nizam-ud-Din, tomb of, 249.
Nogi, General, 38.
Nueva Caceres, in the Philippines, 162.

Oahu, Hawaii, 7.
Oiran Duchu, procession of the
courtesans, 34.
Okayama, 72.
'Old Buddha,' the, the Empress
Dowager of China, poisons
Kwang Hsu, 92, 93, 101;
deserts Peking at time of
Boxer Rebellion, 96, 97; an
able ruler, 100, 101; her fortune, 111, 113; her final burial-place, 139.
'Open door,' the, China protected by, 110, 139.
Opium, Great Britain and the
trade in, 141–43, 190–96.
Orloff Diamond, the, 275.
Osaka, 72.
Osmeña, Sergio, Philippine Senator, 148.

Pacific Mail Line of steamships, 6.
Page, Walter H., Ambassador
to Great Britain, 129.

Pagoda, Shwe Dagon, the, at Rangoon, 213.

Pagodas, Chinese, 123, 136.

Palawan Island, Iwahig Penal Colony on, 197, 198.

Pamplona, in the Philippines, 162.

Parang, Mindanao, 166.

Parsees, 268–70.

Parvati. *See* Siva.

Pasacao, in the Philippines, 162.

Pasig River, 153, 154.

Peacock Throne, at Delhi, 236, 245, 250.

Pearl River, the, 130–32.

Pechili, Gulf of, 85, 86.

Peking, arrival at, 87; oldest city in the world, 88; picturesquenes of, 90, 95, 96; wall of, 90, 91, 121; hotels in, 91, 124; the three cities of, 91, 92, 94; reminder of Boxer Rebellion in, 96, 97; Temple and Altar of Heaven, 97–99; Temple of Agriculture, 99; Summer Palace, 100, 101; Temple of Confucius, 101, 102; Astronomical Observatory, 102; Lama Temple, 102; Examination Hall, 102, 103; University, 103, 104; Union Medical College and Hospital, 104; shopping in, 105–09; the gates of, 121; to Shanghai from, by boat, 126, 127.

Penang, 213.

Peradeniya, Botanical Garden at, 287.

Pershing, General John J., at Zamboanga, 177, 178.

Phallic worship in India, 227, 229, 233, 271–73, 276–79.

Philæ, temple, 303.

Philippine Archipelago, a cruise in, 156–201; original inhabitants of, 201; the present-day inhabitants of, 202, 203.

Philippine Independence Mission, 149, 159.

Philippines, the, Manila, 144–55; the question of the independence of, 147–50, 157–61, 165, 169, 170, 178, 186, 199, 202, 203, 209, 210; bird life in, 167; animals of, 171, 172; Baguio, 203–05; Lake Taal, 206; a sunset at Mount Mariveles, 207, 208. *See* Philippine Archipelago.

Pi Hsiao Li, 93.

Pichola Lake, 259.

Pilgrimages, Japanese, 57.

Pilgrims at Benares, 227–29.

Pillar of Rajah Dhava, 248.

Pipal, oldest historical tree in existence, 288.

Porcelain, at Shanghai, 127.

Port Arthur, 84, 85.

Port Said, 292.

Powell, Colonel E. Alexander, his *Where the Strange Trails Go Down* quoted on the British North Borneo Company, 195.

Prayers, Japanese, 58, 63.

Puerto Princesa, Palawan Island, 198.

Punt, Land of, 303.

Putnam-Weale, B. L., his *Indiscreet Letters from Peking*, 97.

Pwé, national Burmese amusement, 217.

Pyramids of Egypt, 294, 295.

Quézon, Manuel, President of Philippine Senate, a Spanish *mestizo*, 148; an opportunist, 152; moving spirit of Philippine Independence Mission, 149, 203; *Independencia* virus distributed by, 156, 158, 162–65; 170, 176; his antics, 203.

Raffles, Sir Thomas Stamford, established Great Britain's foothold in Singapore, 210.

Rajah Dhava, the Pillar of, 248.

Rajputana, Jeypore, 253–58; Udaipur and Chitor, 258–62; Mount Abu, 262–65.

Rajputs, character of, 259–62.

Rameses II, 301, 303, 304.

Ramesseum, temple, 303.

Rangoon, the Shwe Dagon Pagoda at, 213–15; sight of elephants piling teak logs at, 215, 216; the bazaars of, 216; a *Pwé* at, 217; drives of, 217; a statue of Buddha at, 217, 218.

Red Fort, Agra, 240, 241.

Red Sea, the, 291.

Rice, Emery, commander of the *Mongolia*, 6.

Rigadon, native Philippine dance, 170.

Rizal, José, Filipino martyr, his statue, 151, 152; an intelligent patriot, 203.

Rockefeller Foundation, Union Medical College and Hospital in Peking built by, 104.

Romblon Island, 200.

Rubies, of Burmah, 216.

Russo Japanese War, 84, 85.

Sakkara, 295, 296.

Saliguri, 225–27.

Salim Chishti, 242, 243.

Samurai, the, 109, 110.

Sandakan, 189–96.

Sarnath, the ancient site of Benares, 233.

Sati custom forbidden by British Government, 232, 233.

Scindia Ghat, at Benares, 231.

Seoul, appearance of, 78, 79; inhabitants of, 79–81; attractions of, 81; tomb of Korean kings near, 81, 82; spot where Korean Queen was assassinated in, 82, 83; eating in, 83; monument in public square of, 83.

Shah Jehan, founder of Delhi, 236, 250; builder of the Taj Mahal, 236–40.

Shah Jehangir, 255.

Shampooers, Japanese, 65.

Shangdu, 124, 125.

Shanghai, from Peking to, by boat, 126, 127; the Shanghai Club, 127; the appearance of, 129, 130,

Shanghai Club, the, 127.

Shanhaikwan, good view of the Great Wall of China at, 116, 117.

Shinyo Maru, of the Toyo Kisen Kaisha Line, 130.

Shoguns, 36, 56.

Shopping, in Kyoto, 52–55; in Peking, 105–09.

Shwangti, first Emperor of China, 114.

Shwe Dagon Pagoda, the, at Rangoon, 213–15.

Siasi, 187, 188.

Sikandra, Akbar's tomb at, 244, 245.

Sikri. *See* Fatehpur-Sikri.

Silks, at Shanghai, 127.

Singapore, establishment of Great Britain's foothold in, by Sir Thomas Raffles, 210, 211; attractions in, 211, 212.

Singleton, Esther, her *Egypt*, 297.

Siva, phallic worship of, 227, 229, 233, 271–73, 276–84.

Smith, Reverend Dr. Arthur H., his *Chinese Characteristics* quoted, 89.

Smoking, in Japan, 67.

Snake-charmers, Indian, 245, 246.

Southern Cross, the, 219.

Spear-fight, of Moros, 178.
Sphinx, 294.
Squatting, the Japanese habit of, 24, 25.
'Squeeze,' the Chinese custom of, 111–13.
Sri Rangam, Vishnu Temple of, 274–76.
Steel, Flora Annie, her *On the Face of the Waters*, 235.
Stevenson, R. L., quoted, 1.
Subrahmanya, 276–78.
Suez Canal, 292.
Sulu, the Moros of, 179–86; appearance of, 179; the Sultan of, 179, 185, 186, 194; the officers' quarters of, 186, 187.
Sunset, a, at Mount Mariveles, 207, 208.
Surajah Dowlah, 223.
Swift, Jonathan, quoted, 112.

Tagun, Mindanao, 170.
Taj Mahal, the, 236–40.
Tamil, the southern Hindu, 272.
Tanjore, 276–79.
Tawi Tawi Islands, 188, 189.
Taylor, Colonel Wallace C., of the Philippine Constabulary, in charge of *El Aguila* cruise, 157, 188; visits the Ifugaos with Congressman Miller, 205; conducts party to Lake Taal, 206.
Temple and Altar of Heaven in Peking, 97–99.
Temple of Agriculture in Peking, 99.
Temple of the Great Bell, near Peking, 123.
Temple Sengakuji, 27–30.
Temple of the Tooth, Ceylon, 286, 287.
Temples, at Nikko, 36; at Kyoto, 57–65; at Nara, 72; Chinese, 97–99, 101, 102, 121–23; in Burmah, 217; at Be-

nares, 231–33; at Mount Abu, 263–65; near Bombay, 271; of Southern India, 272–83, 286, 287; in Egypt, 293, 296, 298–305.
Thebes, 302.
Thuparama Dagoba, the, 288.
Tientsin, 85–87.
Tiger-hunting, Jeypore a center of, 258.
Tod, James, his *Annals of Rajasthan*, 258, 260.
Tokaido Road, 16.
Tokyo, traveling from Yokohama to, 22–25; character of, 25, 26; attractions of, 26–30; the Yoshiwara, 30–34; rivalry with Kyoto, 51.
Tongka, 87.
Torii, significance of, 20, 21.
Tower of Victory, Delhi, 248.
Towers of Silence, of the Parsees, 268–70.
Trade winds, antics of, 10.
Trans-Pacific steamship lines, 6.
Tree-dwarfing, practiced by the Japanese, 44–46.
Trichinopoly, 273.
Trout-fishing, in Japan, 47–50.

Udaipur, 259, 260.
Ustad Isa, architect of the Taj Mahal, 239, 240.

Valley of the Tombs of the Kings, 304.
Visayan Islands, 198.
Vishnu Temple of Sri Rangam, 274–76.

Wanderlust, 1, 2.
Water-buffalo, the Philippine, 150.
Wei-hai-wei, 127.
Whitman, Walt, quoted, 239.
Whitney, Vernon, Civil Governor at Sulu, story of his

wound, 182–84; his story of two Moros, 184–86.

Wood, General Leonard, Governor-General of the Philippines, 163; aims to raise fund to drive leprosy out of the Philippines, 199, 200.

Wrestling, in Japan, 69, 70.

Wusung, 127.

Yalu River, 83.

Yamada, 72.

Yellow Sea, the, 127.

Yelow Temple, near Peking, 122.

Yokohama, 15–17; traveling to Tokyo from, 22–25.

Yosemite Valley, 4.

Yoshiwara, Tokyo, 30–34.

Yuan Shih-kai, Viceroy of China, 93, 94, 98.

Yunglo, tomb of, 118, 119.

Zamboanga, Mindanao, 177, 178.

Zebu, the, 212.